D1291716

INTERNATIONAL SERIES IN
EXPERIMENTAL PSYCHOLOGY
GENERAL EDITOR: H. J. EYSENCK

VOLUME 27

The Wechsler Enterprise

AN ASSESSMENT OF THE DEVELOPMENT, STRUCTURE, AND USE OF THE WECHSLER TESTS OF INTELLIGENCE

OTHER TITLES IN THE SERIES IN EXPERIMENTAL PSYCHOLOGY

NOTICE TO READERS

Dear Reader

If your library is not already a standing order customer or subscriber to this series, may we recommend that you place a standing or subscription order to receive immediately upon publication all new issues and volumes published in this valuable series. Should you find that these volumes no longer serve your needs your order can be cancelled at any time without notice.

The Editors and the Publisher will be glad to receive suggestions or outlines of suitable titles, reviews or symposia for consideration for rapid publication in this series.

ROBERT MAXWELL
Publisher at Pergamon Press

The Wechsler Enterprise

AN ASSESSMENT OF THE DEVELOPMENT, STRUCTURE, AND USE OF THE WECHSLER TESTS OF INTELLIGENCE

BY

GEORGE FRANK
New York, USA

PERGAMON PRESS
OXFORD · NEW YORK · TORONTO · SYDNEY · PARIS · FRANKFURT

BF
432.5
.W4
F7
1983

U.K.	Pergamon Press Ltd., Headington Hill Hall, Oxford OX3 0BW, England
U.S.A.	Pergamon Press Inc., Maxwell House, Fairview Park, Elmsford, New York 10523, U.S.A.
CANADA	Pergamon Press Canada Ltd., Suite 104, 150 Consumers Road, Willowdale, Ontario M2J 1P9, Canada
AUSTRALIA	Pergamon Press (Aust.) Pty. Ltd., P.O. Box 544, Potts Point, N.S.W. 2011, Australia
FRANCE	Pergamon Press SARL, 24 rue des Ecoles, 75240 Paris, Cedex 05, France
FEDERAL REPUBLIC OF GERMANY	Pergamon Press GmbH, Hammerweg 6, D-6242 Kronberg/Taunus, Federal Republic of Germany

First edition 1983

Library of Congress Cataloging in Publication Data

Frank, George.
The Wechsler enterprise.
(International series in experimental psychology; v. 27)
Includes bibliographical references.
1. Wechsler adult intelligence scale. 2. Wechsler intelligence scale for children. 3. Psychology, Pathological—Diagnosis.
4. Brain damage—Diagnosis.
I. Title.   II. Series. [DNLM: 1. Wechsler scales. W1 IN835JE v. 27/BF432.5.W42 F828w]
BF432.5.W4F7 1983   153.9'32   83-2305

British Library Cataloguing in Publication Data

Frank, G.
The Wechsler enterprise. − (International series in experimental psychology)
1. Wechsler adult intelligence scale—History
2. Wechsler intelligence scale for children—History
I. Title   II. Series
159.93   BF432.5.W

ISBN 0-08-027973-2

Printed and bound in Great Britain by
Redwood Burn Ltd., Trowbridge, Wiltshire.

Contents

v

Prologue

WHILE this book is meant for clinicians it is not a clinical book. By that I mean that this book on the Wechsler tests does not aim at an explication of how to administer or interpret Wechsler test data. Rather, this is a book the purpose of which is to evaluate the development, structure and clinical utility of the tests Wechsler developed.

Although David Wechsler began to work on his test in 1932 (Wechsler, 1932), he formally introduced his test of intelligence 7 years later (Wechsler, 1939). Since that time a variety of forms of this first test have been developed, both for adults [the Wechsler–Bellevue, Form II Wechsler, 1946), the Wechsler Adult Intelligence Scale (Wechsler, 1955)] and for the children [the Wechsler Intelligence Scale for Children (Wechsler, 1949) and the Wechsler Preschool and Primary Scale of Intelligence (Wechsler, 1963)]. Essentially these tests are all of the same mold in terms of structure; Form II of the Wechsler test and the Wechsler Adult Intelligence Scale are but modification in some of the content of Form I; the Wechsler Intelligence Scale for Children is a downward extension of Form II, and the Wechsler Preschool and Primary Scale is a downward extension of the Wechsler Intelligence Scale for Children.

Since the original presentation of the text in 1939, at this writing there have been over 40 years of work done with the Wechsler tests. It is the express purpose of this study to examine that work as a means of assessing the heuristic value of the tests Wechsler developed. Thus we will be looking at the structure of the tests and the validity of Wechsler's assumptions about it and the degree to which the tests can be used to assess attributes other than the intellective. In the end, we should have a good idea of the value of the tests Wechsler developed, the use to which they can be meaningfully put, and suggestions for future research.

If psychology is to be a science, and clinical work scientific, not only

1

must we develop interesting instruments but we must also assess the value of these instruments. So let it be with the Wechsler.

This is not the first time that the body of research reflecting on the clinical use of the Wechsler tests has been looked at critically. Albert Rabin, a psychologist who was a pioneer in the research assessment of the clinical utility of the Wechsler test (Rabin, 1941), wrote the first summary of the published research with the Wechsler—Bellevue Scale (Rabin, 1945b). This same psychologist was instrumental in insuring that reviews of the growing body of research were done about every 5 years, viz., Rabin and Guertin (1951), Guertin, Frank and Rabin (1956), Guertin, Rabin, Frank and Ladd (1962), Guertin, Ladd, Frank, Rabin and Hiester (1966, 1971) (see also, the review by Littell, 1960). And as the reader can see, this is not the first time I have looked at this research in an evaluative way. I have been privileged to have been able to participate along with Rabin and Guertin in these periodic reviews of Wechsler research as well as to look at such data by myself, viz., Frank (1970b, 1976). Why, then, you ask, should there be yet another look at these studies? The answer to that question is that the previous reviews have looked at time-limited segments of this research. It is time to look at the totality of the (published) research with the Wechsler tests relevant to an assessment of how well the tests do what Wechsler and others purport that they can. As anyone who has followed the conclusions drawn from the periodic reviews of the approximately 5-year segments of studies, common themes could be seen to be emerging, both in terms of the kind of studies being conducted as well as the evaluation of that research and the suggestions and recommendations born therefrom. If this broader view of the "terrain" only reiterates these findings, that, in and of itself, could be considered a contribution, lending a degree of stability to whatever conclusions have been drawn from the data in the 5-year reviews. Hopefully, however, from this broader perspective some new insights will eventuate, views not as possible when looking at the findings more "close up."

As anyone who has undertaken such a venture as this knows, such a task is, at best, difficult. Trying to bring together such disparate research into a meaningful gestalt is no easy task. To cover the sheer number of published studies is a monumental task in and of itself (as anyone can see just by glancing at the reference section of this book). Such a venture is nothing short of a labour of love, and I dedicate the fruits of my labour to my fellow clinicians, primary amongst them, my budding colleague, Bette Mills, who was kind enough to read the drafts of the manuscript to ensure that the communication would be solely in secondary process form.

CHAPTER 1

The Psychometric Development of the Wechsler Scale

IT TOOK about 20 years for the world to come to appreciate that psychology might have something to offer with regard to practical issues. When Wundt first established his psychology laboratory at Leipzig in 1879, the emphasis was on finding the laws of human reactions to stimuli; his focus was primarily on sensory—motor behavior. Galton and Kulpe, on the other hand, were investigating what had come to be known as "higher mental functions," viz., thinking (e.g. reasoning, judgment and imagination). It took some time before such studies were introduced into Wundt's lab. Just before the turn of the century, a number of experimental psychologists were asked to apply their knowledge of these "higher mental functions" to assist educators in the assessment and placement of school children. This happened with Ebbinghaus in Germany (Breslau), Witmer in America (Philadelphia), and Binet in France (Paris). And thus applied psychology was born.

The world is most acquainted with the contribution to this effort made by Alfred Binet, and the psychometric roots for Wechsler's work in the testing of intelligence are in the work Binet did in the area of testing intelligence. As most of us know by now, Binet, an experimental psychologist with his Laboratory at the Sorbonne, was appointed in October of 1904, by the Minister of Public Instruction of Paris, to a commission whose task was to help identify those children in the public school system who could not benefit from ordinary instruction (Binet, 1905).

Binet was one of those experimental psychologists who was interested in studying the so-called "higher mental processes" and, as with other French psychologists before him (e.g. Esquirol, Pinel, Seguin), he was interested in the study of intellectual functioning. As with Piaget (who studied the "higher mental functions" some 20 years after Binet), Binet began by studying (observing) his own children. The consequence of that was the first test of intelligence Binet developed, a 30-item questionnaire (to be answered "yes" or "no"), graded on the number of total points attained, that is, a point scale. The test assessed: memory, imagination, expectations and fears, moral feelings and muscular force (Binet and Henri, 1895). It was not until later that Binet organized the material of his test in terms of age level and developed the concept of mental age (Binet and Simon, 1908).

As we now know, from a psychometric point of view, there were considerable problems with the structure of the Binet test. Much had been written about these issues (e.g. Ayres, 1911; Cattell, 1937; Krugman, 1939; Kuhlmann, 1911a, b; Stern, 1914; Terman, 1911, 1913a, b). Apart from the issue of the inadequate standardization, the criticism of Binet's test revolved around the following aspects:

(1) the test was too heavily weighted with tasks which involved verbal ability;

(2) some of the tests rely too heavily on scholastic experience;

(3) the sampling of the psychological functions presumed to be involved in the performance of the tests was too narrow; therefore there was an inadequate sampling of psychological functions;

(4) because of the narrow range of functions assessed, the test is inadequate to measure intelligence at the higher mental levels;

(5) the test is too easy at the lower levels, too hard at the upper;

(6) tests are misplaced at the various mental age levels;

(7) items are misplaced within the subtests as to difficulty;

(8) there are an unequal number of tests for different age levels;

(9) the same number of psychological functions are not assessed at each age level; and

(10) the same mental age arrived at differently for each person means that the same mental age does not mean the same thing from person to person.

Binet himself was aware of some of these difficulties and tried to address himself to them in revisions he made of his test in 1908 and 1911. In these revisions: tests which seemed redundant were removed; tests which seemed too heavily weighted with scholastic learning were pruned; the test was reorganized in order to effect a better organization age-level-wise, the number of tests at each age level were equated, and new tests were added (Binet and Simon, 1916). Still unsatisfied, many psychologists (beginning with Terman [Terman and Childs, 1912; Terman, 1913a, b, 1916; Terman and Merrill, 1937]) attempted revisions of the Binet in an effort to correct some of its apparent psychometric weaknesses (e.g. Herring, 1924; Wallin, 1929; McNemar, 1942). However, in spite of these several revisions by Binet and others, the psychometric problems with the test remained, to one degree or another.

As has been noted, one of the glaring problems with the Binet which remained in spite of the many revisions was that the test tended to be weighted with non-verbal items at the lower end, but as soon as it is expected that a child should be comfortable verbalizing (e.g. some time around 5 years old), the test becomes increasingly weighted with tests which require verbal skills. At the upper end of the mental age continuum, when adolescents and adults may be tested, the test is virtually a test of verbal skills. For a variety of reasons, such a test becomes a handicap to a psychologist. Logically, it makes sense that since school is a situation which requires that a child learn to deal with concepts, verbally presented, and with verbal concepts, a test of intelligence dominated by tasks which involve the understanding and manipulation of verbal concepts seems reasonable. However, what of the child who is uncomfortable communicating on a verbal level, e.g. the withdrawn, shy, anxious, uncommunicative, schizoid or autistic child? To attempt to assess the conceptual ability and the reasoning ability of such children via a technique which requires that they utilize the very modality (speaking, using words) with which they have difficulty, would not only put these children at a disadvantage with such a test, but actually would penalize them. Undoubtedly, the intellectual assessment of such children, if it is going to be based on the overall datum — the mental age — could not be accurate. The same consideration obtains with regard to adults who, likewise, have difficulty communicating on a verbal plane or for whom English was not the primary language. A similar problem is involved in the testing of adolescents and adults who come from backgrounds which underplayed school learning or whose experience in school did not emphasize high-level, verbal–conceptual learning, as would be the case with individuals who, perhaps until the Second World War, came from rural school situations, families which tended to underevaluate scholastic endeavours, or those who went to trade schools. To deal with these situations, psychologists began developing a host of non-verbal, performance tests (e.g. Seguin, 1866) whereby individuals might be able to demonstrate their reasoning and problem-solving abilities and their fund of knowledge and information without recourse to speaking or verbally-conceptualized concepts. The consequence of such efforts were such comprehensive sets of tasks as the Army Beta Test, developed for use during the First World War (Yoakum and Yerkes, 1920), and performance scales developed by Grace Arthur (Arthur, 1930), the Cornell–Coxe Performance Scale (Cornell and Coxe, 1934), Healy and Fernald (1911) and the Pintner–Patterson Performance Scale (Pintner and Patterson, 1917), to mention a few of the more popular ones.

Whilst the Binet also included non-verbal tasks (Binet and Henri, 1895), the idea that tests of intelligence should be composed of tasks of verbal *as well as* non-verbal skills could be found in the work of Healy and Fernald (1911), Knox (1914), Terman and Chamberlain (1918), Doll (1920), Wells and Martin (1923), Davey (1926), Alexander (1935) and the National Intelligence Tests (Whipple, 1921). When Wechsler developed his test, he did so with the express purpose of continuing this development, that is, of assessing intellectual ability by both verbal and non-verbal tasks simultaneously.

The ultimate structure of the Wechsler tests include 11 subtests, 6 of them verbal tasks, five of them non-verbal ones (what Wechsler refers to as Performance tests). The subtests included in the Scale are:

Verbal Scale:
   Information
   Comprehension
   Similarities
   Arithmetic
   Digits (Forward and Backwards)
   Vocabulary
Performance Scale:
   Picture Completion
   Picture Arrangement
   Object Assembly (hand, profile, car)
   Block Design
   Digit Symbol

When Wechsler presented his Scale to the public (Wechsler, 1939) he wrote, "Our aim was not to produce a set of brand new tests but to select, from whatever source available, such a combination of them as would meet the requirements of an effective adult scale" (Wechsler, 1939, p. 78). The structure of the Wechsler Scale indicates that Wechsler remained true to his statement. We should, thus, examine from where Wechsler selected these tests.

Information

By Wechsler's own statement the Information test was a task he found as part of ordinary clinical examinations and was a part of the Army Alpha Test (used in the First World War) (Yoakum and Yerkes, 1920). Actually, an information test was developed by Whipple (1909) and included by him in what was called the "National Intelligence Tests" (Whipple, 1921). An information test was also included in the series of tests put together by Healy and Fernald (1911), Knox (1914), Terman and Chamberlain (1918), Thorndike (1920), Thurstone (1921, 1931), Wells and Martin (1923), Manson (1925) and Babcock (1930).

Comprehension

As with Information, Comprehension questions were also part of the traditional clinical examination for intelligence used, as well as the Army Alpha (Yoakum and Yerkes, 1920). A Comprehension subtest was to be found in the Binet, and the tests Terman and Chamberlain (1918) and Whipple (1921) put together.

Arithmetic

An Arithmetic subtest was to be found in the Binet and the Army Alpha tests (Yoakum and Yerkes, 1920) and the tests put together by Healy and Fernald (1911), Terman and Chamberlain (1918), Thorndike (1920), Manson (1925) and the National Intelligence Tests (Whipple, 1921).

Digits

In the 1890s Ebbinghaus had included memory for digits in his test of intelligence (Pintner, 1923) as did Bolton (1892). Repetition of digits was to be found in the Binet and in tests developed by Terman and Chamberlain (1918), Thorndike (1920), Wells and Martin (1923), Manson (1925) and Babcock (1930).

Similarities

A task found in the Binet, the Army Alpha (Yoakum and Yerkes, 1920) and the National Intelligence Tests (Whipple, 1921).

Vocabulary

A standard test of intelligence used, as well, by Binet, Terman and Chamberlain (1918) and in the National Intelligence Tests (Whipple, 1921).

Picture arrangement

A picture arrangement subtest was to be found in the Army Beta (Yoakum and Yerkes, 1920), the Pintner (1919) and the Cornell–Coxe (1934).

Picture completion

Healy (1914) had developed the Picture completion test, and this task was to be found not only in the Binet but in the Scales put together by Knox (1914), Pintner and Patterson (1917), Thorndike (1920), the Army Beta Test (Yoakum and Yerkes, 1920) and the Grace Arthur (Arthur, 1925, 1930).

Block design

Healy and Fernald (1911) had developed the Block design test, whose use was to be amplified by Kohs (1920) and to be found in the Scales put together by Knox (1914), Pintner and Patterson (1917), the Army Beta Test (Yoakum and Yerkes, 1920), Arthur (1925, 1930) and Cornell and Coxe (1934).

Object assembly

Healy and Fernald (1911) had developed the object Assembly test, and this was to be found in the Scales put together by Knox (1914), Pintner and Patterson (1917), the Army Beta Test (Yoakum and Yerkes, 1920), Arthur (1925, 1930), and Cornell and Coxe (1934).

Digit symbol

The Digit symbol test had been used by Healy and Fernald (1911), Woodworth and Wells (1911), Pintner and Patterson (1917) and found in the Army Beta Test (Yoakum and Yerkes, 1920), and the National Intelligence Tests (Whipple, 1921).

Thus it can be seen that all of the tests Wechsler included in his Scale had, indeed, been in use before, and to facilitate our understanding of their previous use, Table 1 presents these data.

One must note that of the tests Wechsler selected to include in his Scale, the Information, Comprehension, Arithmetic, Digits, Similarities and Vocabulary subtests were taken from the Binet, and Picture completion, Object assembly, Block design and Digit symbol subtests were taken from the Pintner—Patterson (1917). From Table 1 we can see that not only were the tests Wechsler selected to use, used before, and, virtually, in the same combination, but that having set themselves the task of developing an omnibus test of intelligence composed of verbal and non-verbal tasks, the tests that Wechsler finally adopted for his Scale was nearly the same as that used by Alexander and virtually identical to that found in the Army Alpha and Beta Tests (Yoakum and Yerkes, 1920). In short, then, while Wechsler appears to have made some selection from previously developed scales to constitute an entirely new Scale, it would appear that essentially what he did was to take into his Scale the tests of the Army Alpha and Beta Tests (adding to them Digits).

While, on the one hand, one might question a procedure which simply borrowed the tasks from another Scale and, by adding one more task, give it a new name and present it as a new Scale, on the other hand, one has to acknowledge that Wechsler was merely following the pattern adopted by other test constructors of the era some 20 years before him. For example, to compensate for the heavily verbal orientation of the Binet, Healy and

TABLE 1. *Multiple subtest scales prior to the Wechsler scale*

Scale Author(s)	Verbal Tests	Performance Tests
Alexander (1935)	Binet	Picture completion Object assembly Block design Digit symbol
Healy and Fernald (1911)	Information Arithmetic Digits	Object assembly Block design Digit symbol
Knox (1914)	Information Digits	Picture completion Block design Object assembly
Pintner and Patterson (1917)		Picture completion Object assembly Block design Digit symbol
Terman and Chamberlain (1918)	Information Comprehension Arithmetic Digits Vocabulary	
Wells and Martin (1923)	Information Digits	Picture completion Object assembly Block design Digit symbol
Whipple (1921)	Information Comprehension Arithmetic Digits Vocabulary	
Yoakum and Yerkes (1920)	Information Comprehension Similarities Arithmetic Vocabulary	Picture arrangement Picture completion Object assembly Block design Digit symbol

Fernald (1911) assembled a variety of non-verbal tasks into a Scale. Then, in an attempt to develop a Scale to assess the intelligence of immigrants passing through Ellis Island, Knox (1914) borrowed some tasks from the Binet and from the Healy–Fernald Scale, added a few different ones and presented this as his own Scale. The Pintner–Patterson Scale (Pintner and

Patterson, 1917), the first attempt at a really standardized set of non-verbal tasks (with age norms and an overall I.Q. score), was constructed by borrowing tests from the Healy—Fernald and Knox Scales (as well as others) and reassembling them to suit their own purposes. The Army Performance Scale (Yoakum and Yerkes, 1920) was composed of tests borrowed from the Pintner—Patterson series, and the Cornell—Coxe Performance Scale (Cornell and Coxe, 1934) and the Arthur Performance Scale (Arthur, 1930) were both based on the Pintner—Patterson Scale (indeed, the Scale Grace Arthur developed was but a better standardization of the Pintner—Patterson Scale, much as we could say that the Scale Wechsler developed was but a better standardized version of the Army Tests). While Stern (1914) was calling for selection of test tasks on a more theoretical basis, the prevailing attitude in the field of test construction was the one Wechsler adopted, viz., that which seemed "good" would be chosen. And except for the work of Healy and Fernald who developed some of the tests they used in their Scale, all other Scale developers constructed their scales by borrowing from the ones which came before. So it was with Wechsler. When we add to this that Yerkes (Yerkes, Bridges and Hardwick, 1915) had called for the raw scores of a subtest to be converted into weighted scores, a sentiment echoed by Thorndike, Terman, Freeman, Colvin, Pintner, Ruml, Pressey, Henmon, Peterson, Thurstone, Woodrow, Dearborn and Haggerty (1921), Oates (1928), and West (1924), and the weighted scores transformed into standard scores suggested by Thorndike, Bregman and Cobb (1920), Thurstone (1925, 1928) and Stephenson (1931), one gets a sense of how the Wechsler Scale was, in fact, developed.

Summing up the psychometric position of the psychologists who were developing tests to assess intelligence, Conrad (1931) commented that a good general test of intelligence should:
(1) be a point scale with a definite zero point,
(2) provide scores on scales made up of equal units or should be scales so as to be converted into equal parts,
(3) include an adequate sample of tasks,
(4) measure general intelligence as well as specific aspects of intelligence,
(5) be reliable and valid, and
(6) measure verbal and non-verbal factors separately but equally.

From these statements it seems clear that the direction in which

Wechsler went in developing his Scale was dictated by the currents in the field of intelligence testing. The form of the test seemed determined by what the field of intelligence testing deemed necessary, but we still do not know why Wechsler chose to simply borrow the tasks from the Army Tests for his own Scale. As Cronbach commented in his critical assessment of the Wechsler Scale,

> one can point to numerous shortcomings. Most of these arise from Wechsler's emphasis on clinical utility rather than upon any theory of mental measurement. (Cronbach, 1949, p. 158)

While we might wish to question Wechsler, we cannot fault him in the sense that what he did was simply to follow tradition in the field of intelligence testing, for better or worse, for richer or poorer.

Different Forms of the Scale

Over the years Wechsler has developed different forms of his Scale all constructed, in form and content, on the model of the first one, Form I. Since, basically, both the structure and, to a great extent, the content of the Scales remain the same from form to form, we would expect that this essential similarity would be reflected in meaningful comparisons between the different forms. For example, since Form II is a revision of Form I we would expect that the overall I.Q. measures derived from Form I of any one individual would correlate well with the overall I.Q. measures derived from Form II for that same person. In the same manner we would expect that the performance of any one individual on the subtests of Form I would correlate well with the performance by that same individual on the subtests of Form II. Since the WAIS (Wechsler Adult Intelligence Scale) is a restandardization of Form I, we would expect the same relationship to obtain between Forms I and II and the WAIS, and since the WISC (Wechsler Intelligence Scale for Children) is a downward extension of Form II, we would expect a relatively high correlation between Form II and the WISC. By definition, we should expect a high correlation between scores on the WISC and the WISC-R, and since the WPPSI (Wechsler Preschool and Primary Scale of Intelligence) is a downward extension of the WISC, we should expect scores on the WISC-R and the WPPSI to be similar.

With regard to the comparison of performance on Form I with that from Form II, the data indicate that there is no consistent relationship between performances on these two Forms even when the same kind of subjects are involved. Thus, for example, in comparing the performance of college students on Forms I and II (Gerboth, 1950) while the correlations between the overall I.Q. measures derived from each of these two tests were relatively (modestly) high (Verbal I.Q.: .86, Performance I.Q.: .71, Full Scale I.Q.: .71), this group of subjects consistently achieved higher scores on Form I than on Form II. And in comparing the performance of adults of the same age range (20–40), the performance of individuals on Form I was found not to be consistent with regard to performance on Form II (Barry, Fulkerson, Kubala and Seaquist, 1956; Gibby, 1949). Sometimes the subjects would receive higher scores on a particular set of subtests of Form I while doing better on other subtests on Form II. Table 2 presents the data of these correlational studies.

From Table 2 we can see that the degree of the relationship of the measures from Form I as compared to Form II vary significantly from study to study. Thus, while in the study by Gibby the relatively high (particularly: Full Scale I.Q., Performance I.Q., Arithmetic, Similarities, Block design, Picture arrangement, Object assembly and Picture comple-

TABLE 2. *Correlation of Form I with Form II*

	Study	
Variable	Barry *et al* (1956)	Gibby (1949)
Verbal I.Q.	.66	.76
Performance I.Q.	.62	.82
Full Scale I.Q.	.66	.87
Information	.48	.56
Comprehension	.42	.20
Digits	.60	.65
Arithmetic	.47	.76
Similarities	.42	.71
Vocabulary	–	.93
Picture completion	.10	.87
Picture arrangement	.16	.49
Block design	.63	.87
Object assembly	.38	.53
Digit symbol	.70	.81

tion), the same relationship as found in the study by Barry *et al.* was quite low. Only with regard to Verbal I.Q. and performance on Information, Digits and Digit symbol were the data of the two studies consonant. The only study I could find where the data from Form I and II were truly alike involved the performance of institutionalized mental defectives (Hays and Schneider, 1951). It is possible to conclude, therefore, that where the performance of the subjects is inherently so unvariable (as with the institutionalized retardates), the two Forms produce similar data, but that when variability is possible, individuals demonstrate that the two Forms of the Scale are not really similar enough as to be able to say that they are generating comparable information regarding the intellectual behavior of the same individuals.

Since the WAIS is a restandardization of Form I of the Wechsler Scale, we should expect a relatively high degree of agreement on the measures for individuals taking both tests. In some studies (Goolishian and Ramsay, 1956; Karson, Pool and Freud, 1957; Prado and Schnadt, 1965) individuals achieved higher overall scores on Form I of the Scale than on the WAIS. In those studies which examined people's performance on the subtests as well (e.g. Cole and Weleba, 1956; Fitzhugh and Fitzhugh, 1964; Goolishian and Ramsay, 1956; Karson *et al.*, 1957), performance on the subtests was found to vary from test to test. The comparison of Form I and the WAIS is presented in Table 3.

When we look at the correlations between performance on Form I and the WAIS (Duncan and Barrett, 1961; Karson *et al.*, 1957; Neuringer, 1963a) we find that it appears that in general it looks like some of the I (Information, Digits) and that some of the subtests of the Performance part of Form I are easier than those same subtests of the WAIS (Digit Symbol, Object assembly, Block design and Picture completion). In reworking Form I in the construction of the WAIS, Wechsler made some changes within subtests (see the discussion of such changes by Sinnett and Mayman (1960), changes which included revising order of presentation, substituting new items for the older ones, etc.); apparently these changes affected the difficulty of the new Scale selectively, making some of the Verbal tasks more difficult, some of the Performance ones less difficult. Thus we can possibly account for the less than adequate correlations between the overall I.Q. scores and the scores on the subtests when comparing these WAIS items with those on Form I of the Scale.

TABLE 3. *Correlation of Form I with the WAIS*

	Study			
	Karson *et al* (1957)		Duncan and Barrett (1961)	Neuringer (1963a)
Variable	WBI-first	WAIS-first		
Information	.75	.58	.64	.81
Comprehension	.33	.50	.35	.51
Digits	.69	.90	.69	.70
Arithmetic	.61	.07	.58	.58
Similarities	.58	.86	.41	.56
Vocabulary	.45	.81	.72	.66
Picture arrangement	.40	.51	.18	.44
Picture completion	.70	.51	.38	.65
Block design	.75	.51	.62	.62
Object assembly	.37	.26	.49	.04
Digit symbol	.73	.67	.81	.51
Verbal I.Q.	.76	.67	.83	.89
Performance I.Q.	.56	.12	.45	.44
Full Scale I.Q.	.69	.15	–	.77

From Table 3 we can see that there is, at best, a modest relationship between performance on Form I and the WAIS, but with regard to some of the variables, the relationship is, in fact, rather low. The degree of the relationship for the same variables (that is, the correlations) varies significantly depending upon which test was administered first (Karson *et al.* 1957). From this latter finding we could conclude that the practice effect, that is, the degree of carry-over from one subtest to another, differs (probably for each person). From the former set of data we can conclude that Form I and the WAIS are not comparable sets of tasks.

When we look at the relationship of Form II and the WAIS (Quereshi and Miller, 1970) we find (as presented in Table 4) an even more modest relationship.

Light and Chambers (1958), using a relatively stable population intellectually (institutionalized mental retardates), found a .62 correlation between the Verbal I.Q. and a .77 correlation between the Full Scale I.Q. of these subjects between Form II and the WAIS. Thus, from these data it can be concluded that the adult forms of the Wechsler scales are not as comparable as intended, that is, they do not generate comparable informa-

TABLE 4. *Correlation of Form II*
with the WAIS

Variable	Correlation
Information	.68
Comprehension	.40
Arithmetic	.60
Digits	.60
Similarities	.34
Vocabulary	.71
Picture completion	.41
Picture arrangement	.24
Block design	.68
Object assembly	.35
Digit symbol	.63
Verbal I.Q.	.80
Performance I.Q.	.66
Full Scale I.Q.	.78

tion regarding an individual's intellectual performance. This would suggest that the tests cannot be used as alternate forms (as they had been intended to be).

When we look at the children's forms of the Wechsler (WISC vs the WISC-R), where we would expect similarity of performance, we find that in some studies subjects achieve higher scores on the WISC than they do on the WISC-R (e.g. Doppelt and Kaufman, 1977; Larrabee and Holroyd, 1976); sometimes the reverse is true (e.g. Hamm, Wheeler, McCallum, Herrin, Hunter and Catoe, 1976), and sometimes the relationship of performance on the WISC or the WISC-R comes out higher on the WISC-R (particularly as regards Information, Comprehension, Arithmetic, Picture completion, Picture arrangement, Object assembly or Coding (Pristo, 1978; Wheaton and Vandergriff, 1978)) with higher scores on Similarities, Digits, Vocabulary, Block design and Coding for the WISC (Pristo, 1978). In some studies, the correlation between performance on the WISC and the WISC-R is high (i.e. between the .80s and .90s (Covin, 1977a, b; Hartlage and Boone, 1977)); sometimes it is low (i.e. in the .40s and .50s (Wheaton and Vandergriff, 1978)). When we look at the obtained correlations between performance on the WISC and the WISC-R, Table 5 presents the findings from two studies: Covin (1977a) and Hamm *et al.* (1976).

TABLE 5. *Correlation of WISC with WISC-R*

Variable	Study	
	Covin (1977a)	Hamm *et al* (1976)
Information	.80	.65
Arithmetic	.52	.68
Comprehension	.40	.49
Similarities	.68	.76
Vocabulary	.55	.74
Picture completion	.44	.57
Picture arrangement	.38	.63
Block design	.49	.77
Object assembly	.64	.79
Coding	.53	.67
Verbal I.Q.	–	.86
Performance I.Q.	–	.83
Full Scale I.Q.	–	.89

From Table 5 we can conclude that while the format of the WISC-R is identical to that of the WISC and 75% of the items of the WISC-R and the WISC are identical, there are sufficient differences between these two forms of the test so as to yield different information with regard to the same set of subjects. Moreover, the nature of the information comparability differs dependent upon the kind of individual being tested. As we found when looking at the data derived from the adult forms of the Wechsler Scales, the forms for children (the WISC and the WISC-R) can not be conceived of as alternative forms.

While the WISC is a downward extension of Form II of the Wechsler Scale, I could not find any studies which related performance on the WISC and Form II. We are limited to looking at data derived from an assessment of the relationship of performance (by adolescents, where we would expect similarity of performance on the two Scales) on the WISC and Form I of the Wechsler Scale (as found in the studies by DeLattre and Cole, 1952 and Knopf, Murfett and Milstein, 1954).

From Table 6 we can conclude that while we might have expected the performance of individuals at an age where the standardization groups for both tests overlap (i.e. adolescence) to be similar, they are not. Thus, from these data we can conclude that the WISC and Form I of the Wechsler

TABLE 6. *Correlation of WISC with Form I*

	Study	
Subtest	DeLattre and Cole (1952)	Knopf *et al* (1954)
Information	.53	.70
Arithmetic	.54	.63
Digits	.71	.71
Comprehension	.48	.54
Similarities	.68	.55
Vocabulary	.55	.83
Picture completion	.69	.63
Picture arrangement	.19	.22
Block design	.49	.66
Object assembly	.56	.01
Digit symbol/coding	.65	.41

Scale yield different information regarding the intellectual performance of individuals of an age range where similarity of performance would be expected. Moreover, the WISC tended to be the easier task (that is, generated higher I.Q.s) for the adolescent than Form I of the Scale (Knopf *et al.*, 1954; Price and Thorne, 1955; Vanderhost, Sloan and Benberg, 1953).

With regard to the comparison between the WAIS and the WISC, sometimes subjects (high school students) achieved higher scores on the WISC (Barclay, Friedman and Fidel, 1969; Quereshi, 1968a) and sometimes no differences were found (Ross and Morledge, 1967). Hanon and Kicklighter (1970) found that, with regard to their sample of 16-year-olds, individuals with I.Q.s below average achieved higher scores on the WAIS; individuals with average or above average intelligence achieved higher scores on the WISC; as did Webb (1973) and Wesner (1963) Quereshi (1968a or b) found the correlations shown in Table 7 between items on the WAIS and the WISC.

From Table 7 we can see that while the overall I.Q. measures reflect consonance, the relationship (correlation) between the subtests on the WAIS and the WISC, except for a few items (e.g. Information and Vocabulary), is really quite low. Thus, even though the age-range of the subjects (adolescents) overlap with regard to the standardization groups for the WAIS and the WISC, and, hence, we should expect similarity of their performance on each test, their performance does not demonstrate that (Silverstein, 1968d; Simpson, 1970a).

TABLE 7. *Correlation of the WISC*
with the WAIS

Variable	Correlation
Information	.86
Arithmetic	.57
Digits	.67
Comprehension	.54
Similarities	.54
Vocabulary	.93
Picture completion	.61
Picture arrangement	.17
Block design	.53
Object assembly	.55
Coding/Digit symbol	.76
Verbal I.Q.	.94
Performance I.Q.	.84
Full Scale I.Q.	.95

With regard to the relationship of the WPPSI to the WISC, since the WPPSI is a downward extension of the WISC (with some modification) we might expect a reasonable degree of relationship between performance on these two forms of the Wechsler, and that is what we find (e.g. Yater, Boyd and Barclay, 1975).

What can we conclude from this overview of the assessment of the relationship between the various forms of Wechsler's Scale? In the first place, we can see that the changes Wechsler instituted in constructing new forms of his Scale introduce significant enough differences between the tests such that, as for example, with regard to the three adult forms of the Scale (i.e. Forms I and II and the WAIS) and the three forms of the Scale for use with children (i.e. the WISC, WISC-R and WPPSI), individuals do significantly different on one form of the Scale as compared to their performance on the other form of the Scale (within the same age range). Thus, the different forms of the Scale cannot be considered alternative forms of the Scale; test—retest correlations would be affected by the built-in, at best modest, relationship of the data derived from one form of the Scale as compared to another. Moreover, it seems clear from the research that the differences in the performance of the same individuals on different forms of the Scale are obscured by examining the overall I.Q. measures (i.e. Verbal, Performance, and Full Scale I.Q.s), but are highlighted when looking at the performance of individuals on the subtests. It would appear that the different forms of the test generate somewhat different information regarding the intellectual behavior of individuals.

Yankee Ingenuity

There is something about Americans which prompts us to want to "get down to basics," as it were. Perhaps it has something to do with the rapid way our country developed; "streamlining," alleviation of unnecessary "frills" seems to characterize our life — socially, artistically, politically, and philosophically. This need to find the least amount of time and effort to accomplish the task has found its way into the field of intelligence testing, in general, and with regard to testing with the Wechsler Scales, in particular. One such direction has been to devise a method of testing groups of individuals at the same time. Eme and Walker (1969) utilize four of the subtests (Information, Similarities, Picture completion and Digit symbol) to test groups. They have found a respectable correlation (.88) between the I.Q. derived from this group administration as compared to the traditional individual mode. Elwood (Elwood, 1969, 1972a; Elwood and Griffin, 1972) and Mishra (1971) have devised automated ways of administering parts of the Scales (again, with respectable, i.e. correlations between the machine- and clinician-administered versions of the tests in the .90s). Another direction has been to abbreviate the Scales.

Doll (1917) had offered an abbreviated form of the Binet, so the idea is neither new nor unique to the Wechsler Scales. This method of abbreviation involved giving only selected tests at each age level. Correlation of the overall assessment of I.Q. from this method with the same assessment made from the traditional mode of administration was relatively high (in the .80s). On the other hand, Terman (1918) had found that just using the Vocabulary subtest of the Binet yielded high (in the .90s) correlations with the I.Q. as derived from the administration of the Full Scale.

Abbreviations of the Wechsler Scales have basically followed these two models, viz., single subtests being administered in isolation, or selection of items from the total Scale. As regards the singling out of individual subtests, Brown (1942) had suggested that an individual's performance on Arithmetic could substitute for an estimate of the Full Scale I.Q., and following Terman's example with the Binet, Rabin (1944a) recommended the utilization of the Vocabulary subtest of the Wechsler as an alternate to administering the entire Scale when an estimate of intellectual level is all that is needed. To demonstrate the effectiveness of the Vocabulary subtest in this regard, Rabin correlated the performance of patients on the Vocabulary subtest with their Full Scale I.Q. The results were that the correlations for patients were: neurotics, .68; schizophrenics, .75; manic-depressives, .77; patients without psychosis, .86; and luetics, .98. There was, therefore, at least a modest relationship found with some of the patients, and a good relationship with others, between Vocabulary and Full Scale I.Q. Perhaps it might be safe to presume that patients with greater manifest psychopathology did more poorly on Vocabulary thereby diluting what in other instances turned out to be a respectable relationship between performance on Vocabulary and overall performance.

Subsequent studies exploring the relationship between Vocabulary and Full Scale I.Q. on the Wechsler test (e.g. Patterson, 1946b; Wildman and Wildman, 1977) have only confirmed Rabin's findings, yielding a correlation between Vocabulary and Full Scale I.Q. in the .90s. The relationship between Vocabulary and Full Scale I.Q. is so substantial that individuals have selected only a part of the Vocabulary subtest (e.g. Armstrong, 1955, Brown, 1968; Burton, 1968; Finkelstein, Gerboth and Westerhold, 1952; Jastak and Jastak, 1964) and found correlations between scores on even this abbreviated Vocabulary subtest and Full Scale I.Q. in the .90s. The correlations of the other subtests with Full Scale I.Q. were not as high (e.g. Wechsler 1949); thus it is not surprising that researchers have not offered other subtests of the Wechsler Scale as adequate alternatives to the Full Scale when an estimate of that Full Scale I.Q. is needed. Unlike the Binet, which we saw had been criticized for being too heavily loaded with verbal items throughout, the Vocabulary subtest of the Wechsler Scale constitutes but one eleventh of the total Scale. Thus, while the relationship of a person's performance on the Vocabulary subtest with the overall I.Q. derived from the Binet could be viewed as an artifact, a function of the fact that the Binet constituted, in the main, tests of verbal functions, one cannot make this claim with the Wechsler. The correlation of Vocabulary with Full Scale I.Q. of the Wechsler can be taken to mean that Vocabulary correlates well with performance on the non-verbal, Performance subtests as well.

Doll had selected various parts of the Binet and considered them as an abbreviated form of the Test. Similarly, with the Wechsler, a variety of such abbreviated forms have been offered. Wechsler, himself, discussed the issue of abbreviated forms of his test (Wechsler, 1944, p. 145). He thought the Scale could be shortened to five subtests, "provided a judicious choice of subtests is made." Wechsler suggested that since the Verbal I.Q. correlated so highly with the Full Scale I.Q., that it would seem meaningful that if an abbreviated form of the test was warranted, the full test be reduced to the Verbal subtests. Rabin (1943) was the first to recommend a short form of the Wechsler composed of but three subtests: Comprehension, Arithmetic and Similarities. He chose these subtests based on "clinical experience and observation." Rabin correlated a score derived from performance on these three subtests with Full Scale I.Q. for nurses and patients in a state hospital (both psychotic and neurotic). With the nurses, Rabin found that performance on these three subtests correlated .51 with their Performance I.Q. (not an unexpected finding since the three subtests are part of the Verbal Scale items), .88 with their Verbal I.Q., and .80 with the Full Scale I.Q. The findings with the patients were even better; for them, the C-A-S correlated .76 with their Performance I.Q., .95 with their Verbal I.Q., and .96 with their Full Scale I.Q. Cross-validation of Rabin's work (Franklin, 1945; Springer, 1946) substantiated his findings.

The relationship to Full Scale I.Q. of all manner of combinations of subtests has been examined. Gurvitz (1945) for example, offered a combination of performance on Digits and Picture arrangement which he found correlated in the .80s and low .90s with Full Scale I.Q. Cummings, MacPhee and Wright (1946) offered performance on Comprehension and Arithmetic as a substitute for the Full Scale I.Q. (with correlations in the .80s). Hunt and French (1949) offered Picture arrangement and Picture completion; Simpson and Bridges (1959), Block design and Vocabulary (supported by subsequent research, e.g. Silverstein, 1967a–d, 1970a, 1971; Wight and Sandry, 1962), and Information and Picture completion (Nickols, 1962). Following Rabin's utilization of a combined score from three subtests, Hunt (Hunt, French, Klebanoff, Mensh and Williams, 1948a; Hunt and French, 1952) utilized a combination score from Comprehension, Vocabulary and Similarities; Bay and Berks (1948), Comprehension,

Similarities and Digit symbol; Hafner *et al.* (1978), Similarities, Picture arrangement and Block design; Murphy and Langston (1956), Information, Comprehension and Block design; Schneyer (1957), Comprehension, Block design and Digits; Sloan and Newman (1955), Similarities, Picture arrangement and Block design. Altus (1945) offered a score composed of performance on four subtests (Information, Comprehension, Arithmetic and Similarities), while Geil (1945) offered Comprehension, Similarities, Digits and Block design. Kriegman and Hansen (1947) found high correlations between Vocabulary, Information, Block design, Similarities and Full Scale I.Q. (a finding supported by subsequent research, e.g. Caldwell and Davis, 1956; McKenzie, 1951). Other four-subtest combinations have been: Vocabulary, Comprehension, Block design and Object assembly (Britton and Savage, 1966); Arithmetic, Similarities, Picture arrangement, and Object assembly (Clements, 1965); Information, Comprehension, Picture arrangement and Vocabulary (Cole, Williams, Nix and Litaker, 1967); Comprehension, Similarities, Picture arrangement and Block design (Cotzin and Gallagher, 1950), Information, Comprehension, Similarities and Vocabulary (Dana, 1957a); Information, Digits, Vocabulary and Picture completion (Dorken and Greenbloom, 1953); Similarities, Vocabulary, Block design and Picture arrangement (Duke, 1967); Arithmetic, Vocabulary, Block design and Picture arrangement (Himelstein, 1957a); Information, Arithmetic, Digits and Picture completion (Nickols and Nickols, 1963); and Vocabulary, Arithmetic, Block design and Object assembly (Stroud, 1957). Doppelt (1956) intercorrelated each subtest of the Verbal Scale with every other subtest of the Verbal Scale and then selected the four which correlated the highest: Arithmetic, Vocabulary, Block design and Picture arrangement, and found a high correlation between these subtests and Full Scale I.Q., a finding supported by subsequent research, e.g. Bassett and Gayton (1969), Clayton and Payne (1959), Feldman (1968), Fisher and Shotwell (1959), Himelstein (1957b, c), Kaufman (1972), Levinson (1957), McKerracher and Watson (1968), McKerracher, Watson, Little and Winter (1968), Monroe (1966), Olin and Reznikoff (1957), Sines and Simmons (1959), Smith (1971), Sterne (1957), Whitmyre and Pishkin (1958).

Patterson (1948) had offered a combination score composed of five subtests: Vocabulary, Comprehension, Block design and Picture completion. Other five-subtest combinations were: Information, Picture arrangement,

Picture completion, Block design and Coding (Finley and Thompson, 1958) (cross-validated by Thompson and Finley, 1962); Coyle and Bellamy, 1970), Arithmetic, Digits, Vocabulary, Picture arrangement and Object assembly (Karras, 1963), and Karras found high correlations between Full Scale I.Q. and a six-subtest abbreviation comprised of Information, Comprehension, Similarities, Digit symbol, Block design and Picture completion.

The amazing aspect of all of these studies is that *any* of the combinations of the subtests were found to correlate with Full Scale I.Q. in the .90s with any kind of subject: normal, psychiatric or mentally retarded. As the research mounted, it became clear that perhaps there was no difference in the estimation of the Full Scale I.Q. made from *any* combination of the subtests and investigators began examining this hypothesis. Gurvitz (1951) experimented with all possible combinations of two of the subtests; Osborne and Allen (1962) experimented with all possible three-subtest combinations; Hunt, Klebanoff, Mensh and Williams (1948b) compared the relationship of some two- and three-subtest combinations with Full Scale I.Q., McNemar (1950) examined the relationship of *every* possible combination of subtests — every two-, three-, four-, and five-subtest combination — and found all of them adequate to estimate Full Scale I.Q. McNemar found correlations of .80 with Full Scale I.Q. for the two-subtest combinations, correlations in the .90s for all the rest, a finding that was to be found by all other investigators who replicated the paradigm established by McNemar (e.g. Carleton and Stacey, 1954; Cotzin and Gallagher, 1949; Enburg, Rowley and Stone, 1961; Herring, 1952; Hilden, Taylor and DuBois, 1952; Howard, 1959; Jones, 1962, 1967; Maxwell, 1957; Schwartz and Levitt, 1960; Silverstein, 1967e, 1968a, b, 1975; Stricker, Merbaum and Tangeman, 1969).

Wolfson and Bachelis (1960) developed an abbreviated form of the Wechsler in a unique manner to that which has been described up until now. Instead of selected *subtests*, Wolfson and Bachelis selected selected *items* from each of the subtests of the Verbal Scale. This short form of the WAIS was composed of every third item of the Information and Vocabulary subtests, the odd-numbered items of Comprehension, Arithmetic and Similarities, and all of the Digits subtest. Saltz and Mogel (1962) followed this pattern of item selection, but whereas Wolfson and Bachelis limited themselves to items of the subtests of the Verbal Scale, Satz and Mogel expanded that to include samplings from all of the subtests. Thus, the short form developed by Satz and Mogel consisted of every third item of Information, Vocabulary and Picture completion, and odd-numbered items of Comprehension, Arithmetic, Similarities, Block design, Picture arrangement and Object assembly, leaving Digits and Digit symbol intact. They found that this short form correlated with Full Scale I.Q. in the .90s, a finding that has been corroborated by subsequent research (e.g. Adams, Kobos and Preston, 1977; Estes, 1963; Finch, Childress and Ollendick, 1974a; Finch, Thornton and Montgomery, 1974b; Goebel and Satz, 1975; Holmes, Armstrong, Johnson and Ries, 1965, 1966; Luzki, Laywell, Schultz and Dawes, 1970; Marsh, 1973; Meikle, 1968; Mogel and Satz, 1963; Resnick and Entin, 1971; Satz, Van De Riet and Mogel, 1967b; Silverstein, 1968b, c; Tipton and Stroud, 1973; Watkins and Kinzie, 1970; Watson, 1966; Zytowski and Hudson, 1965). Following Satz and Mogel, Yudin (1966) developed a short form for the WISC, while King and Smith (1972) used the same format to develop a short form of the WPPSI. As with adults, these abbreviated forms of the children's form of the Wechsler Scale (WISC) proved to be adequate in estimating Full Scale I.Q. (e.g. Erikson, 1967; Gayton, Wilson and Bernstein, 1970; Preston, 1978; Rasbury, Falgout and Perry, 1978; Reid, Moore and Alexander, 1968; and Tarkington and Ricker, 1969). Finch, Childress and Ollendick (1973a) and Finch, Ollendick and Gino (1973b) developed a short form (the Devereux Short Form) which was, in large measure, a slight modification of the Satz and Mogel short form, which correlated with overall I.Q. in the .90s. Pauker (1963) constructed an abbreviated test by arbitrarily selecting half of the items of every subtest of the Scale. Comparative analysis of the effectiveness of the Doppelt and Satz and Mogel short forms have shown them both to be effective in estimating Full Scale I.Q. (Preston, 1978).

While the obtained relationships between virtually all abbreviated forms of the Wechsler Scale and Full Scale I.Q. appear high (in the .80s and .90s), the real question is how useful these short forms are beyond correlating with the Full Scale I.Q. Stroud (1957) found that a four-subtest abbreviation of the WISC (Vocabulary, Arithmetic, Block design, Object assembly) correlated .73 with reading ability. The relationship of all of the other short forms with some dimension of, for example, scholastic ability, remains to be explored. The assumption is probably being made that if the Full Scale I.Q. correlates satisfactorily with scholastic abilities (a topic which will be covered in Chapter 8), and the abbreviated Scale relates well to the Full Scale measures, then the abbreviated Scale must relate well to scholastic ability as well. Undoubtedly that remains to be tested.

Cummings *et al.* (1946) found that in assessing the intellectual level of mentally retarded adults, the I.Q.s derived from a brief three-subtest form of the Wechsler (Arithmetic, Vocabulary and Similarities) was reliable when the I.Q. was in the 50 to 100 range; with I.Q.s above 100, the brief form becomes unreliable. Luzki *et al.* (1970) found the split-half reliability of the short forms to be high (estimated Full Scale I.Q. in the .90s). That, then, is another aspect of I.Q.s derived from brief forms of the Wechsler — their reliability. I.Q.s estimated from the short forms were slightly higher than I.Q.s estimated from the long form (Luzki *et al.*, 1970).

Probably the most serious criticism of the brief forms of the Wechsler are:

(1) that while the I.Q. derived from the short forms correlates highly with Full Scale I.Q. with regard to group data, the degree of accuracy of identifying a given protocol is, at best, modest (e.g. Finch *et al.*, 1974a, b; King and Smith, 1972; Kramer and Francis, 1965; Love, 1969; Mumpower, 1964; Sines and Simmons, 1959), with the degree of accuracy hovering round 60%, and

(2) while bearing some (60%) relationship to individual Full Scale I.Q. (as noted above), short forms do not lend themselves to clinical use (Gurvitz, 1945; Kaldegg, 1960; Luzki *et al.*, 1970). MacPhee, Wright and Cummings (1947) note that at different I.Q. levels, subtests make different contributions towards the Full Scale estimate, meaning that at each level, the validity (and reliability) of estimates from brief forms of the Wechsler test may vary. In this regard, Paulson and Lin (1970) write about "Age: The neglected variable in constructing an abbreviated WAIS." In the end, those individuals who have surveyed the research on short forms (e.g. Bersoff, 1971; Levy, 1968; Tellegen and Briggs, 1967) waxed unimpressed.

If a rapid estimate of an individual's level of intelligence is needed, Hanna (1950), Sperba and Adlerstein (1961), and Templer and Hartlage (1969) found that an adequate assessment can be made in an interview (back to the consistently high correlation between Vocabulary and Full Scale I.Q., probably being done through the implicit or explicit analysis of an individual's use of language). Bailey and Gibby (1971) found that by the twelfth grade, individuals can estimate themselves what they achieved on a formal test of intelligence (the Otis). Therefore, if a quick assessment of an individual's I.Q. is needed, there seems to be no dearth of ways of attaining that, from administering one subtest of the Scale (e.g. Vocabulary) or any combination of subtests, by interview, or just by asking the subject his own estimate. However, as Mateer (1918) observed long ago about the non-specific informational value of the I.Q. or the M.A., if we are going to use the Wechsler Scale data, we are going to have to look at data derived from an analysis of the Full Scale.

CHAPTER 2

The Clinical Use of the Wechsler Scales

ALTHOUGH Wechsler spent some 7 years at Bellevue Psychiatric Hospital developing his test (Wechsler, 1932), when he finally published his test (Wechsler, 1939) he was very conservative regarding the clinical use of the data. The first book on the test focused on the issues of intelligence, viz., the nature of intelligence, the concept of the I.Q. (as compared to Mental Age), the classification of intelligence, the need for an adult intelligence scale, and a description of the test and the standardization data. There was, however, one chapter on "The Problem of Mental Deterioration." It was Wechsler's observations over the years of experience with his test that intellectual abilities develop to a point (around the age of 25) after which the brain weight and the concomitant functions of the brain begin to decline. It was his observation that some of the tests in the Scale reflected this decline more than others. From this, he developed the notion of the Deterioration Quotient. This Quotient consisted of the ratio of those tests which held up in spite of the aging process (what Wechsler referred to as the "Hold" tests), to those where the aging process induced impairment (what Wechsler referred to as the "Don't Hold" tests). Those tests Wechsler observed to hold up in spite of the aging process were: Information, Comprehension, Object assembly, Picture completion and Vocabulary. Those tests Wechsler observed to manifest decline with aging were: Digits, Arithmetic, Digit symbol (or Picture arrangement), Block design, and Similarities. Wechsler assumed that the intellective decline he observed in response to the aging process constituted a configuration of subtests which would reflect psychological deterioration whatever the cause. Thus, Wechsler employed the Deterioration Quotient to examine the intellectual disability which occurred in a variety of mental disorders: dementia praecox, chronic alcoholism, senile dementia, general paresis as well as organic brain disorder for which the Deterioration

30

Quotient was originally devised. The Table Wechsler constructed to show the relative impairment of specific psychological functions in these different psychiatric disorders were not based on the data of *his* test, but was information extracted from Wells (1927) which reflected the kind of psychological impairment one could expect with each specific psychiatric disorder.

First, as regards the Deterioration Quotient (developed to reflect impairment due to aging) being used to assess intellectual impairment as might be found in various psychiatric disorders. The assumption is being made that impairment, is impairment, is impairment; that the kind of impairment in intellective functions due to aging should be the same as the kind of impairment due to psychological/psychiatric factors. The validity of that notion will be explored later.

As regards the expectation of which psychological functions would be impaired in specific psychiatric disorders, we find Wechsler basing his work on that which he seems to base all of his work on, viz., empirical evidence, either his or that which appears to be traditionally observed by others in the field. Wechsler offers no psychological rationale for why some tests should reflect impairment, whether due to aging or psychiatric disorder; experience dictates that they do (the same *modus operandi* we have seen Wechsler use in selecting the subtests for his Scale). When, in the second edition of his book (Wechsler, 1941a) Wechsler does spell out the use of the subtest data of his test for clinical assessment, he also offers no theoretical rationale; he bases his notions on experience that had been gleaned through the use of his test.

However, Wechsler *could* have established the rationale for the clinical use of his Scale on theoretical/psychological principles *if* he had chosen to. Wechsler might have noted that 19th-century psychiatry in France (Baldwin, 1894) and Germany (Binet and Henri, 1895) had begun to examine psychopathology from the point of view of psychological functions. In this regard, he could have cited the work of such notables in psychiatry who were studying psychiatric disorders from a psychological point of view such as Kraepelin (1902) or Adolf Meyer (1906), and/or he could have cited the work of psychologists who supported this view of psychopathology, e.g. Babcock (1930), Bijou (1942a, b), Bolles (1937), Curtis (1918), Hanfmann (1944), Hunt and Older (1944), Lewinski (1943), Manson (1925), Pressey (1917), Pressey and Cole (1918), Tendler

(1932), Wallin (1917, 1918), Wells and Kelley (1920), Wentworth (1924), Wylie (1902). He could have noted the work of other individuals in the testing movement who, after years of experience, reasoned that non-intellectual factors did, indeed, influence intellectual performance, e.g. Binet and Henri (1895), Binet and Simon (1905), Downey (1917), Pearson (1906), Hart and Spearman (1914), Spearman (1927, 1939), Terman (1916), Thorndike *et al.* (1921), Cattell (1930), Roe and Shakow (1942). He could have cited the summation of ideas in the testing of intelligence as found in the literature:

> The (intelligence) test should, ideally, be more than simply an instrument to measure an individual's specific fields of intellective strength and weaknesses . . . the intelligence tests should, in addition, be at least suggestive of unusual strength or deficiencies in temperamental or character traits. (Conrad, 1931, p. 80)

and the psychological research which supported this idea, e.g., Alexander (1935), Brown (1923, 1924), Cattell (1930), Poffenberger and Carpenter (1924), Webb (1915). Wechsler could have based a rationale for the expectation that intelligence test data would/should reflect personality characteristics from a psychoanalytic point of view (as did Rapaport (Escalona and Rapaport, 1944; Rapaport, 1942, 1946) or Schafer (1946)) or from a gestalt psychology point of view (as did Allport (Allport and Vernon, 1933; Allport, 1937), William Stern (1938) or Martin Scheerer (1946)). Wechsler could have cited research which supported the subjective nature of cognition (beginning with the seminal work of Henry Murray (1933), and including the related studies by Ansbacher (1937), Barker (1938), Brady (1933), Neff (1937), Sanford (1936, 1937), Sears (1936, 1937), and Sherif (1935)), or the non-clinical psychologists who demonstrated the influence of motivation and motivational factors on perception (e.g. Lewin (1935) and Heidbreder (1945)). Wechsler's discussions of the non-intellective factors in intelligence (e.g. Wechsler (1940, 1943, 1950)) make but passing reference to a very small number of studies. However, as is consistent with his generally non-theoretical, pragmatic approach, Wechsler bases the use of the data from his tests for clinical assessment on experience; the different subtest configurations proffered for different psychiatric groups is based purely on experience, that which has been found, is.

In eschewing a theoretical orientation for the clinical use of the data from his intelligence test, Wechsler forces us to either accept his pragmatic position or to develop a rationale of our own. However, from what has just been presented, such a rationale should not be hard to develop. From the afore-stated theoretical as well as pragmatic positions it seems clear that:

(a) what we call intelligence or intelligent behaviour is a function of the application of learning, experience, and natural endowment and cognitive ability to problem solving, and

(b) research precludes isolating thinking and perceiving from emotional or attitudinal factors, so that

(c) we would/could/should expect that a test of cognitive functions should be affected by other aspects of an individual's personality than "efficiency," thus

(d) the Wechsler test, as a test of cognitive functioning, can be expected to yield information regarding personological factors.

It did not seem to take great effort to establish a psychological rationale for the clinical use of Wechsler test data; the problem is not in the rationale, but how the assumption has been stated. Basically, while accepting the fact that factors other than intellectual level influence an individual's performance on a test of intelligence, clinicians (including Wechsler) seem to have committed the error of isomorphism in doing so. There seems to be an expectation that there will be a direct, undiluted, one-to-one relationship between emotional and attitudinal factors, on the one hand, and cognitive factors, on the other, and/or that a universal law can be developed which will describe this relationship as it would be expected to be found in all individuals. A second assumption seems to be that once the intellective factor is extracted from an individual's performance on a test of intelligence, that which is left is personality (normal or pathological). The validity of these assumptions will affect what we will find as regards the performance of clinical groups on the Wechsler tests, data we will be exploring in subsequent chapters. With what clarity, directness and uniqueness personality factors emerge from an analysis of subtest performance remains to be seen.

The Deterioration Quotient

As we have already noted, when Wechsler embarked upon the clinical use of his test of intelligence (that is, for the assessment of non-intellective aspects of the performance on the subtests) he was quite conservative.

Moreover, whether in constructing his test or analyzing test data clinically, he seemed to follow established trends in the field. As we have noted the most notable clinical application of the data from his test was in terms of the assessment of intellectual deterioration due to aging. On the basis of his experience and the work of his predecessors such as Babcock (1930), Wechsler, we have seen, noted that some tests seemed to hold up in spite of aging (viz., Information, Comprehension, Vocabulary, Object assembly, and Picture completion) while others seem to become impaired more easily as a function of aging (viz., Digits, Similarities, Block design, and Digit symbol). The ratio of the "Don't Hold" to the "Hold" tests Wechsler termed the Deterioration Quotient.

The notion that only some aspects of psychological functioning are significantly influenced by the aging process had been part of clinical lore; failing memory and temporal disorientation are but two examples of processes that reflect deterioration due to aging. Such a clinical observation was supported by the research. Babcock (1930), for example, noted that while other psychological functions declined with age, Vocabulary did not. Indeed, Babcock utilized performance on Vocabulary as the standard against which to plot the performance of an individual on other intellectual tasks as a measure of deterioration. In general, the research appears to uphold that assumption (e.g. Berkowitz, 1953; Berkowitz and Green, 1963; Bersoff, 1970; Birren and Morrison, 1961; Cleveland and Dysinger, 1944; Fox, 1947; Jones and Conrad, 1933). Thus it is not surprising that Wechsler should include Vocabulary in his category of subtest performances which hold up in spite of aging. However, Wechsler's notions about the influence of aging on intellective behaviour is more complex than that proffered by Babcock; Wechsler, we see, presupposes that functions other than world knowledge and word usage also hold up in spite of aging.

The research findings are equivocal with regard to what degree of support can be given to Wechsler's notion regarding the nature of the intellectual deterioration due to aging. Thus, while some studies support the validity of the Deterioration Quotient (e.g. Blum, Fosshage and Jarvix, 1972 Botwinick and Birren, 1951a, b; Fox and Birren, 1950; Kraus, 1966; Kraus and Selecki, 1965; Levi, Oppenheim and Wechsler, 1945; Rogers, 1950a; Sloan, 1947), we can point to other studies wherein Wechsler's assumptions regarding which subtests hold up with age and which do not, are not supported (e.g. Bensberg and Sloan, 1950; Botwinick and Birren, 1951a, b; Corsini and Fassett, 1952; Hunt, 1943; Jackson, 1955; Norman and Daley, 1959). And Bolton, Britton and Savage (1966) found that the deterioration index for the WAIS data and that computed from the data from Form I do not yield comparable results, thereby complicating cross-validational studies which may utilize different forms of the test.

Wechsler assumed that the intellectual deterioration reflected in aging could also be reflected in other forms of psychopathology where mental deterioration is manifest clinically. Explorations of the validity of the notion that the Deterioration Quotient was more a measure of general mental deterioration have yielded findings which do not support this hypothesis (e.g. Bersoff, 1970; Garfield and Fey, 1948; Schlosser and Kantor, 1949). The performance of psychiatric groups with differing degrees of severity of psychopathology (e.g. neurotic vs psychotic) were not differentiated by the Quotient. Boehm and Sarason (1947) concluded that Wechsler's formula did not distinguish intellectual deterioration from mental deficiency. The Deterioration Quotient was found to correctly identify mental deterioration only approximately 75% of the time (Blake and McCarty, 1948; Rogers, 1950a), and Dorken and Greenbloom (1953) found that the Deterioration Quotient did not identify as deteriorated a large number of patients who were, in fact, clinically diagnosed as deteriorated.

Some of the problems with the Deterioration Quotient appear to relate to some of the functions Wechsler assumes to hold up with age. For example, while Wechsler assumes that performance on the Object Assembly subtest held up in spite of the aging process, Allen (1948a) and Krauss (1966) found otherwise. The sex of the subject is sometimes seen to influence intellectual decline (e.g. Norman, 1966), sometimes not (Howell, 1955b). Another issue pertains to the assumption that performance of the Vocabulary subtest holds up with age. Capps (1939) demonstrated that if one looks critically (more intensively) at the definitions offered by subjects in defining the words, significant qualitative differences, though scored the same, could be discerned in the responses given. Thus a stringent analysis of the meanings of words does reveal changes that a less critical assessment misses (e.g. Capps, 1939; Orme, 1957). Of course, grouping subjects with different degrees of deterioration in the same clinical group because of a common diagnosis, as well as grouping a variety of kinds of cerebral dysfunction into one group, thereby ignoring the particular contribution to psychological impairment different conditions make, cannot help but influence the outcome of studies trying to assess the validity of Deterioration Quotient. Since most studies attempting to assess the validity of the Deterioration Quotient ignore these factors, in all fairness to Wechsler, one could conclude that most of the research assessing the validity of the Deterioration Quotient as a measure of psychological impairment characteristic of cerebral disorders or of psychiatric impairment, *sui generis*, is invalid.

The Discrepancy Between Verbal and Performance I.Q.s

Rather than draw inferences from performance of different psychiatric types on specific subtests, Wechsler chose to remain at a more general level of analysis of these data. We have seen how Wechsler looked at those tests which did not reflect deterioration due to aging and those which did (the Hold/Don't Hold differentiation). Another such general measure for Wechsler was the discrepancy between the Verbal and Performance I.Q.s. "Apart from their possible relation to vocational attitudes," wrote Wechsler, "different verbal and performance test scores, particularly when large, have a special interest for the clinician because such discrepancies are frequently associated with certain types of mental pathology" (1944, p. 146). Of the clinical groups who fared better on the Verbal tests, Wechsler listed: people with organic brain disease, psychoses, and neuroses. Those who fared better on the Performance part of the Scale were adolescent psychopaths and mental defectives. With regard to the differential performance of individuals from different cultural groups, Wechsler noted that Jewish children do better on the Verbal subtests, Italian children on the Performance subtests, and he noted research on the performance of Blacks was still needed.

Once again, the expectation of this differential performance on the Verbal and Performance tasks by these various clinical groups rests not on some theoretical formulation, but on clinical experience. I dare say Wechsler could have attempted a rationale (even *post hoc*) in terms of differential cognitive functions affected by various psychopathological conditions, but he remains consistent with the pragmatic approach which so typifies his work.

Another problem regarding the discrepancy between the Verbal and Performance tasks is: what constitutes "large"? Wechsler suggested that "For subjects with I.Q.s not far from the average, a variation of 8 to 10 points between verbal and performance in either direction is within the normal range" (1944, p. 147). For a definition of "large" Wechsler stated that a large Verbal-Performance difference was 10 to 15 points or more. What of individuals whose I.Q. is far from the average? Wechsler states, "the amount (of discrepancy between the Verbal and Performance I.Q.s) as well as the direction of the difference also varies with the age and intelligence level of the individual" (1944, p. 147). However, we are not provided with any guidelines with regards to the discrepancy between Verbal and Performance functioning at levels beyond (in both directions) the average, nor of different age groups. We are, therefore, limited to discover what groups perform better on the Verbal and Performance parts of the Scale and whatever else the research done on the discrepancy between better performance on verbal vs the non-verbal tests demonstrates.

To review, Wechsler posited that the following clinical groups would do better on the Verbal tasks: organics, psychotics, and neurotics. Studies with patients with organic disorders (e.g. Angers, 1958; Black, 1974a; Ladd, 1964) support the V > P pattern. Harwood and Naylor (1971), Overall, Hoffman and Levin (1978), and Rust, Barnard and Oster (1979) found the V > P in the aged as well, individuals who we can assume have cerebral dysfunction also. As regards the performance of psychotics, Brown (1967) and Rabin (1941, 1942a) found that schizophrenics yielded the V > P patterns of performance as Wechsler anticipated.

As regards cultural factors, Wechsler posited that Jewish individuals would do better on the Verbal tasks than on the Performance ones, and the research supports his notion (e.g. Levinson, 1958, 1959, 1962, 1963b; Wendt and Burwell, 1964). The research also demonstrates that Blacks also do better on the verbal than on the non-verbal tasks (Levinson, 1963).

Wechsler postulated that the adolescent psychopath and the mental defective would do better, in general, on the Performance tasks. The research demonstrates that the majority of delinquent (or sociopathic) youths do do better on the non-verbal tasks (e.g. Andrew, 1974; Bernstein and Corsini, 1953; Corotto, 1961; Fisher, 1961; Manne, Kandel and

Rosenthal, 1962; Saccuzzo and Lewandowski, 1976; and Wiens, Matarazzo and Gaver, 1959). In addition, Army and Air Force prisoners (Clark and Moore, 1950), conduct disorders (Dean, 1977), adult criminals (Kahn, 1968) also do better on the non-verbal tasks than the verbal ones. Newman and Loos (1955) and Warren and Kraus (1961) found that mental defective individuals did, indeed, yield the P > V pattern as Wechsler predicted. The research also indicated that individuals with learning disabilities performed (as might be expected) better on the non-verbal than the verbal tasks (e.g. Holroyd, 1968; Rourke *et al.*, 1971, 1973). The research also demonstrated that individuals from the lower socioeconomic groups also fared better on the Performance part of the Scale (e.g. Marks and Klahn, 1961; Ravenette and Kahn, 1962; Telegdy, 1973). The research also indicates that Northern Blacks not only did better on the Verbal tasks than Southern Blacks (Teahan and Drews, 1962) but they also showed a greater degree of similarity between their Performance and Verbal I.Q.s than did Southern Blacks, who demonstrated a marked discrepancy in their Verbal and Performance I.Q.s.

Thus far we could state that Wechsler's assumptions regarding the ratio of Verbal to Performance I.Q.s in different psychiatric groups has been validated. However, there are those inevitable studies that can be cited which do not support Wechsler's hypotheses. For example, athough we have seen that some individuals diagnosed as organic did do better on the verbal subtests, there are studies wherein organics did not function in that manner on the Wechsler Scale (e.g. Parsons and Kemp, 1960; Rowley, 1961; Woody, 1968). Whereas we did find that some studies supported Wechsler's notion that psychotics would perform better on the Verbal subtests than the Performance, studies can be cited where this effect did not obtain (e.g. Bolton *et al.*, 1966; Holmes, 1968; Loro and Woodward, 1976; Olch, 1948; Schoonover and Hartel, 1970; Weider, 1943). And while some researchers had found that the aged follow the expected pattern for organics, some (e.g. Eisdorfer *et al.*, 1959) did not.

While some support (cited above) was found for Wechsler's idea that adolescent psychopaths would do better on the non-verbal as compared to the verbal tasks, research can be cited which presents data contrary to that finding (e.g. Camp, 1966; Fernald and Wisser, 1967; Field, 1960b; Foster, 1959; Frost and Frost, 1962; Henning and Levy, 1967; Manne, Kandel and Rosenthal, 1963; McHugh, 1963; Solway, Hays, Roberts and

Cody, 1975; Sutker, Moan and Allain, 1974). And whereas the performance of some individuals diagnosed as mentally defective followed Wechsler's expectations, some did not (e.g. Atchison, 1955; Fisher, 1960; Fisher, Dooley and Silverstein, 1960). Individuals with learning disabilities, where we would expect that they might do more poorly on the Verbal tasks, do not do so with any consistency (e.g. Rourke, Dietrich and Young, 1973; Vance, Gaynor and Coleman, 1976; Wener and Templer, 1976); some do, some do not. In the same way while we expect individuals who are from academically unstimulating backgrounds would perform more poorly on the Verbal than the Performance tasks, again, some do and some do not (e.g. Seashore, 1951; Young and Pitts, 1951).

There appears to be no area of research in clinical psychology that is free from the disturbing effect of studies which tend to present contradictory findings. Obviously, even subtle changes in design, population studied, and/or mode of data analysis can account for what, on the surface appears to be "random" contradictory results. On the other hand, it is also probably scientifically naïve to consider that individuals who have been assigned to a particular diagnostic or personality category should function homogeneously intellectually and/or cognitively. For example, the diagnosis of psychopath which Wechsler employs must include a wide variety of behaviors which range from rather minimal antisocial acts to major antisocial crimes. Trying to find commonalities within such a heterogeneous grouping of individuals (and styles of thinking) would (should) seem improbable. To analyze test data, therefore, ignoring this (not to mention other facts such as age, education, I.Q., socioeconomic level, all of which influence performance on the Wechsler Scale) would seem to constitute unsound research. In the same way the diagnosis of "schizophrenia" covers such a wide variety of pathologies, personalities, and even cognitive styles that homogeneity of performance on the Wechsler tests, even with regard to so gross an assessment as the comparison between the Verbal and Performance parts of the Scale is (ought) not to be expected. Variations in the outcome of research studying, essentially, different kinds of individuals who, nevertheless, are diagnosed similarly, thus, can be expected. This is particularly true when one is dealing with individuals who are identified as having some form of cerebral pathology. "Organic brain disease" Wechsler called these individuals, but brain *disease* and brain *damage* are not the same; we would not expect their intellectual performance to be the same; just as we would expect locus and degree of brain involvement to influence test results. As we have seen, Wechsler stated that we should expect individuals with cerebral pathology to perform more poorly on the Performance tasks. As the research demonstrates, that pattern of performance (i.e. V > P) turns out *not* to be characteristic of the patient with cerebral pathology *sui generis*, but only of individuals where the cerebral involvement is either limited to the right hemisphere or involves both hemispheres in some nonspecific way. Individuals with cerebral pathology restricted to the left hemisphere produce the reverse effect; they do *better* on the Performance tasks than on the Verbal ones (e.g. Balthazar and Morrison, 1961; Balthazar, Todd, Morrison and Ziebell, 1961; Doehring and Reitan, 1962; Doehring, Reitan and Kløve, 1961; Fitzhugh and Fitzhugh, 1964; 1965; Fitzhugh, Fitzhugh and Reitan, 1962; Heilbrun, 1956, 1959; Kløve, 1959; Kløve and Fitzhugh, 1962; Kløve and Reitan, 1958; Lansdell and Smith, 1975; McFie and Piercy, 1952; Parsons, Vega and Burn, 1969; Pihl, 1968; Reed and Reitan, 1963, 1969; Reitan, 1955; Reitan and Fitzhugh, 1971; Rourke and Telegdy, 1971; Todd, Collidge and Satz, 1977). Ignoring the locus of the cerebral pathology and, indeed, the specific nature of that pathology, must have led the early users of the Wechsler test, who followed Wechsler's assumptions regarding the comparative performance of individuals with cerebral pathology on the Verbal and Performance tasks, into a significant number of diagnostic errors, not to mention being productive of contradictory research findings.

The situation with regard to the discrepancy between performance on the Verbal and Performance parts of Wechsler's tests is even more complicated when we note, again, what is to be considered a significant discrepancy between these two measures. As we have seen, Wechsler posited that a discrepancy of between 8 and 10 points between the Verbal and Performance I.Q. should be considered significant. Again, that figure was probably arrived at through Wechsler's experience with his test and test data gathered by his staff at Bellevue. Those who have investigated this dimension have come up with a somewhat different assessment. For example, Piotrowski (1978) found that with regard to performance on the WISC-R, a difference between the Verbal and Performance I.Q. would have to be as large as 18 in order to be significant; Black (1974a) found that, with regard to the WISC, 15 or more points was a minimum. In a most unique and valuable contribution to an understanding of what constitutes a meaningful Verbal—Performance I.Q. discrepancy, Wolfens-berger (1958) presented us with Z scores regarding probable levels of significance for a range of V—P differences, and Field (1960b) presents us with tables of probabilities for expected discrepancies for the range of age from 7—12 to 75+, with regard to the WISC, Form I of the Wechsler, and the WAIS. I have yet to see these studies repeated in order to cross-validate the findings, nor the data utilized in either research or clinical endeavours. When one notes that Verbal—Performance I.Q. differences may be inherent in the WAIS (Pickering, Johnson and Stary, 1977), the importance of such base line data becomes even more apparent. In light of the contradictory findings regarding Verbal and Performance I.Q. discrepancies, the absence of base line data having been utilized in assessing what should be considered a significant difference beyond which clinical significance might be assumed, nor the psychological meaning of such differences, we are left with not being able to know what to do with Verbal—Performance I.Q. differences and/or what conclusions can be drawn from the research in this area.

Subtest Patterning

The expectation that specific psychological functions would be impaired in specific psychiatric conditions (that is, with regard to specific forms of psychopathology) can be traced back at least as far as the work of Kraepelin (1902). Following Kraepelin's line of reasoning, Binet wrote that, "the various psychological processes arrange themselves in a different configuration with each individual" (Binet and Henri, 1895), and that psychopathology influenced intellectual performance in unique ways, and that this "irregularity" in test performance can be meaningful and should be studied (Binet and Simon, 1916). By the time Wechsler began develop-ing his test this notion that psychopathology produced unique patterns of intellectual performance was part of common lore (e.g. Wells, 1927) and was certainly shared by the most respected psychologists of Wechsler's era (e.g., Bijou, 1942a, b; Jastak, 1937; Schafer, 1944; Schafer and Rapaport, 1944; Rapaport, Gill and Schafer, 1945). While the study of the clinical meaningfulness of this "irregularity" was intensively studied through the use of the Binet test (e.g. Pressey, 1917; Pressey and Cole, 1918) a survey of over 20 years of that research with the Binet indicated that while little real support was found for the presence of systematic differences in performance by varied psychiatric groups (Harris and Shakow, 1937), a major source of difficulty was presumed to be the structure of the Binet. By organizing the various tasks an individual would have to perform by age level, and by not having an equal number of tasks between psychological functions that were being assessed (e.g. memory, judgment, problem solving, abstract thinking, word knowledge, etc.), and by not assessing the same psychological functions at every age level, comparative analyses of the pattern of performance on the various psychological tasks in the Binet was hampered. The search for the influence of psychopathology upon intellective functions, therefore, went on, sparked by the idea that the way the Wechsler data were arranged, comparative analyses of patterns of intellective behavior would be feasible.

Wechsler, himself, was at the forefront of such exploration (Wechsler, 1941b; Wechsler, Halpern and Jaros, 1940; Wechsler, Israel and Balinsky, 1941), and by the time the second edition of his book was forthcoming (in 1944), a host of studies existed which reflected on the clinical use of the Wechsler test data (e.g. Brown and Partington, 1942; Gilliland, Wittman and Goldman, 1943; Hunt, 1943; Levi, 1943; Lewinski, 1943; Machover, 1943; Magaret, 1942, 1943; Rabin, 1941, 1942a, b, 1943; Weider, 1943). From his own studies and the studies of these other psychologists, Wechsler began generating more specific ideas about the performance of psychiatric patients on the subtests. As we have already noted, while the first edition of the book (in 1939) did not transcend a discussion of the intellectual aspects of performance on the Scale, by the second edition (in 1944) we find Wechsler writing that he expected that the patient with cerebral pathology would manifest difficulties in the visual-motor sphere, a loss of the capacity to shift conceptual frames of reference (i.e. set) and difficulty in cognitive organizational ability. He posits that these difficulties should interfere with performance on such tests as Block design, Object assembly, and Similarities, and a memory difficulty should interfere with performance on Digits. The schizophrenic's inability to pay attention to the details of reality should produce difficulty in Similarities and/or Picture completion. He expected psychopaths to do poorly on Similarities, Arithmetic, and Information, reflecting disinterest in the world outside of themselves. Neurotics were expected to do poorly on tasks which require immediate effort "and everywhere their sense of inadequacy may interfere."

It is to Wechsler's credit that he remained relatively conservative with regard to the expectation of the performance of specific psychiatric groups on specific subtests. Other clinicians, waxed enthusiastic believing that they were now, with the Wechsler, able to do something better (that is, make comparative analyses regarding psychological functions) than the Binet had permitted them to do. Thus, we find other clinicians expecting to find very unique and specific patterns of performance on the subtests for different groups of patients (e.g. Rapaport *et al.*, 1945). In this regard when we look at the research reflecting on the degree to which certain psychiatric groups *do* reflect specific subtest patterning, we must separate out Wechsler's predictions and observations from those of other clinicians.

The following four chapters will focus on the degree to which the performance on the Wechsler tests does reflect uniqueness. We will examine the performance on the Wechsler tests of patients with specific kinds of difficulties, trying to determine to what extent the specificity hypothesis obtains.

CHAPTER 3

The Use of the Wechsler in the Assessment of Intellectual Difficulties

IN THAT the Wechsler tests are tests of intelligence it would not be unreasonable to expect that the tests could be effective in discerning whatever unique pattern of performance is manifested by individuals who demonstrate difficulties which are primarily intellectual (rather than more manifestly emotional). Here I am referring to individuals who have been diagnosed as being mentally retarded and those who have been diagnosed as having problems reading (i.e. comprehending the written word).

As regards the pattern of performance of individuals who have been diagnosed as being mentally retarded, Wechsler (1944) noted that they could be expected to do particularly poorly (relative to their own performance on all of the subtests) on Arithmetic, somewhat less poorly on Digits and Picture completion, somewhat better on Information, Similarities, and Picture arrangement, and (again, relative to their own performance) relatively well on Comprehension, Object assembly, and Vocabulary. A number of studies have been conducted to determine whether the person identified as mentally retarded evidenced some unique pattern of subtest performance. Some studies (e.g. Lewinski, 1943, 1944) seem to support Wechsler's ideas regarding the performance of the mentally retarded on the subtests. Altus (1956) found that retarded readers performed rather poorly on Information, Arithmetic, and Coding, and relatively well on Digits, Picture completion, and Object assembly. Baroff (1959) found that endogenous mental retardation manifests itself in relatively good performance on such Performance tasks as Object assembly, Block design, Picture completion, and Coding, and rather poorly on such Verbal tasks as Vocabulary and Similarities. Belmont and Birch (1966) found that their retarded readers performed relatively more poorly on the Verbal than the Performance tasks in general. Sternlicht, Siegel and Deutsch (1968)

44

found that their group of (institutionalized) retardates showed no great scatter at all, but did more poorly on such Verbal tasks as Arithmetic, Similarities, and Vocabulary, relatively better on such Performance tasks as Picture completion and Object assembly, but also Comprehension.

As regards Wechsler's predictions regarding the performance of mentally retarded individuals on the subtests, the research reflects partial support for his ideas. With regard to their performance on Object assembly, he appears to have been "right on": the mentally retarded individuals did, indeed, do well on this task. Wechsler seems not to have been correct about their performance on Picture completion; mentally retarded individuals seem to do relatively (relative to their own performance on the other subtests) well on the Picture completion task. But he seems to have been correct about their relatively poor performance on: Arithmetic, Information, and Similarities. Mentally retarded individuals, however, did not seem to manifest any unique and/or specific pattern of performance on the subtests (Alper, 1967; Baumeister, 1964; Cook and Solway, 1974; Fisher *et al.*, 1960).

Individuals diagnosed (identified) as being poor readers (though not necessarily mentally retarded) were not studied by Wechsler. Burks and Bruce (1955) found that poor readers did relatively more poorly on Information, Arithmetic, and Comprehension, and relatively well on Picture arrangement and Block design. Coleman and Rasof (1963) found that individuals who were underachievers (that is, manifested a learning disorder as opposed to an intellectual limitation) did poorly on Information, Arithmetic, and Object assembly. Corwin (1967) found that poor readers did poorly on Information, Arithmetic, Digits, and Coding, Graham (1952) found that poor readers did significantly poorly on Arithmetic, Vocabulary, and Digit symbol, while doing relatively well on Similarities, Object assembly, Block design, Picture arrangement, and Picture completion. Huelsman (1970) also found poor readers to do poorly on Information, Arithmetic, and Digits, and to do rather well on Picture arrangement and Block design.

Using the WISC-R, Vance, Singer and Engin (1980) found no significant subtest pattern which could identify learning-disabled children nor which would satisfactorily differentiate the younger from the older learning disabled youngster. Thompson (1980) found that V–P I.Q. differences did not differentiate the learning disabled child from the mentally retarded child nor the child manifesting a behavior disorder. And Bloom and Raskin (1980) compared VIQ-PIQ discrepancies for learning disabled children and normal children. They found that while 53% of learning disabled children showed at least a nine-point discrepancy between V and P I.Q.s, so did 48% of the normal group. In fact, the results of their study indicated that the amount of VIQ-PIQ discrepancy found in a group of learning disabled was virtually matched by a similar amount of VIQ-PIQ discrepancy among normal children. Thus, while 41% of the learning disabled group manifested a twelve-point VIQ-PIQ discrepancy, 34% of the normal group did, and so it went (e.g. fifteen-point discrepancy: LD 31%, normals 24%; twenty-point discrepancy: LD 17%, normals 12%; twenty-five point discrepancy: LD 8%, normals 4%). "These findings indicate," write Bloom and Raskin, "that the incidence of significant Verbal—Performance I.Q. discrepancies among LD children may not be substantially different from what is observed to occur in the general population" (1980, p. 323).

From a review of the studies on individuals identified as poor readers, a number of observations can be made as regards their performance on Wechsler's test. The first observation that can be made is that, as with the mentally retarded individuals, those with significant reading problems do better on the Performance tasks than the Verbal ones. More specifically, the poor reader (in almost every study) seems to do most poorly on Information and Arithmetic, and, to some extent, Digit symbol (or Coding). In that the "poor reader" does relatively well on the Performance tasks and relatively poorly on tasks which might seem to involve scholastic learning (Arithmetic, Information), we should wonder whether such a pattern constitutes a pattern of subtest performance which is unique to these individuals. There is no research to test out this hypothesis. Whether or not there is a unique pattern of performance on the subtests remains obscure; while the research reviewed above might suggest that there is, other research would seem to suggest that there is not (e.g. Kallos, Grabow and Guarino, 1961; Kender, 1972; Maxwell, 1972; Muzyczka and Erickson, 1976; Ramanauskas and Burrow, 1973; Reed, 1967; Reid and Schoer, 1966).

We are left with the conclusion from this overview of the performance of individuals with intellectual disorders (i.e. mental retardates and poor readers) that they do more poorly on the Verbal tasks than the Performance ones, and, more specifically, on Information and Arithmetic, both school-oriented subjects. However, beyond that, no specific subtest pattern for mentally retarded individuals or those identified as poor readers seem to exist. Moreover, since both the retarded individual and the poor reader do poorly on the Verbal tasks, and, more specifically, those most influenced by scholastic learning, given that a child who is doing poorly in school does poorly on the Verbal tasks, and given that the child did most poorly on Arithmetic and Information, a clinician would not be able to discern whether the performance was that of a retarded child or a child with reading difficulty. Perhaps the relatively good performance on the Performance tasks would differentiate the problem reader from the retarded child, but that comparison seems not to have been tested in the literature. Indeed, what we would still seem to need is research clarifying the differences between these two groups so that they *are* more readily differentiable.

CHAPTER 4

The Use of the Wechsler in the Assessment of Cerebral Pathology

AS WE have noted, a more psychologically sophisticated conception of intelligence and/or intellectual behavior states that intelligence involves the utilization of cognitive functions. Binet (Binet and Henri, 1895; Binet and Simon, 1916) subscribed to that notion, and Spearman (1904) made it the central idea of his conceptualization of intelligence (indeed, entitling his book, *The Nature of "Intelligence" and the Principles of Cognition* [Spearman, 1923]). To the extent, therefore, that we can consider any test of intelligence as an opportunity to assess a variety of cognitive functions, then we can consider the Wechsler test as a test of the individual's capacity to utilize his or her cognitive abilities towards the kind of problem solving and reasoning that is required to accomplish the tasks with which the Wechsler tests confront one. Thus, wherever we have impairment of cognitive functions we should expect the Wechsler test to be able to reflect that, to one degree or another, in one way or another. One of the central characteristics of most forms of cerebral pathology (except, perhaps, those which involve disturbances of sensory and/or motor functions primarily) is the interference with one or more cognitive function: of attention, memory, perception, thinking, and the judgments that are based therefrom. Wechsler was adamant that individuals with cerebral pathology would manifest serious disturbance in their subtest performance in areas where conceptualization and memory, in particular, were entailed.

However, to diagnose a person as having "brain damage," or any other such diagnostic generalization (e.g. organic brain disease, brain disorder, or even cerebral pathology), commits a most grievous error diagnostically. While Wechsler uses the term "organic brain disease" it is clear that not all cerebral pathology is due to a disease process. Whatever general term might be used, in fact, possesses little communication value as regards what condition the patient really has. Part of the problem in this area of exploration is that prior to the research exploring the performance of individuals with specific hemispheric or lobal difficulties (which, we have found, produce selective impairment of intellective/cognitive functions), clinicians (including Wechsler) believed that brain dysfunction (regardless of locus of the brain or amount of the brain involved) leads to disturbances in either memory or abstract ability. Subsequent research has proven such expectations to be inaccurate. Much of the early research with the Wechsler and cerebral pathology did not make a differentiation as regards area involved or extent of involvement. Thus when Wechsler (1944) examines the intellective performance of patients with "organic brain disease" his group includes a wide variety of cerebral pathologies. Examining the intellective performance of this group, Wechsler concluded that the patient with "organic brain disease" manifests disturbance in the sphere of visuo-motor functioning, a loss of the abstract attitude (involving a loss in the capacity to make conceptual shifts and of conceptual organizational ability), and memory. These patients do poorly on the Performance tasks in general, in particular, on Digit symbol, Block design, and Object assembly. Memory impairment is manifested in their poor performance on Digits. Similarities would also be low to the extent that there is loss of the capacity for abstraction. Digit symbol would be low because of a presumed impairment in the capacity for new learning.

Looking at the research done subsequent to Wechsler we find that, as compared to a general sample of psychiatric patients (excluding patients with known cerebral pathology), patients with cerebral pathology do do poorly on Digit symbol, Block design, Object assembly, and the Performance tasks in general (e.g. Burgess, Kodanaz, Ziegler and Greenburg, 1970; Klatskin, McNamara, Shaffer and Pincus, 1972; Morrow and Mark, 1955). As compared to schizophrenics, patients with cerebral pathology do more poorly on Digits and Block design (but better than the schizophrenics on Comprehension and Picture completion) (DeWolfe, Barrell, Becker and Spaner, 1971). Reed, Reitan and Kløve (1965) and Reitan (1959) found that diffuse brain pathology affects all subtest scores. Holroyd and Wright (1965) found that a 25-point discrepancy (where the Performance I.Q. is lower than the Verbal I.Q.) is diagnostic of cerebral pathology.

For children with cerebral pathology, no unique pattern of intellective deficits were found (Bortner and Birch, 1969; Hopkins, 1964), nor could the intellective/cognitive deficit due to cerebral pathology be differentiated from that due to mental retardation (Birch, Belmont and Belmont, 1967; Jansen, 1973). Moreover, children with known cerebral pathology do not show the same pattern of intellective functioning as adults (Beck and Lam, 1955). And in contrast to the findings with regard to adults (as noted above), Davis, Becker and DeWolfe (1971a) did not find that adults with cerebral pathology demonstrated any unique pattern of performance on the subtests.

Following Wechsler's model of developing ratios with regard to the subtests, Allen (1948b), Hewson (1949), Hunt (1943), Norman (1966), Reynell (1944), and Saunders (1958) all developed their own ratios to attempt to illuminate the performance of individuals with cerebral pathology. The problem with all of these ratios is while they do separate patients with cerebral pathology from those without, the efficiency of that separation is not sufficient for clinical use (Gutman, 1950; Rogers, 1950b; Vogt and Heaton, 1977; Wheeler and Wilkins, 1951; Wolff, 1960). Even a multiple regression equation to estimate the degree of cerebral pathology (Hirt and Cook, 1962) was effective only about 75% of the time.

Moving in the opposite direction of more objective analyses of test data (viz., ratios), some investigators reasoned that the performance of individuals with cerebral pathology would be more meaningfully illuminated through a *qualitative* analysis of their performance (e.g. Ben-Yishey, Diller, Mandelberg, Gordan and Gerstman, 1971; Hall and LaDriere, 1969; Rappaport, 1953; Reitan, 1958; Spence, 1963; Watson, 1965c). In such analyses of responses to the Wechsler stimuli, patients with cerebral pathology were found to make more errors which reflected concrete conceptualizations and tended to respond to questions with "I don't know" rather than offer a wrong answer (as the schizophrenic might).

It should not be surprising that the research exploring the performance of individuals with cerebral pathology on the Wechsler test should turn out disappointing. The criterion for selection of individuals to be studied, e.g. "cerebral pathology," "brain damage," "cerebral or brain dysfunction" are much too global. Such categories are so broad that they include a wide variety of cerebral disturbances such that it would have been surprising *if* the research would have demonstrated that such groups perform uniquely on the Wechsler. To get a better assessment of the ability for the Wechsler test to reflect the performance of individuals with cerebral pathology with some uniqueness, we should look at that research where the subjects under study were described, diagnostically, by some more specific criterion, that is, where a more specific diagnosis has been made.

Wechsler, it should be remembered, referred to all individuals with cerebral pathology of whatever kind as "organic brain diseased." On the assumption that brain "diseased" and brain "injured" constitute two different groups, Allen (1947, 1948a, 1948b, 1949) tried to discover the difference between groups of individuals diagnosed as "brain diseased" (e.g. those patients with lues, meningeal pathology, cerebral atrophy, and hemorrhage) and "brain injured" (those individuals with head trauma or epilepsy). Allen found that the major difference in the performance on the Wechsler tests between these two groups was one of degree rather than kind. The two groups both manifested difficulties in analysis and synthesis of information, attention and concentration, visual planning, and speed of arithmetic computation. Both showed the $P < V$ performance Wechsler anticipated. Where the two groups did differ was that the "brain diseased" manifested greater intellectual impairment than the "brain injured."

Further in the direction of specificity, Morrow and Mark (1955) looked at the differential performance on the Wechsler of patients diagnosed (on autopsy) as having focal versus diffuse cerebral pathology. Patients with diffuse cerebral pathology showed greater impairment on the Performance I.Q. than patients with focal pathology, doing particularly more poorly on Comprehension, Picture arrangement, and Object assembly. Patients with focal pathology showed greater impairment on the Digit Symbol subtest than patients with diffuse cerebral pathology.

Some of the more recent findings in neurophysiological research point to the fact that the two halves of the brain of the human function, to some extent, uniquely (in terms of psychological/cognitive functioning) (e.g. Gazzaniga, 1976; Kimura, 1976; Luria, 1976). In sum, this research has demonstrated that the left side of the brain tends to have control over verbal behavior, the right, spatial—temporal. In light of these findings we would/should expect that cerebral pathology focused in one or the other hemisphere should eventuate in the interference of different cognitive/intellective functions, and, indeed, that is what the research demonstrates.

Beginning with the seminal work of Andersen (1950, 1951), many studies of the performance of individuals with lateralized cerebral pathology have demonstrated that disturbance in the left side of the brain does, in fact, eventuate in different cognitive deficits than disturbances localized in the right side of the brain (e.g. Balthazar and Morrison, 1961; Balthazar *et al.*, 1961; Blakemore, Ettinger and Falconer, 1966; Dennerll, 1964; Doehring and Reitan, 1962; Doehring *et al.*, 1961; Fitzhugh and Fitzhugh, 1964, 1965; Fitzhugh *et al.*, 1962; Heilbrun, 1956, 1959; Kløve, 1959; Kløve and Fitzhugh, 1962; Kløve and Reitan, 1958; Lansdell and Smith, 1975; Leli and Filskov (1981); McFie and Piercy, 1952; Meyer, 1959; Meyer and Jones, 1957; Milberg, Greiftenstein, Lewis and Rourke (1980); Parsons *et al.*, 1969; Pihl, 1968; Reed and Reitan, 1963, 1969; Reitan, 1955; Reitan and Fitzhugh, 1971; Rourke and Telegdy, 1971; Satz, Richard and Daniels, 1967a; Simpson and Vega, 1971; Smith, 1966; Todd *et al.*, 1977; Vega and Parsons, 1969). In all of these studies with the Wechsler, patients with left-sided cerebral involvements did more poorly on the verbal tasks of the Wechsler; patients with right-sided cerebral involvement did more poorly on the tests involving spatial orientation, that is, the Performance tasks. Admittedly, not all of the research done in this area reflect the above-stated results (e.g. as in the studies by Black, 1976; Bolter, Veneklasen and Long, 1981; Matthews and Reitan, 1964; Meier and French, 1966; Russell, 1972, 1979). However, what is amazing is that so much of the research reflects consistent findings. In spite of ignoring such diverse factors which could influence their performance on the Wechsler test over and above the presence of the cerebral pathology such as age, sex, education, level of intelligence, cultural background, specific site of the cerebral pathology, kind of cerebral pathology, length of time the difficulty existed, amount of brain involved, etc., the effect of left or right cerebral pathology is so dramatic that it comes through, through it all.

The subjects of the studies cited above were all adults. Studies of the effect of unilateral cerebral pathology on Wechsler performance of children consistently did not reveal the left–right effects on Wechsler performance of adults (e.g. Fagan-Dublin, 1974; Hartlage and Green, 1972; McIntosh, 1974; Pennington, Galliani and Voegele, 1965). In response to this, Pennington *et al.* concluded that, "The relationship observed in adults by other investigators did not appear to be directly applicable to children" (1965, p. 545).

Kraus and Selecki (1967) found only modest differences in the assessment of the left–right cerebral damage in chronically impaired subjects; Balthazar (1963) did not find significant differences in the performance of individuals with left vs right cerebral damage on the Object assembly subtest.

Other investigators have studied the performance on the Wechsler tests of individuals with frontal, temporal, or parietal lobe pathology. As compared to the results with the performance of patients with unilateral hemispheric pathology, the results are less clear cut. In one study (Giannitirapini, 1969), patients with frontal lobe involvement were found to do poorly on the verbal tasks. In another study (Woo-Sam, Zimmerman and Rogal, 1971), patients with any kind of cerebral involvement (frontal, occipital, or parietal) were found to do more poorly on the Verbal tasks than the Performance ones. As regards specific subtests, McFie (1960) looked at the effect of lobe *and* hemisphere involvement. Patients with left frontal lobe involvement were found to do particularly poorly on Digits; patients with left temporal lobe involvement were found to do particularly poorly on Similarities and Digits; patients with left parietal lobe involvement were found to do particularly poorly on Arithmetic, Block design, and Digits. Patients with right frontal lobe involvement were found to do more poorly on Picture arrangement; patients with right parietal lobe involvement were found to do particularly poorly on Picture arrangement and Block design. To some extent, the previously noted left/right, verbal/performance difficulties emerge here, too.

Given the rather consistent finding that, with regard to adults, cerebral pathology generally limited to the left side of the brain is generally manifested in impairment on the Verbal tasks, while cerebral pathology generally limited to the right side of the brain is generally manifested in impairment of performance on the Performance tasks, the question should be asked: what is the clinical-diagnostic value of such a finding? If a patient with suspected cerebral pathology is tested and produces a Wechsler pattern where the Performance tasks are significantly lower than the Verbal tasks, can the clinician conclude that there is unilateral (in this instance, right-sided) cerebral pathology? Such a question might be of import if neurosurgery is being contemplated. Unfortunately, on the basis of Wechsler data alone, the answer much be given in the negative, since both diffuse (bilateral) *and* right cerebral pathology produce a P < V pattern. Only left-sided cerebral pathology is uniquely reflected in a V < P pattern. Thus, given a P < V pattern of performance on the Wechsler tests a clinician could not tell whether the pathology is limited to the right cerebral hemisphere or involves both hemispheres. It is clear, however, that Wechsler's observations that patients with cerebral pathology do more poorly on the Performance tasks refers only to patients with right-cerebral or bilateral cerebral pathology; the P < V pattern would not identify patients with left cerebral pathology as having cerebral pathology, since they would produce the opposite pattern. Moreover, unless the clinician knows or is pretty certain that the patient has identifiable cerebral pathology, a V < P *or* a P < V pattern of performance does not necessarily confirm the presence of cerebral pathology; a V < P or a P < V pattern could be a function of a variety of factors, not limited to cerebral pathology. Even *degree* of impairment (Kløve and White, 1963; Kraus and Selecki, 1965; Reed and Fitzhugh, 1966) is not reflected in some unique pattern of Wechsler performance. Thus, although the research lends a very strong support to the notion that a differential locus of cerebral pathology eventuates in rather significant and unique Verbal/Performance difficulties, given a specific V:P relationship, this does not enable the clinician to decide whether or not cerebral pathology *is* present since neither pattern is limited to patients with cerebral pathology. In this regard, performance on the Wechsler by itself, is not helpful in differentiating neurological from psychiatric difficulties. In this regard, Russell wrote, "the WAIS by itself cannot assess either the existence or location of brain damage. It must be supported by other tests that are designed specifically to determine the existence and location of damage" (1979, p. 619), and Bolter *et al.* wrote:

> making diagnostic decisions regarding the presence or absence of temporal lobe seizure disorder based upon . . . WAIS subtests may not be in the best interest of the patient. It would appear that if a clinician is in a position where such decisions are important to a referring physician or to the planning of treatment strategies, more careful diagnostic procedures would be warranted . . . there would appear to be considerable danger in using this type of data exclusively in order to recommend or not recommend extensive neurological workup or specific treatment approaches depending on the outcome of the patient's WAIS performance. (1981, p. 553)

The question can further be raised: what is the value of the Wechsler test in identifying cerebral pathology due to known source: trauma or disease? The examination of the Wechsler performance of individuals who have undergone frontal lobotomy (e.g. Markwell, Wheeler and Kitzinger, 1953; McCullough, 1950) indicated that postoperative patients manifested improvement in performance on Digits, and, sometimes, Picture arrangement and Block design. Wehler and Hoffman (1978) did not find such results but they compared the performance of lobotomized and nonlobotomized *chronic* schizophrenic patients, thereby probably precluding finding the aforementioned improvement after surgery.

Patients with epilepsy were found, in one study, to perform poorly on Similarities, Digits, and Picture arrangement, while performing well on Object assembly, Block design, and Picture completion (Lewinski, 1947). In another study (Schwartz and Dennerll, 1970), epileptics were found to do poorly on Information, Similarities, Vocabulary, Picture arrangement, Picture completion, Block design, and Coding. Obviously differences in subjects (the first study involved adults, the second, children), degree of involvement, age of the subject, duration of involvement, uncontrolled variables from one study to another, can also account for the nonspecific findings of this particular aspect of study of patients on the Wechsler test.

Patients with paresis (Fisher, 1958) showed greatest impairment on Digits and Similarities, least on Vocabulary. Although patients with multiple sclerosis show impairment in psychomotor coordination (which we would expect) their higher level cognitive functions remain intact (Hirschenfang and Benton, 1966; Ivnik, 1978). No specific impairment or improvement was noted in the Wechsler performance of patients who suffered from a concussion (Becker, 1975).

Hartlage (1970) found that the WISC was not helpful in differentiating dyslexic children from children with minimal brain damage from children with non-organically-based emotional disturbances.

Alcohol abuse and aging are two conditions which are known to produce cerebral pathology. The question should be asked as to whether these two conditions produce unique and/or specific cognitive deficits which would be reflected in the Wechsler test data.

As regards the study of alcoholism (e.g. Halpern, 1946; Kaldegg, 1956; Teicher and Singer, 1946; Wechsler, 1941b), the one test which stands out which individuals who abuse alcohol do poorly on is Object assembly. In her study, Halpern found that alcoholics also did poorly on Digit symbol; Kaldegg, Arithmetic; and Teicher and Singer, Picture arrangement. In his study, Wechsler examined the performance of younger (35–42) and older (45–55) alcoholics. As compared to younger alcoholics, the older alcoholics performed more poorly on Arithmetic, Comprehension, Similarities, Picture arrangement, and Digit symbol, but better on Picture completion. Chronic use of alcohol seems to interfere with some aspects of cognitive organizational ability (Object assembly), but differing aspects of the various populations under study obviously contribute to the difference in the results of each study.

Amongst other things, the aging process is characterized by a decline in neurophysiological functioning, sensory, motor, as well as cognitive. As a test involving the assessment of motor- and hand/eye coordination as well as cognitive functioning, the Wechsler tests should be able to reflect the cognitive and motor difficulties the aging person manifests. There should be little doubt that the Wechsler tests can do that. The problematic question is: is there a unique and/or specific pattern to the aging process which gets reflected in a unique and/or specific pattern of performance on the subtests? We will look at the research to determine to what extent both expectations are viable.

In his chapter on "The Problem of Mental Deterioration" (Wechsler, 1939 and all subsequent editions of his book), Wechsler discusses the problem of aging and its vicissitudes. Therein, Wechsler indicates which of the subtests his experience has taught him reflect the aging process (that is, manifest impairment), and those which do not. He labels these two sets of subtests those which hold up with age and those which do not. Of the subtests which Wechsler found to hold up in spite of the aging process, there were Information, Comprehension, Vocabulary, Object assembly, and Picture completion. Those subtests which Wechsler found to be sensitive to (reflective of) senescent decline, there were Digits, Arithmetic, Block design, Similarities, and sometimes Picture arrangement.

Dorken and Greenbloom (1953), Green and Berkowitz (1965), and Overall et al. (1978) found that the aged with clinical signs of cerebral pathology perform differently on the subtests than the aged individuals without manifest signs of cerebral pathology. The aged without clinical signs of cerebral pathology show loss of conceptual flexibility and slowing in perceptual-motor speed, but their cognitive abilities in general remain unimpaired. Aged individuals with clinical signs of cerebral pathology do poorly on all the subtests. Performance on the WAIS was found to vary (negatively) with EEG findings and cerebral blood flow (Wang *et al.*, 1970). Botwinick and Birren (1951b) found that the institutionalized aged could be differentiated from the non-institutionalized aged on Information, Comprehension, Arithmetic, Object assembly, and Picture arrangement. The institutionalized aged did more poorly on those tests than did the non-institutionalized. One wonders whether such lowering of cognitive alertness as the performance on these subtests might suggest, is the cause of these individuals having to be institutionalized or the result of their having been institutionalized. While Howell (1955a) found that there is an observable progression of percentage of deterioration, beginning with 10% at ages 30–40, with about 5% deterioration normally occurring every 5 years until age 70 when the percentage of deterioration each 5 years increases, McKeever and Gerstein (1958) found that level of intelligence, *per se*, affects the curve of deterioration, while Doppelt and Wallace (1955) found marked individual differences in the performance of the aged. Studies of the Wechsler test performance of individuals with premature signs of senescence (Crookes, 1974; Perez, Gay and Taylor, 1975) showed that these individuals, in general, did most poorly on Block design. Crookes also found that these patients also had difficulty with Digit symbol, but not with Vocabulary. Perez *et al.* found that their subjects also performed poorly on Information, Arithmetic, Picture completion, and Picture arrangement. Crookes also found male/female differences, with the female aged performing significantly more poorly on all the subtests than the male aged.

While Babcock (1930) had found that Vocabulary seemed to hold up in spite of any kind of deterioration, whether neurological or psychological, Fox (1947) found that performance on Vocabulary does hold up with age; Fisher (1958) found that it did not always hold up with age, and Orme (1957) found that it did not hold up with aging when there is accompanying dementia. Obviously, we cannot afford to make such simplistic statements that, for example, Vocabulary does hold up with age, when aging is not the only factor which influences an individual's performance on the Wechsler test.

In the conclusion to his study, Whitehead wrote, "the pattern of subtest scores on the WAIS gives little information relevant to a differential diagnosis in elderly patients" (1973, p. 436), a conclusion which seems to point out the fact that the intellectual performance of the aged is obviously influenced by more factors than just the aging process, and, moreover, that people change in quite individual ways during aging. Table 8 will illuminate this point.

TABLE 8. *The effect of aging on subtest performance*

Study	Hold	Don't Hold
Wechsler	I, V, C, OA, PC	BD, DSym, S, D[a]
Berkowitz (1953)	I, V, C, D, S, OA	BD, DSym, PA
Berkowitz and Green (1963)	I, V, C	BD, DSym, PA
Blum *et al* (1972)		BD, DSym, D, S
Corsini and Fassett (1952)	I, V, C, D	BD, DSym, OA, PC
Dibner and Cummins (1961)	I, C, S, A, PC, OA	BD, DSym, PA, D
Fox and Birren (1950)	I, V, C	BD, DSym, PA
Howell (1955)	I, V, PC, OA	BD, DSym, A, D
Hulicka (1962)	I	S
Hunt (1943)	I, C	BD, DSym, A, D
Hunt (1949)	I, C	
Jackson (1955)	C, S, D, PA, DSym	BD, OA, I, PC, A
Madonick and Solomon (1947)	I, C, S	PA, DSym
Norman and Daley (1959)	C, S, D, OA, PC	DSym, A
Rabin (1942)		OA, PC
Rabin (1945)	I, C	BD, DSym, PA, PC, OA

[a]In this and several of the subsequent tables the subtests will be identified by their first letter; thus, I will indicate the Information subtest, C (Comprehension), S (Similarities), A (Arithmetic), D (Digit span), V (Vocabulary), PA (Picture arrangement), PC (Picture completion), BD (Block design), OA (Object assembly), DSym (Digit symbol), COD (the notation for the Digit symbol task in the WISC).

From Table 8, we can see that performance on Information seems to hold up with age quite consistently. The idea that Vocabulary and Comprehension hold up with age seems to happen with regard to some individuals, but not all. Wechsler's idea that Object assembly and Picture completion hold up with age receives rather weak support; only with a very few individuals did this seem to be the case. Block design and Digit symbol seem to be subtests where most aged individuals do poorly. And while some individuals do poorly on Digits, contrary to expectation, performance on Similarities was found, quite frequently, to remain unimpaired in the aged.

Norman (1966) found that there was a sex difference in terms of which subtests hold up with age and which do not. As regards men, Norman found that Similarities, Digits, Block design, and Digit symbol hold up with age, while Information, Arithmetic, Picture completion, and Object assembly did not. With regard to women, Similarities, Digits, Digit symbol, and Picture arrangement did not hold up with age, while Vocabulary, Information, Object assembly, and Block design did. Clearly the use of which subtests hold up with age and which do not is a lot more complex than Wechsler anticipated.

If we look at the research reflecting upon the search for the unique and/or characteristic performance of individuals with cerebral pathology, that search seems to have been futile. Undoubtedly, individuals with cerebral pathology show difficulties on the subtests, but the search for specific patterns of performance for specific kinds of cerebral pathology did not prove to be successful. The only relatively consistent positive finding with regard to individuals with cerebral pathology was with regard to unilateral hemispheric involvement, but even that finding turned out to be useless diagnostically. While the relationship of Verbal and Performance tasks seemed consistently related to left and right cerebral involvement, given a V:P relationship was not, in and of itself, information enough for the clinician to conclude, in the absence of other clinical and test data, that an individual had left- or right-cerebral pathology. Performance on none of the Wechsler material, looked at any level (subtest or with regard to Verbal/Performance differences) stood in isomorphic relation with any kind of cerebral pathology.

To expect that cerebral pathology should affect an individual's intellective/cognitive behavior isomorphically is obviously naïve. Too many factors must be taken into consideration to understand how an individual performs intellectually. It seems apparent that cerebral pathology affects individuals' intellective/cognitive behavior individually. Loss of or interference with intellective/cognitive functions might bother some individuals, might not bother others; the age of individuals, their sex, their level of education, their capacity to compensate, the amount of involvement, the locus of involvement, the length of time of the involvement, etc., *all* of these factors act in concert to determine how individuals will perform, for example, on a test of intelligence such as the Wechsler test. The specificity hypothesis, i.e. the expectation that specific kinds of cerebral pathology would eventuate in consistently specific kinds of performance on the intellective/cognitive functions assessed by the Wechsler test, turned out to be incorrect.

A novel approach to the effect of cerebral pathology on intellectual functioning has been utilized by, e.g. Goldman, Greenblatt and Coon (1946) and Kraus and Walker (1968). Rather than starting with the nature of the cerebral pathology and trying to find the psychological functioning which corresponds to particular pathology, these investigators began by trying to identify just the kind of cognitive pathology empirically found on the Wechsler. Goldman *et al.* isolated seven different patterns of functioning on the Wechsler with regard to cerebral pathology (regardless of type):

(1) marked lowering of Comprehension and Information
(2) Comprehension holding up uniquely well
(3) poor performance on the Performance tasks and poor performance on Digits
(4) poor performance on the Performance tasks and poor performance on Arithmetic
(5) poor performance on the Performance tasks and poor performance on Arithmetic and Digits
(6) good performance on Block design and poor performance on Digits and Similarities
(7) poor performance on all the subtests.

Beginning with these intellective/cognitive types, Goldman *et al.* found that clinical findings seem to correlate with the types. For example, Type 1 cognitive/intellective pathology seemed correlated with individuals who were given to marked aggressivity, irritability and explosiveness, especially when under the influence of alcohol, an aggressive type of psychopath. Type 2 did not seem to be associated with any clearcut clinical picture. Type 3 seemed to be associated with brain atrophy. Type 4 seemed to be associated with psychopaths who committed sex crimes. Type 5 seemed to be associated with epilepsy. Type 6 manifested no clinical evidence of brain disorder, and Type 7 manifested clinical evidence of defective memory, confusion, clouding of consciousness, disturbance of speech, and deterioration of conduct.

Kraus and Walker isolated six intellective/cognitive types:

Type 1 was characterized by impairment in rote memory (Digits),

Type 2 was characterized by impairment in visuo-motor abilities (Digit symbol, Block design),

Type 3 was characterized by impairment in constructional activity (Block design, Object assembly),

Type 4 was characterized by impairment in judgment (Comprehension),

Type 5 was characterized by impairment for making closure (Object assembly), and

Type 6 was characterized by impaired verbal abstraction (Similarities).

Since the research exploring the errors certain cerebrally impaired types made on the Wechsler seemed to have been fruitless, perhaps research beginning with what might be called "error types" (to borrow from Watson [1965c]) might lead to more meaningful results. If we begin with examining what cognitive/intellective difficulties are manifested in individuals with cerebral pathology, *sui generis*, as determined by factor analysis, these intellective/cognitive types might be found to relate more consistently to clinical data than we found when we looked at the data the other way around, beginning with the clinical types and trying to find the consistent cognitive/intellective patterns associated with them.

CHAPTER 5

The Use of the Wechsler in the Assessment of Schizophrenia

SINCE we are maintaining that a test of intelligence is a test of cognitive functions (being put to use in service of problem solving and reasoning), then we surely should expect that schizophrenia, a form of psychopathology that has been shown to be characterized by disordered cognitive functioning (e.g. Bolles and Goldstein, 1938; Bychowski, 1935; Cameron, 1938a, b, 1939; Goldstein, 1939; Kraepelin, 1902; Rawlings, 1921; Vigotsky, 1934; and White, 1926), should manifest this cognitive disorder on the Wechsler tests in an identifiable way. However, we have seen (in Chapter 4) that while cerebral pathology involves cognitive dysfunctioning, the question: do patients with cerebral pathology manifest disorder in their cognitive/intellective functioning? had to be made more specific. So, too, with schizophrenia. As we did with regard to cerebral pathology, we will examine the data that reflect on how the cognitive disorder of the schizophrenic becomes reflected in their intellectual behavior.

Not on the basis of any theoretical rationale but solely on the basis of their performance on the subtests, Wechsler (1944) maintained that the schizophrenic should be expected to do poorly on Picture arrangement, Picture completion, Object assembly, Digit symbol and Similarities, relatively well on Information and Vocabulary, and moderately well on Digits and Block design. Rapaport (Rapaport et al., 1945) noted that the schizophrenic should be expected to do relatively well on Information and Vocabulary, moderately well on Digit symbol and Block design, and poorly on Comprehension, Arithmetic, Picture arrangement, Picture completion, and Object assembly (in many aspects, similar to the suggestions by Wechsler). Schafer (1948) indicated that the schizophrenic does poorly on Comprehension, Arithmetic, and Picture completion. From all of these extensive clinical studies, therefore, we have some expectation that schizophrenics should be expected to do poorly on Arithmetic, Similarities, Comprehension, Picture arrangement, Picture completion, Object assembly, and Digit symbol, while doing relatively well on Information and Vocabulary.

Maloney, DeYoung and Majovsky (1975) found that Vocabulary does, indeed, remain relatively undisturbed in schizophrenia, and Price and Gentry (1968) found that acutely disturbed schizophrenics do, in fact, do poorly on Comprehension. Wechsler and Jaros (1965) delineated five signs they thought were characteristic of schizophrenic patterning (on the WISC):

(1) any three subtests deviating by three or more scale score points from the mean,
(2) performance on Picture Arrangement better than Picture completion, and performance on Object assembly better than Coding, both by three points or more,
(3) performance on Comprehension and Similarities better than Arithmetic by three or more points,
(4) Verbal I.Q. different from Performance I.Q. by sixteen points,
(5) Sign #1 plus any one of the other three.

However, it must be noted that while Wechsler indicated that the first sign seemed to differentiate best, he also noted that, at its best, it was effective in identifying the person as schizophrenic only 50% of the time.

Other research in search for the unique subtest patterning for schizophrenia has not eventuated in enthusiastic support for its existence. Garfield (1949) and Kogan (1950) could not find any unique subtest patterning for schizophrenics in general, while Frank (1956), Harper (1950a), and Kay (1979) could not find any unique subtest pattern for any of the clinical subgroups of schizophrenia (e.g. paranoids, catatonics, hebephrenics, etc.). When comparing the pattern of subtest performance to that of normals, Harper (1950b) found that the schizophrenics were differentiated from the normals on: Information, Block design, and Digit symbol, but even then he noted that the discrimination is not adequate for clinical use. Holzberg and Deane (1950) found that the schizophrenic shows greater scatter on Comprehension, Picture completion, and Block design. Garfield (1948), however, did not find that his sample of schizophrenics showed any unique subtest performance as distinguished from normals. Neither in comparison to the performance of a general population of psychotics (Rabin, 1944b), neurotics (Kissel, 1966a; Kraus, 1965a; Monroe, 1952), or mental defectives (Magaret and Wright, 1943) did schizophrenics perform uniquely enough so as to define a specific pattern of subtest performance for themselves. In comparison to the performance of patients with known cerebral pathology, schizophrenics were found to do better than some (paretics) on Block design and Digits, but more poorly on Comprehension and Picture arrangement (Magaret, 1942).

Several investigators have attempted to develop formal ratios to identify the performance of schizophrenics. One of the first of such ratios was developed by Rabin (1941). His ratio of subtests representative of the performance of schizophrenics was:

$$\frac{\text{Information} + \text{Comprehension} + \text{Block design}}{\text{Digit symbol} + \text{Object assembly} + \text{Similarities}}$$

The numerator was composed of subtests Rabin believed to hold up in schizophrenia (that is, where the schizophrenic would do well), the denominator, subtests which did not. While Rabin had relative success with his Index differentiating the performance of schizophrenics from normals (nurses) and neurotics, subsequent tests of the effectiveness of Rabin's Index have not been positive (e.g. Brown, 1949; Rogers, 1951; Webb, 1947). DeWolfe (1971) developed a pattern of subtest variation which he·thought differentiated schizophrenics from those with cerebral pathology. DeWolfe found that a pattern of Digit symbol being greater than Comprehension correctly identified subjects as having cerebral pathology 82% of the time, a pattern of Digit symbol being less than Comprehension correctly identified subjects as schizophrenics 75% of the time. However, a cross-validation of the effectiveness of the DeWolfe signs (Watson, 1972) demonstrated that it proved effective in only one hospital but not in another. The source of such instability of findings was not explored. Rogers (1951) compared the signs of schizophrenia on the Wechsler offered by several investigators (Rapaport, Schafer, Rabin, and Wechsler) and found that Rapaport's predictions were substantiated most of all (basically, that in schizophrenia, vocabulary would hold up, particularly in relation to Comprehension, Similarities, Arithmetic, Picture arrangement, and Digit symbol).

Rather than compare the subtest performance of schizophrenics with but one other group, some investigators have elected to make multi-group comparisons, comparing the performance of schizophrenics with the performance of several other psychiatric groups simultaneously. Wittenborn (1949), for example, performed an analysis of the distribution of correlations with regard to the data presented by Rapaport (Rapaport *et al.*, 1945) to determine whether patients with the same diagnosis produced similar subtest patterns. Wittenborn selected five patients each from each of Rapaport's eleven major clinical groupings. An analysis of the distribution of correlations with each group indicated marked variability within each group. In another analysis of these data by Wittenborn, one patient from each of the eleven diagnostic groups were selected at random, and the performance of each one was correlated (rank order) with each other one. It was found that the performance of patients with different diagnoses was intercorrelated to as high a degree as patients with the same diagnoses. Kaldegg (1950) found no unique patterns amongst a variety of psychiatric groups. Frank (Frank, Corrie and Fogel, 1955) analyzed the Wechsler data of patients diagnosed as schizophrenic, brain-damaged, and neurotic. The data were drawn from Rapaport, Cohen (1950) and other published data, grouping the performance of these patients on the Wechsler according to the diagnosis they had received. Thirty-six different diagnostic groups were formed, but analysis of variance indicated that only the test performance of eight groups revealed significant homogeneity of subtest performance. These groups were all found in the data presented by Rapaport. The diagnostic groups which revealed such homogeneity of performance were: Maladjusted Patrol, acute paranoid schizophrenia, deteriorated paranoid schizophrenia, deteriorated unclassified schizophrenia, coarctated preschizophrenia, involutional depression and a group labeled anxiety and depression. The rest of Rapaport's twenty-one groups, Cohen's three groups of schizophrenics, neurotics, and brain-damaged subjects, and the groupings derived from the other published research all proved to reflect such heterogeneity of performance that the data from each group could not be said to constitute samplings from the same kinds of populations. Travers (1939) had reported that Fisher had suggested to him to use the multiple regression technique and discriminant function analysis on psychological problems, which he did. In like manner, Garrett (1943) argued for the use of multiple regression techniques in psychology as a more meaningful way of differentiating between groups through the weighting of individual items, and research workers in government demonstrated the effectiveness of multiple regression techniques for differentiating profiles of tests of different diagnostic groups (Staff Personnel Research Section, 1946). Following these trends Klein (1946, 1948) utilized the multiple regression equation to help determine a meaningful pattern of subtest performance for schizophrenics, but found that basically even that technique did not permit of individual prediction or identification. Frank (1953) compared the effectiveness of the Klein and Harper (1950b) regression equations in identifying the performance of schizophrenics. While the Klein regression equation identified 19% of the non-schizophrenics as schizophrenic, the Harper equation mis-identified 47% (of the non-schizophrenics as schizophrenic) of the time. Patterson (1946a) found that correct diagnoses could be made from test patterns by clinicians 70% of the time, but subsequent multiple group comparisons (e.g. by Johnson, 1949; Winne and Schoonover, 1972) failed to yield unique patterns of subtest performances for the different psychiatric groups.

Thus, while the schizophrenic does manifest impairment in cognitive/ intellective functioning, it seems clear no *one* area of cognitive impairment seems involved (at least as far as the data from the Wechsler test are concerned) in schizophrenia. In light of the inability to identify a unique pattern of intellective performance for schizophrenia, or with regard to the subtypes of schizophrenia, it must be that individuals, though being diagnosed as schizophrenic, manifest sufficient individual differences in intellective/cognitive functioning so as to preclude finding a common subtest pattern for all schizophrenics or all people diagnosed as one of the subtypes.

In the absence of research which supported the hypothesis that specific psychiatric groups would yield unique patterns of subtest performance, research has turned towards analysis of scatter (which does not imply any particular fixed pattern of subtest performance, it merely notes how much overall difference there is amongst subtest performance) and more subjective modes of data analysis.

The concept of scatter in intelligence test analysis has existed since the early days of psychometric analysis of psychological functioning. Binet, himself, was aware of scattering of performance on the various subtests of his Scale (e.g. Binet and Henri, 1895; Binet and Simon, 1916); he wrote: "the various psychological processes arrange themselves in a different configuration with each individual" (Binet and Henri, 1895, p. 411). Clinicians focused on analyzing performance on the Binet Scale in terms of the scattering of functioning (e.g. Wallin, 1917, 1918, 1922, 1927). However, a review of some 40 years of research with the Binet evaluated in the following comment, "Research up to now has failed to demonstrate clearly any clinical use for numerical measure of scatter" (Harris and Shakow, 1937, p. 148).

Despite the failure of this research with scatter analysis, clinicians remained convinced of the meaningfulness of individual variation in psychological functions (e.g. Wells and Kelley, 1920; Wells 1927), and, hence, the interest continued. Rather than question this notion, clinicians criticized the Binet for not being structured in such a way so as to facilitate inter-test comparisons. When the Wechsler test appeared on the psychometric scene, hope was re-kindled that because of the structure of the Wechsler test, such inter-test comparisons could be made more meaningfully and scatter analysis made more fruitful.

While Wechsler became involved in pattern analysis only, Rapaport (Rapaport et al., 1945) focused on both pattern and scatter analysis, and the concept of scatter re-assumed a position of import in the clinical analysis of test data (e.g. Schafer, 1944; Schafer and Rapaport, 1944).

Scatter presumes some baseline against which to plot the positions of the subtests. Rapaport (Rapaport et al., 1945; Schafer and Rapaport, 1944) utilized three such baselines, viz., mean scatter (where the baseline is the mean of all the subtest scores), a modified mean scatter (where the baseline value is the mean of all the subtests in which the subtest falls, e.g. (Verbal or Performance)), and Vocabulary scatter (where the baseline value is the subject's own Vocabulary score). The search for some significant degree of interest scatter for specific psychopathological conditions has also proved futile (e.g. Bradway and Benson, 1955; Gilliland et al., 1943). Indeed, while one would expect that the cognitive disorganization of the schizophrenic would be reflected in significant inter-test scatter, this is clearly not always the case. Gilliland et al., for example, found that their sample of schizophrenics manifested less inter-test scatter than their normal controls, and Frost (1960) found no degree of subtest deviation related to any diagnosis. Clearly one of the uncontrolled factors in such research is length of hospitalization. The effect of institutionalization is such that even individuals with the exact same diagnosis can look quite different psychometrically if length of hospitalization is not equated for. The effect of institutionalization on Wechsler test scores has been amply charted (e.g. Bernstein, Klein, Berger and Cohen, 1965; Davis, Dizzonne and DeWolfe et al., 1971; Watson, 1965a, b).

The most comprehensive analysis of scatter was done by Rapaport (Rapaport et al., 1945). The data were analyzed according to which psychiatric groups manifested most scatter (overall subtest scatter, Verbal or Performance scatter, Vocabulary scatter). Each psychiatric group was analyzed exhaustively in terms of how they scatter on the Wechsler and where. And while a tremendous amount of psychological insight might be gleaned as to how certain individuals function on the Wechsler subtests, a careful reading of this monumental work reveals that whatever insights are gained have nothing to do with psychiatric differentiation. Poor performance on any particular subtest or a particular degree of scatter was not found to be related to any specific psychiatric type. Thus, for example, poor performance on a given subtest might be characteristic of either a depressive, a schizophrenic, or a neurotic. Perhaps the overall amount of scatter could be seen to bear some relationship to deterioration, but nothing more specific than that. Subsequent analyses of the diagnostic utility of intra-test scatter have substantiated this conclusion (e.g. Watson, 1965b; Wentworth-Rohr and Macintosh, 1972).

Rather than search for inter-test scatter, some investigators have reasoned that whatever cognitive disorganization an individual might have, might better be reflected within any one given cognitive modality. Thus, investigators have looked at intra-test scatter. As reasonable as the expectation might appear that cognitive disorganization should be reflected in considerable intra-test scatter, the data do not support the hypothesis.

From other research (e.g. Frank, 1975) the argument could be made that since psychiatric diagnoses do not constitute groupings of individuals according to psychological functioning anyway, the search for some common psychological pattern of intellective/cognitive performance was, perforce, due to failure. A differentiation within schizophrenia that Frank's research showed to be defined by psychological dimensions was the process-reactive differentiation. Too few studies exist which have explored the intellectual performance of these two groups for any definitive statement to be made regarding performance on the Wechsler tests. That which has been done (e.g. Davis, DeWolfe and Gustafson, 1972; Royer and Janowitch, 1973) do not indicate that the two groups perform significantly differently on the Wechsler. And research on the borderline groups (e.g. Frank, 1970a) did not reveal any unique pattern of subtest performance on the Wechsler (their uniqueness in psychological functioning became evident on the Rorschach).

While the development of the research covered reflects analysis of the test data by increasingly more sophisticated "objective" methods (e.g. formal ratios, analysis of variance, multiple regression equations), another group of investigators have explored the relationship of schizophrenia to subtest performance from a more subjective and/or qualitative point of view. For example, one early study (Patterson, 1946a) had clinicians make diagnoses just from viewing the subtest patterns. The most correctly identified subtest pattern was that of paranoid schizophrenia; this contributed to the overall "hit" rate by the clinicians of 70%. Subsequent explorations of the ability of clinicians to correctly identify the patient's diagnosis from just viewing their subtest performance (e.g. Cohen, 1955; Hunt and Walker, 1962, 1971; Hunt, Walker and Jones, 1960; Levine, 1949) eventuates in modest (at best) results. Both Cohen and Hunt found that not all clinicians possessed the ability to correctly identify patterns from the Wechsler data equally; some psychologists could correctly identify the patient's diagnosis from the subtest pattern, others could not. Thus, one uncontrolled aspect of this research is the variable of the skill of the clinician to accomplish the task.

Another more "subjective" approach to the clinical use of the analysis of Wechsler test performance has been to examine individuals' performance qualitatively, that is, with regard to content. This certainly was the recommendation of clinicians in the face of the absence of the success of the more "objective" methods of subtest analysis (e.g. Brecher, 1946). Following the lead of such individuals as Capps (1939), Feifel (1949), Gerstein (1949), and Yacorzynski (1941), researchers such as Blatt (1959), Chodorkoff and Mussen (1952), Fox (1947), Hunt (Hunt and Arnhoff, 1955; Hunt and Jones, 1958b; Jones, 1959), Moran (Moran, 1953; Moran, Moran and Blake, 1954), Richman (1964), Sigel (1963, 1967), and Stacey and Portnoy (1950) analyzed the responses to Vocabulary in detail in order to ferret out clinically useful material. Jortner (1970) analyzed responses to the Similarities subtest, and Norman and Wilensky (1961) analyzed responses to the Information subtests in detailed fashion. Hunt developed a scale of schizophrenicity to determine the presence of this dimension in the responses to the Vocabulary and Comprehension subtests. Moran applied a bi-dimensional analysis to responses to Vocabulary, exploring the degree to which the answers could be rated with regard to two dimensions: public—private and concrete—abstract performance. Norman and Wilensky analyzed the reasoning errors and recall problems inherent in patients' responses to Information, and Jortner analyzed the level of abstraction of the answers on the Similarities subtest. Essentially this more qualitative analysis, viewing the answers from a psychological point of view, rather than a psychometric one (i.e. whether the answer is merely correct or not) is still in the early stage of usage, but appears promising.

In summary, while we would have expected the cognitive disorder of the schizophrenic to be reflected in a systematic patterning of subtests and/or degree of scatter, we have found that the data do not substantiate such an expectation. And the expectation that the different subtypes of schizophrenia would produce significantly different patterns of subtests was not found. Indeed, *psychometrically* (that is, with regard to subtest patterns and scatter analysis) sometimes the schizophrenic could not be differentiated from the non-schizophrenic. Clearly, the person diagnosed as "schizophrenic," or even "paranoid schizophrenic," for example, function sufficiently individually so as to make the search for the common patterns-by-diagnosis futile. Looking only at the subtest performance from a pattern-analytic point of view does not even enable the clinician to differentiate the patient with cerebral pathology from that of the schizophrenic; if both have difficulties in conceptualization (for their own reasons), tests which entail capacity for conceptual thinking will be impaired *in both* instances. The way a more accurate clinical differentiation, both within schizophrenia, and between schizophrenia and cerebral pathology, can be made was through analysis of the content of an individual's answers to questions and a qualitative analysis of their performance on the non-verbal tasks. While it might have lent an air of legitimacy and scientificness of the work that clinicians do had we found these psychometric patterns, we are left with the impression that a differentiation between schizophrenics and any other group must still be made by the analysis of the data by the clinician, not a statistic or a machine (computer).

CHAPTER 6

The Use of the Wechsler in the Assessment of Other Psychiatric Disorders

Affective Disorders

Very little research has been done on the intellectual/cognitive functioning of the manic, the manic-depressive, or the depressive through the use of the Wechsler intelligence tests. Waldfogel and Guy (1951) found that Rabin's index (Rabin, 1941) did not differentiate the affective disorders from schizophrenia, and Rapaport's signs of depression were primarily for the 50-year-old person rather than the 30-year-old depressive. Wechsler did not posit any particular pattern of subtest performance for the affective disorders.

Neurosis

Wechsler (1944) reasoned that the neurotics' feelings of inadequacy would make them do poorly on tasks requiring immediate effort. Thus, he expected that the neurotic would do poorly on Object assembly and Digits. He also expected them to do poorly on Picture arrangement because of their lack of "social alertness and reflects their common inability to deal with social situations" (Wechsler, 1944, p. 156).

Hewson (1949) developed several ratios which she felt could differentiate the psychiatric person from the non-psychiatric; these were:

(1) $\dfrac{\text{Picture completion} + \text{Picture arrangement}}{\text{Arithmetic} + \text{Digit symbol}}$

(2) $\dfrac{\text{Comprehension} + \text{Picture arrangement}}{\text{Digits} + \text{Digit symbol}}$

(3) $\dfrac{\text{Comprehension} + \text{Similarities}}{\text{Digits} + \text{Digit symbol}}$

71

(4) <u>Object assembly + Block design</u>

Digits + Similarities

A person's performance matching one or more of these signs would be indicative of psychopathology. But as regards neurotics, Hewson concluded, "Some types of neurotics are detected by these methods but many neurotic persons are found to have normal patterns" (Hewson, 1949, p. 265).

Warner (1950) found that as compared to normal controls, neurotics do poorly on Similarities and Block design, but (contrary to what Wechsler predicted) better than controls on Picture arrangement and Object assembly. Warner did not find that either inter-test variability, scatter, or the V : P ratio differentiated the neurotics from the normals.

Wittenborn and Holzberg (1951) correlated subtest performance with diagnoses. Of the ninety-nine correlations, only one, Hysteria and Digits, reached significance (.42); all the rest hovered around .10 to .25. Bloom and Entin (1975) found the same relationship: relating WAIS performance and MMPI scores, only Digits correlated significantly with scores on the Hysteria scale (.35). L'Abate (1962) found no significant relationship of scatter to any of the MMPI scales, and Heyer (1949) found no significant relationship between scatter and diagnosis for neurotics.

Harwood (1967) found no specific subtest pattern for introverted individuals.

Sociopathic Personality

Wechsler (1944) posited that the performance of the sociopathic personality on the subtests would be characterized as:

(1) Performance I.Q. greater than Verbal I.Q.

(2) Object assembly + Picture arrangement > Block design + Picture completion

(3) low scores on Information and Arithmetic

(4) relatively low scores on Comprehension, Digit span, Similarities and Digit symbol, but

(5) relatively good scores on Picture arrangement and Object assembly.

As regards these predictions, Sloan and Cutts (1945) and Cutts and Sloan (1945) found that their group of sociopathic personalities (mental defectives committed for delinquent behavior) showed a pattern of subtest performance which conformed to Wechsler's expectations. As predicted, their subjects performed well on Object assembly, poorly on Arithmetic, and their Verbal/Performance ratio was in the expected direction. The data presented by Altus and Clark (1949) demonstrated that their sample of army behavior problems performed on the subtests remarkably similar to Wechsler's adolescent psychopathic group, both in terms of which subtests they performed well on as well as which ones they performed poorly on, and the Verbal/Performance ratio. In examining the subtest performance of "well-behaved" and "problem" children, Woody (1968) found that the "problem" children performed poorly on most of the tests Wechsler would predict: Information, Arithmetic, and Digit span. On the other hand, Walters' (1953) group of sociopaths (prisoners) did most poorly on Object assembly and Picture arrangement (subtests on which Wechsler predicted sociopaths should do well). The group Walters studied also did well on Picture completion and Information (the latter, contrary to prediction from Wechsler's data). Purcell (1956) found that his group of sociopaths did more poorly on Comprehension than Similarities or Vocabulary, in accord with the pattern of performance in Wechsler's data. However, Hale and Landino (1981) examined the Wechsler performance of one hundred boys (aged 7–16) who had been referred by their classroom teacher for psychological evaluation. They utilized the Quay–Peterson Behavior Problem Check List (Quay and Peterson, 1979) to differentiate the one hundred students into four sub-groups: those students who were identified by the Quay–Peterson Behavior Check List as conduct problems, those identified as withdrawn, a mixed group (conduct problems and withdrawn), and a non-problem group. Discriminant analysis was performed with the result being that no subtest pattern was found by which these groups could be differentiated. Haynes and Bensch (1981) tried to differentiate recidivists from non-recidivist delinquents in terms of a $P > V$ pattern (on the WISC-R). Only 70% of the recidivists showed the $P > V$ pattern, but so did 42% of the non-recidivists.

Some research exists which has attempted to differentiate subtest patterns within the range and variety of sociopathic personalities. Thus, Randolph, Richardson and Johnson (1961) found that solitary (asocial) delinquents score higher on the WAIS (Full Scale I.Q. 105) than the more social delinquents (Full Scale I.Q. 93), and Kissel (1966b) found that asocial delinquents fared better on Picture completion than the more social delinquent. Kahn (1968) found that burglars and murderers could be differentiated on their performance on Block design only, but Hays and Solway (1977) found that no subtest differences existed between violent and non-violent juvenile offenders.

As regards the relative position of Verbal to Performance I.Q. as predicted from Wechsler's data (P > V), Wiens *et al.* (1959) found that while the performance of 74% of their group of sociopaths conformed to this expectation, 26% did not, and Kingsley (1960) found that the P > V pattern existed in some normals as well. Other research (e.g. Brown and Partington, 1942; Craddick, 1961; Deiker, 1973; Gurvitz, 1950; Lewandowski and Saccuzzo, 1975; Panton, 1960) fails to confirm expectations based on Wechsler's data with regard to specific subtest patterning as well as V : P ratio. Graham and Kamano (1958) and Henning and Levy (1967) found that the performance of sociopaths on the Wechsler were being unduly influenced by reading difficulties more so than the factor of sociopathy, *per se.*

Except for the research on the sociopathic personality, there is little in this section to support the notion of unique subtest patterns for unique psychiatric types.

Anxiety

Clinicians have come to expect that anxiety interferes with intellective/ cognitive functioning in specific ways, for example, in reducing the capacity for attention and concentration and by reducing psychomotor efficiency. Thus, we have come to expect that anxiety will interfere with performance on such subtests of the Wechsler as Digits, Arithmetic, and the timed subtests. Research exploring the relationship of anxiety to subtest performance has employed a variety of criterion measures for anxiety, viz., diagnosis (anxiety neurosis), and psychometric measures (e.g. the Taylor Scale, the Cattell Scale, and the "neurotic triad" of the MMPI). Clustered in the same body of research are studies which examine the effect of stress (both real and induced) on subtest performance.

In terms of psychometric criteria of anxiety, the most frequently used is the Taylor Scale (Taylor, 1953). Correlating subjects' performance on every subtest with their Taylor Scale score, Calvin, Koons, Bingham and Fink (1955) found that while the Taylor Scale correlated modestly with Digits (.37) and Block design (.36), correlations with the other subtests were, in most instances, insignificantly different from zero. Hafner, Pollie and Wapner (1960) and Rowley and Stone (1963) correlated Taylor Scale scores with WISC subtest performance. For the children (both sets of whom were from clinics), Taylor Scale data correlated modestly with Block design and Digit symbol only, or with none of the subtests (Matarazzo, 1955; Mayzner, Sersen and Tresselt, 1955; Rowley and Stone, 1963). Looking only at the relationship between Taylor Scale scores and scores on Block design, Digits, and Arithmetic, Boor and Schill (1968) found that Taylor Scale scores correlated with Digit span only. Looking at performance on Comprehension, Vocabulary, and Similarities only, Matarazzo, Ulett, Guze and Saslow (1954) did not find that Taylor Scale scores related to scores on these subtests. And while Siegman (1956) found Taylor Scale scores to relate to the timed tasks only, Edwards (1966) did not. Kraus (1965b) did not find any significant relationship between Cattell's Anxiety Scale (Cattell, 1957) and any subtest performance. Dana (1957b) examined the relationship of the so-called "neurotic triad" (Hysteria, Depression and Hypochondriasis) of the MMPI and Wechsler data, and Jurjevich (1963) and Shoben (1950) explored the relationship of MMPI data and Wechsler performance, all without positive results.

Lewinski (1945) examined the subtest performance of white, male military personnel diagnosed as anxiety neurotic. Although he found that Digits was significantly low, Block design was high, but no psychometric pattern emerged which seemed unique to this group.

Ordinarily, we have made the assumption of an isomorphic relationship between anxiety and disruption of intellectual performance, the more of one, the more of the other. However, Feldhausen and Klausmeier (1962) found that, at least in children, anxiety influences intellectual performance dependent upon level of intelligence.

While phenomenologically and/or autonomically stress and anxiety might not be distinguishable, generally we make a difference as regards their source: anxiety is the term for that kind of pressure from within, stress, when the pressure emanates from the environment. A number of studies have examined the effect of induced stress upon subtest performance.

Oros, Johnson and Lewis (1972) told subjects, "You did not do very well on the I.Q. test that you took last week. Here are some other tests I would like for you to take. Let's see if you can't do better on these." The children were then given the subtests of the WISC. The experience impaired performance on Information, Arithmetic, Digits, Vocabulary, Block design, and Coding.

Solkoff (1964) induced stress by interrupting subjects (brain-injured children) while they were performing the WISC. Only Coding was affected significantly.

In the study by Walker, Sannito and Firetto (1970) college students were told that they had performed questionably on a personality test and that it was felt that they should be given an intelligence test. After the administration of the Verbal tasks, the subjects were asked how they felt, that being the criterion for the assessment of their level of distress. The experimental group, exposed to this experience, demonstrated significant differences (impairment on Information, Arithmetic, and Digits).

In the study by Davis (1969), the examiner frowned at the subject, acted as though he could not understand the subject's answers, and feigned puzzlement at the subject's responses. The subjects reported that they were made "frustrated" and "nervous" by the experience. Pre- and post-stress experience was assessed via the Arithmetic subtest only. While Davis reported a statistically significant lowering of subjects' Arithmetic subtest scores, in fact, the mean difference pre- and post- was 1½ scaled score points, not a very large actual difference.

Dunn (1968) induced stress in college juniors by telling them that they were going to be given a test, that it was a short form of an intelligence test, and that the results would become part of their academic record. Response to stress was assessed by subject report; level of anxiety was assessed by the Sarason Test of Test-Taking Anxiety (Mandler and Sarason, 1958). Dunn looked at the relationship between subjects' performance on Information and Digit span to the test measure of anxiety and reported stress and nervousness. In the experimentally-induced stress condition, only the subjects' performance on the Information subtest seemed to be affected (-.33).

Morris and Liebert (1969) induced stress by letting subjects know they were being timed while taking the following subtests: Arithmetic, Picture completion, Block design, Picture arrangement and Object assembly. Morris and Liebert felt that the mediating factor would be whether the subject was a worrier or not. Low worriers were spurred on by being aware of being timed; knowing they were being timed lowered the performance of high worriers.

Moon and Lair (1970) showed subjects a stress-inducing film. They then examined the relationship of Digit symbol performance to stress and found a modest relationship.

Some studies examined the influence of real stress on Wechsler performance. In the study by Capretta and Berkun (1962) the stress condition was that subjects were crossing a rope-bridge, 200 feet long, suspended 50 feet above a rocky ravine. The examiner stopped the subjects midway and administered the Digit span subtest. The "control" condition was administration of Digits just before or just after crossing the bridge. The stress condition significantly interfered with performance on Digits. Grisso and Meadow (1967) considered taking the Rorschach a stressful experience. Taking the Rorschach before the Wechsler proved to influence performance on Digits, Comprehension and Similarities.

Purcell, Drevdahl and Purcell (1952) felt that the way one assesses anxiety from the Wechsler test might determine whether the effect is observed or not. They suggested altitude scatter (subtest scatter from the subjects' highest subtest score) as demonstrating a linear relationship to anxiety.

What, now, can we say about the capacity of the Wechsler to resonate with anxiety? In the first place, performance on the Digit span subtest seemed to be the most frequently affected subtest by anxiety or stress; to some extent (that is, in some studies while not in others) response to stress or anxiety affected Information, Arithmetic and Block design. The notion that anxiety or stress would influence the timed subtests more than the untimed ones received variable support (in some studies yes, in some studies no). Stress seemed to influence performance on the subtests more so than test-assessed anxiety, while of the latter measures, the Taylor Scale was seen to bear the most consistent relationship to anxiety.

Clearly some very important dimensions of this methodology are not always considered. For example, actual experience of stress and actual concern with regard to what is posited as a stressful or distressful situation are not always assessed. And there is some question about the relationship of anxiety to stress, where one is internally-determined while the other is more situationally-determined. Usually the clinician would like to be able to determine the presence of the internally-determined state (anxiety) from the patient's performance on the subtests. However, it might also be important to determine an individual's tolerance for pressure as a dimension which influences life adjustment; performance on Digits seems to be the most reliable method of assessing response to stress or anxiety.

CHAPTER 7

Factors which Influence the Clinical Use
of Subtest Patterning

WHEN the Binet was *the* test of intelligence, efforts had been made to extract personality and dimensions of psychopathology from Binet material, but as we have learned (Harris and Shakow, 1937) those efforts came to grief. The conclusion, however, was not that the notion that an assessment of psychopathology could be made from an analysis of intelligence test data was in error, but that the structure of the Binet interfered with such an analysis. We have seen how Yerkes (Yerkes *et al.*, 1915) had tried to reorganize the Binet, grouping the test material by content, not by mental age, but in the absence of sophisticated psychometric knowhow, that revision of the Binet failed. The psychometric world waited for (a) Wechsler who, some 20 years and much psychometric knowledge later, with the model of others in the field of test construction who, in trying to accomplish the very things Wechsler was trying to do, paved the way for him. The signposts were there for Wechsler to follow; he did so, and the test he put together seemed as though it would be the answer to all the clinician's psychometric prayers. However, we have also seen that in spite of the fact that the Wechsler looked like it would be ideal for a comparative study of the intellective/cognitive behavior of various psychopathological types, 40 years of research has failed to support that idea. Analysis of psychopathology from the Wechsler Scale fared no better than that from the Binet. As scientists we should wonder about such outcomes.

The notion that an instrument which assesses intellectual/cognitive functioning should, at the same time, be tapping into other aspects of the personality seems tenable. And we can certainly point to research in personality and psychopathology which demonstrate that other aspects of the individual do, indeed, influence cognitive functioning, to one degree or another, in one way or another. One question remains, therefore, as to why, in the face of what seemed like psychometrically optimum conditions, did the Wechsler test fail to produce results any more encouraging than that with the Binet.

One possible explanation for the fact that the Wechsler test failed to live up to expectations may have to do with the psychologically simplistic and psychometrically naïve manner in which this hypothesis has been stated. Essentially, the assumption has been that once the intellective, more purely cognitive aspects have been extracted from the subtests, that of the variance which is left is contributed by personality factors. However, the research is clear that many non-emotional, non-motivational, non-personality-style factors influence performance on a test of intelligence (see, e.g., earlier comments by Rabin, 1945b; Rabin and Guertin, 1945; Schofield, 1952; Guertin, Frank and Rabin, 1956; Guertin, Ladd, Frank, Rabin and Hiester, 1966, 1971; Guertin, Rabin, Frank and Ladd, 1962; Gurvitz, 1952). We should examine some of these.

From the early days in psychometrics, the fact that men and women, of the same age level, level of intelligence, socio-economic level, etc. perform differently on tests of intelligence has been public knowledge (e.g. Burt, 1911; Goddard, 1911; Stern, 1914). This was noted by Wechsler (1939) and supported by subsequent research (e.g. Brown and Bryan, 1955; Overall *et al.*, 1978). For example, Wechsler noted that boys tended to do better than girls on Arithmetic, girls, on Vocabulary. Boor (1975) found that males scored higher on Information, Comprehension, Arithmetic, Picture completion, Block design and Vocabulary; females scored higher on Digit symbol as well as achieving higher Verbal, Performance and Full Scale I.Q.s. Norman (1953) found that males scored higher than females on Arithmetic, females, on Digit symbol. Shaw (1965) found that males scored higher than females on Arithmetic, Comprehension, Block design, and Picture arrangement, females, on Digit symbol. Silverstein and Fisher (1960) found that males scored higher than females on Information, Comprehension, Picture completion and Block design. Strange and Palmer (1953) found that males scored higher than females on almost all subtests as well as achieved higher Verbal, Performance and Full Scale I.Q.s.

Wechsler had stated that men did better on Information, Arithmetic and Picture completion, while women did better on Similarities, Vocabulary and Digit symbol. Levinson's (1963b) research failed to replicate these findings; while Lewandowski, Saccuzzo and Lewandowski (1977) found that males seem to conform more to Wechsler's presumed patterns for males than females did for females. Turner and Willerman (1977) found that while sex differences did not show up on overall measures of intelligence or specific subtest performance, sex influenced performance on specific subtest items. Quereshi (1968b) found that the influence of the sex of the person taking the test cannot be assessed out of context of the sex of the person administering the test.

Sex itself, therefore, becomes a person-variable which systematically influences the performance on the subtests of the Wechsler of males and females. If clinical studies were done on only one sex, or sex was not incorporated into the design as a factor to be controlled for, patterns of subtests for groups of subjects could be influenced significantly by this variable which such influence would go undetected.

Another factor which influences the pattern of subtest performance is level of intelligence. From early on (e.g. Wallin, 1927), it has been known that level of intelligence influences test patterns, and subsequent research with the Wechsler tests (e.g. Estes, 1946; French and Hunt, 1951; Schnadt, 1952; Shimkunas, Grohmann and Zuibelman, 1971) has confirmed this. Individuals in the superior range of intelligence produce more scatter than those in the mid-range. And as one might expect, level of education influences subtest performance, not only on certain tests, but the higher the education, the greater the scatter.

As one might expect, age is a factor which influences subtest performance. Since the early days of intelligence testing (e.g. Asch, 1936; Bayley, 1933, 1955; Garrett, Bryan and Perl, 1935; Jones and Conrad, 1933; Quereshi, 1973), it has been known that abilities mature at different rates, thereby producing different patterns of cognitive/intellective abilities. Failure to compare groups of comparable ages (commented Foster, 1947) or including a wide range of age in any given sample, automatically means that the age factor will be contributing to the overall pattern which is produced by individuals.

From the early days of testing it has been known that the pattern of performance on tests of intelligence was affected by cultural factors. For example, in 1911, Binet (Binet and Simon, 1916) realized that children's scores on his test were, in part, a function of socio-economic level. In general, Binet found that children from the lower socio-economic group performed less capably on his tests than children of the same age range but from the middle class. This effect has been noted subsequently both as regards intelligence testing, *sui generis* (e.g. Burt, 1911; Neff, 1938; Stern, 1914; Yerkes and Anderson, 1915), as well as with regard to the Wechsler tests in particular (e.g. Appelbaum and Tuma, 1977; Cole and Fowler, 1974; Cole and Hunter, 1971; Crockett, Rardin and Pasewark, 1975; Estes, 1953, 1955; Kaufman, 1973; Laird, 1957). The effect of the differential socio-economic level has been that persons from the lower socio-economic level achieve lower I.Q. scores (Verbal, Performance as well as Full Scale). Estes (1955), however, found that the effect was more pronounced at the second grade than at the fifth. As regards specific subtest performance, Cole and Fowler (1974) and Cole and Hunter (1971) found that socio-economic level most seriously affected performance on Information, Picture arrangement, Object assembly, Block design, and Coding.

Comparative analysis of the performance of British and American individuals reveals that the British tended to stress accuracy at the expense of speed; the Americans emphasized speed (Robertson and Batchelder, 1956). In comparison with the performance of Americans, Puerto Ricans (Brown, 1960), Navaho Indians (Howell, Evans and Downing, 1958), Philipinos (San Diego, Foley and Walker, 1970), and Hawaiians (Tsushima and Bratton, 1977) all performed below the standard American group (perhaps because of language difficulties), and Jewish subjects were found to perform relatively poorly (relative to their own performance) on Picture completion, Picture arrangement, Block design, and Object assembly (Dershowitz and Frankel, 1975). In comparison to other groups, Jewish individuals performed better than Italians on Information, Comprehension, Arithmetic, and Similarities; better than Irish individuals on Comprehension and Similarities, but poorer than both groups on the Performance tasks. Thus one could say that Jewish culture tends to emphasize verbal learning since that seems to be their (intellectual) forte.

Probably the one aspect of cultural differences influencing performance on the Wechsler tests that has been studied most has been Black–White differences. The bulk of the studies in this area note that Blacks consistently achieve lower scores than Whites on the individual subtests (e.g. Carson and Rabin, 1960; Covin and Covin, 1976; Covin and Hatch, 1976, 1977; Davidson, Gibby, McNeil, Segal and Silverman, 1950; Davis, 1957; Hughes and Lessler, 1965; Kaufman, 1973; Kendall and Little, 1977; Levinson, 1964; Munford, 1978; Semler and Iscoe, 1966; Smith and Caldwell, 1969;

Solkoff, 1972; Wysocki and Wysocki, 1969; Young and Bright, 1954, and as reviewed by Dreger and Miller, 1960). Yet if we look at particular subtest performance, as opposed to the overall intellectual measure (i.e. Full, Verbal and Performance I.Q.s, we find that Black (children) do better than Whites on Comprehension, Picture completion, and Object assembly, while doing more poorly than their White counterparts on Information, Similarities, and Vocabulary (Vance and Engin, 1978). However, there are confounding effects to such a finding. For example, as Wysocki and Wysocki (1969) point out, samples of Blacks tend to have less education than White subjects. By looking at overall I.Q. scores, comparative Black–White studies, therefore, may be overlooking the fact that impaired performance on such tests as Information, Similarities, and Vocabulary may reflect differences in scholastic experience, reflecting different levels of education rather than any intrinsic characteristics of either group. This hypothesis receives further support from the observation that Northern Blacks tend to score significantly better on the Wechsler than.Southern Blacks (e.g. Caldwell and Smith, 1968; Carson and Rabin, 1960; Levinson, 1964; Machover, 1943) and Black–White differences wash out when socio-economic level is controlled for (Burnes, 1970). Thus, as Klineberg (1963) has pointed out, Black–White (i.e. racial) differences may, more accurately, be cultural, that is, learned, not genetic. Nonetheless, it seems clear that not only should samples of patients not group Whites and Blacks together (unless they are all from the North or all from the South), but that the performance of (Northern) Whites should not be the criterion group for the comparison of performance of Southern Blacks (and, perhaps, even Southern Whites); regional differences do influence subtest performance.

Thus far in this section we have been focusing on those subject factors which are known to influence performance on the Wechsler tests over and above personality and/or psychopathology. There are also factors in the instrument itself which contribute to "irregularity" in subtest performance. For example, subtest patterning is influenced by the degree each subtest correlates with each other subtest, and the degree to which each subtest correlates with the overall I.Q. measures. Here, we can look at Wechsler's own data (Wechsler, 1944, p. 223). In Table 9 we see the degree each subtest correlates with each other.

This table represents the subtest intercorrelations for Wechsler's sample of adults aged 20–34 (there is another table for the subtest intercorrelations

TABLE 9. *Correlation of each subtest with every other subtest*

Subtest	Subtest									
	I	C	S	A	D	PA	PC	BD	OA	DSym
I		.67	.68	.60	.48	.38	.47	.49	.22	.56
C	.67		.72	.52	.44	.39	.46	.47	.29	.48
S	.68	.72		.60	.38	.49	.46	.54	.31	.51
A	.60	.52	.60		.44	.37	.40	.51	.23	.43
D	.48	.44	.38	.44		.26	.30	.40	.16	.54
PA	.38	.39	.49	.37	.26		.39	.48	.27	.44
PC	.47	.46	.46	.40	.30	.39		.57	.44	.40
BD	.49	.47	.54	.51	.40	.48	.57		.54	.54
OA	.22	.29	.31	.23	.16	.27	.44	.54		.54
DSym	.56	.48	.51	.43	.54	.44	.40	.54	.32	

for Wechsler's samples of adults aged 35—49, which, essentially, resembles the above-noted table [on page 224 of Wechsler, 1944] — the data of which, therefore, will not be reproduced here). What one finds examining this table is that none of the subtests correlate with each other to any great degree nor with any degree of consistency. The relationship of each subtest to the others is quite variable, and it is this variability which makes, inherently, for scattering. This same finding (re inter-test correlation) is reflected in the data for children as presented by Baumeister and Bartlett (1962b) in Tables 10 and 11, or Pilley, Harris, Miller and Rice (1975) in Table 12.

Yet, on the other hand, when the acutal separatedness and uniqueness of the subtests with regard to each other is tested directly (not just inferred from a table of intercorrelations) we find a lack of support for the notion that each subtest constitutes a separate and unique subset of cognitive/ intellective functions, with amazing consistency. Factor analyses of Wechsler's test data with a variety of subjects eventuates in the same factor structure appearing again and again. From the early study by Diamond (1947) to subsequent explorations (e.g. Baumeister and Bartlett, 1962a, b; Belmont, Birch and Belmont, 1967; Berger, Bernstein, Klein, Cohen and Lucas, 1964; Birren, 1951, 1952; Birren and Morrison, 1961; Coates and Bromberg, 1973; Cohen, 1951, 1952a, b, 1957a, b, 1959; Cropley, 1964; Cummins and Das, 1980; DeHorn and Klinge, 1978; DeLuca, 1968; Dennerll, Jen and Sokolov, 1964; Frank, 1956; Gault, 1954; Green and

TABLE 10. *Correlation of each subtest with every other subtest for school children (Baumeister and Bartlett, 1962b)*

Subtest	I	C	A	S	V	D	PC	PA	BD	OA	COD
I		.63	.63	.62	.71	.51	.33	.51	.32	.41	.57
C			.66	.54	.70	.48	.32	.53	.35	.45	.56
A				.57	.56	.64	.38	.49	.42	.37	.62
S					.62	.44	.33	.47	.32	.33	.46
V						.45	.35	.53	.32	.44	.55
D							.30	.53	.42	.36	.53
PC								.38	.31	.33	.28
PA									.53	.53	.53
BD										.55	.44
OA											.52
COD											

TABLE 11. *Correlation of each subtest with every other subtest for institutionalized children (Baumeister and Bartlett, 1962b)*

Subtest	I	C	A	S	V	PC	PA	BD	OA	COD
I		.41	.43	.42	.41	.21	.27	.14	.12	.15
C			.32	.34	.49	.10	.30	.14	.17	.14
A				.31	.30	.25	.37	.24	.16	.28
S					.40	.21	.26	.14	.11	.23
V						.19	.21	.10	.07	.09
PC							.29	.30	.35	.16
PA								.34	.37	.21
BD									.47	.18
OA										.25

Berkowitz, 1964; Hammer, 1949; Hardyck and Patrinovich, 1963; Hollenbeck and Kaufman, 1973; Kaufman, 1975; Kaufman and Hollenbeck, 1974; Lin and Rennick, 1973; McMahon and Kunce, 1981; Matthews, Guertin and Reitan, 1962; Payne and Lehmann, 1966; Phillips, 1979; Radcliffe, 1966; Ramanaiah, O'Donnell and Ribich, 1976; Reed and Fitzhugh, 1967; Reschly, 1978; Reynolds and Gutkin, 1980; Riegel and Riegel, 1962; Rugel, 1974; Russell, 1972; Shaw, 1967; Shiek and Miller, 1978; Silverstein, 1969, 1973; Simkin, 1951; Sprague and Quay, 1966; Vance and Wallbrown, 1977; Wallbrown, Blaha and Wherry, 1973, 1974a;

TABLE 12. *Correlation of each subtest with every other subtest for Southern black school children (Pilley, Harris, Miller and Rice, 1975)*

Subtest	I	C	A	S	V	D	PC	PA	BD	COD
I		.31	.32	.37	.53	.23	.34	.32	.26	.29
C	.31		.37	.26	.45	.21	.34	.36	.34	.17
A	.32	.37		.31	.26	.41	.29	.30	.37	.19
S	.37	.26	.31		.42	.10	.30	.27	.23	.16
V	.53	.45	.26	.42		.21	.24	.34	.25	.09
D	.23	.21	.41	.10	.21		.29	.25	.28	.09
PC	.34	.34	.29	.30	.24	.29		.39	.52	.32
PA	.32	.36	.30	.27	.34	.25	.39		.52	.46
BD	.26	.34	.37	.23	.25	.28	.52	.46		.31
COD	.29	.17	.19	.16	.09	.09	.32	.31	.23	

Wallbrown, Blaha, Counts and Wallbrown, 1974b; Zimmerman, Whitmyre and Fields, 1970), factor analysis demonstrates that the Wechsler test data do not separate into the different subtests, but, rather, two major clusters of subtests emerge: one defined by the Verbal subtests, the other, the Performance ones. Quite often a third factor emerges, comprised of Digit span and Arithmetic, called, alternately, a factor of memory or a factor of distractibility. And while the subtests which emerge in the Verbal and Performance factors are not always exactly the same, these findings can be interpreted as suggesting that the subtests do not measure such highly unique factors, but, rather, that only two factors define what is being assessed by the test. Rather than eleven even relatively unique functions, the eleven subtests sample only two; in terms of Thurstone's primary mental abilities:* a factor of verbal relations and one of spatial relations. Another comment that can be made regarding the factor analytic study of the Wechsler tests is that while there is this basic factor structure which emerges so consistently, the components of those basic factors differ, to one degree or another, at different age levels (Balinsky, 1941; Garrett *et al.*,

*As described in the research by Thurstone (1935, 1936, 1938, 1940; Thurstone and Thurstone, 1941) and as supported by subsequent research, e.g. Green, Guilford, Christensen and Comrey (1953); Hertzka, Guilford, Christensen and Berger (1954), Holzinger and Herman (1938), Kaiser (1960), Kettner, Guilford and Christensen (1956, 1959), Rimoldi (1951), Wilson, Guilford, Christensen and Lewis (1954), Woodrow (1939) and Zimmerman (1953).

1935). In his factor analysis of Wechsler data, Balinsky found three factors to emerge, but differences in the factor structure (that is, the tests which comprised the factor) could vary. Factor I was a "g" factor with virtually all subtests loading significantly in this factor, with minor discrepancies of this factor structure at ages 9, 12, 15, 25–29, 35–44, or 50–59. However, Factors II and III varied considerably at each age level. At age 9, Factor II was composed of Block design and Digit symbol; at age 12, Object assembly and Arithmetic; at age 15, Object assembly, Picture completion, and Arithmetic; at age 25–29, Arithmetic and Information; at age 35–44, Object assembly, Block design, Information, and Digits; and at age 50–59, Object assembly and Information. Clearly, the *meaning* of these factors (as defined by the subtests included in each factor) appears to change at the different age levels. Factors which change in their components and, hence, their psychological meaning, cannot be expected to produce comparable information for subjects of different ages. The psychometric "capriciousness" of the factors cannot be ignored and must be included in those factors which preclude finding stable differences between groups of subjects in terms of their subtest performance. These findings, therefore, place in serious doubt the practice of looking for subtest configurations when the notion of patterning is based on the psychometric independence of the subtests. The factor analytic studies indicate an absence of evidence that such psychometric independence exists.*

Another psychometric factor which introduces a degree of "irregularity"

---

*The only studies which do not support the finding of two or three factors being derived from the analysis of Wechsler data are those by Davis (1956), Osborne (1963) and Saunders (1959). In those studies, the subtests are broken up into two and all of the resultant sub-subtests are intercorrelated and that matrix factor analyzed. The mechanical manipulation of the data in this way eventuates in many more factors, but it is hard to know how to interpret the resultant factor structure in light of the manipulation of the basic data that is performed. Interestingly, factor analyzing the data from several tests of intelligence, Schiller (1934) found three factors, too, viz. a verbal factor, a spatial factor and a numerical factor, exactly that which is found in factor analysis of Wechsler data. Factor analyses of the Binet (e.g. Wright, 1939; Jones, 1954) yield the same three factors plus such factors as: reasoning ability, need for closure and imagery, undoubtedly because of the somewhat different test material in the Binet as compared to the Wechsler different factors are generated. Thurstone's (1938) notion of the existence of primary mental abilities does, indeed, seem to be supported.

into the patterning of the subtests is the variable degree the subtests relate to the overall I.Q. measures. Here again, we can refer to Wechsler's own data. We learn from one of Wechsler's tables (Wechsler, 1944, p. 225) that the correlation of each subtest with the Full Scale I.Q. is as shown in Table 13.

TABLE 13. *Correlation of each subtest with the Full Scale I.Q. (Wechsler, 1944)*

Subtest	Full Scale I.Q.
Information	.67
Comprehension	.66
Digit span	.51
Arithmetic	.63
Similarities	.73
Picture arrangement	.51
Picture completion	.61
Object assembly	.41
Block design	.71
Digit symbol	.67

One notes that basically the correlations of the subtest with the overall I.Q. measure is, at best, modest; moreover, it is quite variable. That variable relationship of each subtest to the overall I.Q. contributes to the unevenness of the subtest patterning.

Another factor which influences subtest patterning is the manner by which scatter is assessed. We have seen that heterogeneity of subtest performance influences subtest *patterning*; this factor also influences the assessment of scatter. Scatter (that is, inter-test variability) seems to be built into the tests (as, as it were, an error factor). How much scatter (and for whom) is "normal" remains to be determined. Moreover, how one extracts the degree of scatter from the subtests would seem to be important, yet we do not know the better way. Wechsler, for example, utilized the mean subtest score as the criterion from which to determine (assess) scattering of the subtests. Rapaport added Vocabulary scatter (that is, taking the person's Vocabulary score as the base line from which to compare all the other subtest scores) as well as a modified mean scatter (relating the Verbal subtests to the mean of the Verbal subtest scores and the same process with Performance tests). Jastak (1948) recommended the individual's highest subtest score be the criterion measure. Kuhlman (1941) noted that there were no norms for scatter. Since that time a number of investigators have offered such norms (e.g. Alimena, 1951, 1961; Kaufman, 1976; Maxwell, 1959; McNemar, 1957; Milliren and Newland, 1968; Newland and Smith, 1967; Piotrowski and Grubb, 1976; Schafer, 1948; Trehub and Scherer, 1958). The problem with these suggested baseline data is that there seems to be little concordance between them; different investigators suggest different degrees of subtest differences which might be considered normal.

If clinicians are going to continue to rely on pattern and scatter analysis of the Wechsler data, in light of what we now know about the many factors which do influence subtest performance, what we would appear to need is a major research undertaking which would chart the amount of scatter, for example, using some tested criterion (baseline) (or, perhaps, several criteria) for men differentiated from women, at a variety of age levels, socio-economic levels, educational levels, as well as geographic area of the country (Eisdorfer and Cohen, 1961). A set of tables would be set up so that the level of scatter expected for each particular kind of person would be available for the clinician. The degree of scatter an individual manifested, then, would be compared to what would be expected for that person as derived from the tables. Only then could one speak about an abnormal amount of scatter. And if the clinician is going to employ pattern analysis, at least some of the mathematically-derived methods of pattern analysis should be employed (e.g. Cattell, 1949; Cronbach and Gleser, 1953; DuMas, 1949; DuToit, 1954; Gaier and Lee, 1953; Horst, 1954; McQuitty, 1956; Meehl, 1954); methods which have virtually gone unused in clinical research.

Another factor in trying to explain why pattern analysis has failed has to do with the method of defining the subjects an investigator is studying. It would seem fair to say that the research on the clinical utility of the Wechsler has focused on the degree to which the data from the Wechsler tests reflect, conform with, or explicate psychiatric diagnoses. Yet it has been demonstrated from a purely research (as opposed to ideological) perspective that psychiatric diagnoses do not define psychological types but behavioral (i.e. symptom) types (e.g. Frank, 1975). To expect that psychological data (a person's response to Wechsler test data) *would* reflect aspects of psychiatric diagnoses might very well be unrealistic and/ or inappropriate. Diagnoses and test data are not the same kinds of data, one being behavioral, the other cognitive, and, hence, maybe we should not expect them to covary (as if there were an isomorphic relationship between the manifest psychopathology and the internal cognitive world of the patient). If symptom (behavioral) and intelligence test data (cognitive) are *not* in the same psychological domain, it would, therefore, seem imperative to find data which *are*. It would seem, therefore, more meaningful to examine the relationship of intelligence test data to other psychological attributes of behavior (e.g. attitudes, motives, emotions, cognitive style) rather than psychiatric which seems to doom our clinical psychological research to failure.

Finally, another factor which is involved in the clinical use of Wechsler test data is the meaning of the subtests, that is, the (psychological) factors involved in each subtest. The more psychometric approach (e.g. Wechsler) is satisfied in charting the pattern of subtests found with regard to a particular type being examined (e.g. schizophrenics, neurotics, etc.); the more psychological approach (e.g. Rapaport) attempts to explain the configuration of subtests which define a particular type in terms of the psychological functions which these subtests would indicate might be impaired. Once again, Wechsler remained conservative with regard to the "meaning" of the subtests. Rapaport, on the other hand, tried to develop a psychological rationale for each subtest (Rapaport *et al.*, 1945). Yet, in spite of Rapaport's noble efforts in this regard, the factors involved in each subtest remain unclear.

Wechsler (1939) outlined the psychological factors involved in the subtests:

Information

Wechsler noted that the Information subtest taps "the subject's range of information" (p. 79). He goes on to state that "One had always to meet the obvious objection that the amount of knowledge which a person possesses depends in no small degree upon his education and cultural opportunities . . . all objections allowed for, the range of man's knowledge is generally a good indication of his intellectual capacity" (p. 80).

Comprehension

Of the Comprehension subtest, Wechsler states, "It is frequently of value in diagnosing psychopathic personalities, sometimes suggests the presence of schizophrenic trends (as revealed by perverse and bizarre responses) and almost always tells us something about the subject's social and cultural background" (p. 82). Wechsler goes on to state, "Precisely what functions the Comprehension Test involves is difficult to say. Off hand it might be termed a test of common sense . . . success on the test seemingly depends on the possession of a certain amount of practical information and a general ability to evaluate past experience" (p. 83).

Arithmetic

Wechsler states, "The ability to solve arithmetic problems has long been recognized as a sign of mental alertness" (p. 84).

Digit span

Wechsler states that Digit span is "a test of retentiveness" (p. 85), and "Low scores on the Memory Span Test are frequently associated with attention defects" (p. 86).

Similarities

Similarities, for Wechsler, "throws light upon the logical character of the subject's thinking process" (p. 88), and Wechsler differentiates two levels of abstraction possible (good and modest, that is, abstract and "superficial").

Picture arrangement

For Wechsler, Picture arrangement "measures a subject's ability to comprehend and size up a total situation. The subject must understand the whole, must get the 'idea' of the story before he is able to set himself effectively to the task. . . . Secondly, the subject matter of the test nearly always involves some human or practical situation. The understanding of these situations more nearly corresponds to what other writers have referred to as 'social intelligence' " (p. 90).

Picture completion

"In a broad way," Wechsler writes, "the test measures the ability of the individual to differentiate essential from unessential details" (p. 93).

Block design

For Wechsler, "The Block design is not only an excellent test of general intelligence, but one that lends itself admirably to qualitative analysis" (p. 94) "[of] synthesizing ability" (p. 93).

Digit symbol

Performance on Digit symbol, for Wechsler, assesses the ability to concentrate and "mental efficiency."

Object assembly

Quoting one of the "field examiners," Wechsler writes about Object assembly, "Various examiners have praised the test repeatedly, because 'it tells you something about the thinking and working habits of the subjects' " (p. 99).

Looking over Wechsler's comments regarding the "meaning" of each subtest, we find Wechsler sticking very closely to intellectual attributes. It is only in a few instances that Wechsler entertains more personality/ psychopathology notions. For instance, the Picture arrangement subtest assesses understanding of social situations, and a qualitative analysis of the content of the responses to Comprehension may reveal psychopathic or schizophrenic traits.

With minor emendations most of those who have speculated about the meaning of the subtests have stayed close to Wechsler's formulations. For example, Reichard and Schafer (1943) added to the basic Wechslerian formulations that Digit symbol involved learning ability. Even Rapaport (Rapaport et al., 1945), while making many more statements than Wechsler regarding the clinical *application* of successful or unsuccessful performance on each of the subtests (as regards psychiatric diagnosis), when it came to spelling out the psychological *rationale* for each of the subtests, in general, the formulations proffered were not unlike Wechsler's. Modification of the basic Wechslerian formulations by Rapaport was with regard to Picture arrangement (which Rapaport said involved the ability to appraise relationships). Zimmerman, Woo-Sam and Glasser (1973) added to Wechsler's ideas about Information that it also involves intellectual curiosity and is affected by perfectionism and chronic anxiety which eventuates in memory gaps; Arithmetic involves problem-solving ability; Picture arrangement involves planning and the ability to see cause-and-effect, and, as with Reichard and Schafer, Digit symbol involves the capacity for learning, the ability to learn unfamiliar material. Matarazzo (1976) in his updating of Wechsler's book basically only adds to Wechsler's formulation that Digits is affected by, and is a good reflector of, anxiety. Essentially, therefore, the hypotheses about the "meaning" of the subtests, the psychological functions they involve, are basically predicated on clinical experience (Wechsler's), except for Zimmerman *et al.* who integrate research findings with the clinical.

Let us look at what research has been done in an attempt to elucidate the psychological functions involved in the subtests.

Information

Clinicians (Wechsler *et al.*) have concluded that Information taps an individual's range of information. Zimmerman *et al.* (1973) thought that it reflected the kind of cultural stimulation to which the individual had been exposed as well as intellectual curiosity. Saunders (1960b) factor analyzed the Information subtest and observed that it involved four different types of information: general information, information regarding contemporary affairs, cultural information and scientific information. In his factor analysis of Wechsler data, Cohen (1952a) observed that Information was primarily loaded with a general Verbal factor rather than possessing any unique variance. And Neuringer (Neuringer, 1963b; Neuringer, Wheeler and Beardsley, 1969) found a near zero correlation of Information with an assessment of diversity of thinking made from the semantic differential.

Clearly, then, Information does entail knowledge of information, but a more refined analysis of the Information subtest might reveal those areas about which the individual is really uninformed, rather than making some general statement which is rather unspecific. Being heavily loaded with a Verbal factor means that it also involves an individual's use of (comfort with) English, a factor which could also account for someone not doing well on Information.

Comprehension

Wechsler was not too certain what the Comprehension subtest measured; most clinicians agreed that it had something to do with applying what has been learned in social situations and the use of common sense. Rapaport thought it involved the use of judgment.

Brannigan (1975) found a low (in the .20s) correlation between scores on the Comprehension subtest and teacher rating of social maturity, and a not-too-significant-from-zero correlation of scores on the Comprehension subtest and social desirability response tendencies (Brannigan, 1976). Cohen (1952a) found that Comprehension reflected judgment. Krippner (1964) found a low (.27) correlation between scores on the Comprehension subtest and scores on the Vineland Social Maturity Scale. Neuringer et al. (1969) found a .09 correlation between Comprehension and a measure of diversity of thinking. Maley (1970) found no relationship between scores on the Comprehension subtest and the assessment of level of social adaptation (of patients in a community mental health center).

While reflecting judgment, the relationship of scores on the Comprehension subtest to a variety of assessments of social knowledge does not seem to have been established. One of the difficulties with the Comprehension subtest is its difficulty re scoring (and, hence, I presume, understanding the nature of the answers) (e.g. Plumb and Charles, 1955; Schwartz, 1966; Walker, Hunt and Schwartz, 1965a).

Arithmetic

Arithmetic has been viewed as a test of the ability to solve problems by Wechsler and Zimmerman et al.; Rapaport thought of it as a measure of concentration abilities.

Marshall, Hess and Lair (1978) found a correlation of .289 between scores on the Arithmetic subtest and scores on the Arithmetic subtest of the Jastak Wide Range Achievement Test. Stroud, Blommers and Laubt (1957) found a correlation of .70 between Arithmetic and scores on the Arithmetic subtest of the Iowa Test of Basic Skills.

As far as personality factors, Cohen (1952a) and Callens and Meltzer (1969) did not find that Arithmetic scores relate to anxiety. Cohen concluded, "The test is virtually useless for diagnostic purposes, since it is necessary to know a patient's diagnosis before it is possible to know what a given score on this test reflects, and even then one cannot be sure. For example, a low score on this test may reflect poor verbal ability, high distractibility, or both, depending on the diagnosis. Also, the score may be an excellent, mediocre, or poor index of the patient's present general intellectual functioning, again depending on the patient's diagnosis" (Cohen, 1952a, p. 274).

Aside from assessing ability to solve arithmetic problems, exactly what Wechsler said it did, performance on Arithmetic bears an uncertain relationship to assessments of anxiety, but the relationship of Arithmetic to problem-solving ability remains to be examined.

Similarities

Most clinicians seem in agreement that Similarities reflects ability to abstract. Both Cohen (1952a) and Furth and Milgram (1965), however, found performance on Similarities to be more a function of verbal abilities and word knowledge. In the light of the limited amount of research on this subtest, it seems unfair to conclude that it might or might not have to do with abstract ability, *per se.*

Digits

Both Wechsler and Rapaport thought that memory for Digits was not so much a test of memory but of attention, the impairment of which would reflect anxiety.

When the assessment of anxiety was made on the basis of paper-and-pencil test data (e.g. the Welsh Anxiety Scale of the MMPI [Callens and Meltzer, 1969], the Taylor Anxiety Scale of the MMPI [e.g. Matarazzo and Phillips, 1955; Pyke and Agnew, 1963; Walker and Spence, 1964]) or subjectively reported levels of anxiety (Firetto and Davey, 1971), no significant relationship was found between scores on the Digit span subtest and these criteria measures of anxiety.

When anxiety was assessed indirectly, in terms of the degree of freedom from distractibility, this research also does not find the presumed relationship between performance on Digits and anxiety. In this research Guertin (1959) distracted subjects with the (recorded) sound of a small *gas*-powered lawn mower "emanating" from outside the examination room and an argument, also "emanating" from outside the examination room; Craddick and Grossman (1962) tried to distract subjects by looking into their eyes as they repeated the digits; Maupin and Hunter (1966) tried to distract their subjects with a flickering light; distractibility was assessed by children's mothers (Nalven, 1967) or teachers (Nalven, 1969; Nalven and Puleo, 1968). One could question the methodology of this research, research which did not show any relationship between Digits and distractibility.

Moldawsky and Moldawsky (1952) tried to induce anxiety by exposing subjects to feelings of inadequacy (they were told that they had done strangely on a previous test) and fear of failure (what they called "situation anxiety"). Performance on Digits was found to reflect the emotional state. This result was replicated when others utilized a similar paradigm (e.g. Dickstein and Weiss, 1972; Walker and Spence, 1964). However, Sherman and Blatt (1968) found that sometimes a failure experience motivated subjects to do better on Digits.

Pyke and Agnew (1963) found that startling a subject (with an electric shock) produced the expected interference with performance on Digits.

The notion that emotional arousal rather than anxiety, *per se*, was the factor which interfered with successful performance on Digits has received support (e.g. Hodges and Spielberger, 1969; Knox and Grippaldi, 1970; Stewart and Davis, 1974).

When anxiety was assessed by paper-and-pencil tests or more indirect subject report, performance on Digits was not found to relate to anxiety. However, when the criterion measure of anxiety was actual experience (e.g. being startled or made to feel insecure), it did. Other research suggests that it is not anxiety, *per se*, which interferes with performance on Digits, but general emotional arousal. However, what *interferes* with performance on Digits and what the Digit span subtest *measures* are two different questions.

Thus in spite of Cohen's (1952a) finding that Digits and Arithmetic seem to form a factor of ease of distractibility, we still cannot be certain whether attention, concentration, or some other variable is involved in performance on the Digit span subtest.

Picture completion

Wechsler considered Picture completion as a test which measures the ability to differentiate essential from nonessential details. Reichard and Schafer thought it measured concentration. Rapaport thought it measured concentration through the capacity to appraise relationships, and Zimmerman *et al.* thought it also reflected accuracy of perception of reality.

Cohen (1952a) found Picture completion to be a subtest which did not reflect one factor, measuring verbal and non-verbal factors simultaneously. And Saunders (1960a) found the Picture completion subtest to be composed of three, not one, factors, viz., questions which reflected contact with reality, maintenance of perspective, and effect of uncertainty. Very little other research has been done with the Picture completion subtest to assess what factors are involved.

Picture arrangement

Wechsler *et al.* assumed that performance on Picture arrangement involved planning ability and knowledge of social situations.

Cohen (1952a) found that Picture arrangement did measure something specifically, but he did not know what that was.

When looked at as a measure of understanding social events, Schill (1966) found a significant positive relationship between social extroversion–introversion (as measured by the Social Introversion Scale of the MMPI) and as measured by degree of participation in actual social events (Schill, Kahn and Meuhleman, 1968). However, when Johnson (1969) replicated Schill's (1966) study (but instead of using college students, as Schill did, used psychiatric patients), Johnson found completely opposite results (introverts performed significantly better on the Picture arrangement subtest than did extroverts). And Maley (1970) found no relationship between scores on the Picture arrangement subtest and assessments of the pre-morbid social adaptation of patients in a community mental health center (as assessed from material in their files). Krippner (1964) found a -.04 correlation between scores on the Picture arrangement subtest and scores on the Vineland Social Maturity Scale, while Brannigan (1975, 1976) found no relationship between scores on the Picture arrangement subtest and assessments of children's social maturity. Burnham (1949) found a near zero relationship between scores on the Picture arrangement subtest and the percent of responses on the Rorschach which involved human percepts. There is some research which suggests that the relationship between scores on Picture arrangement and social factors is better assessed through a content analysis of the stories subjects tell to their arrangement of the cards (e.g. Breiger, 1956; Craig, 1969; Golland, Herrell and Hahn, 1970; Herrell and Golland, 1960; Patalano, 1976), than just from the score a person achieves.

As to whether Picture arrangement is a test of planning ability, Blatt (Dickstein and Blatt, 1967; Blatt and Quinlan, 1967) has defined planning ability in terms of future time perspective. His research seems to support the notion that defined that way, Picture arrangement does seem to involve the (inferred) capacity for anticipation and planning. No other research could be found examining the relationship of the factors presumed to be measured by the Picture arrangement test and what the test "really" measures.

Object assembly

Wechsler *et al.* think that Object assembly assesses psycho-motor behavior and analytic and synthetic thinking.

Cohen (1952a) found that Object assembly, while not measuring any unique factor, was highly loaded on the factor of non-verbal organization.

Sherman, Chinsky and Maffeo (1974) found scores on the Object assembly task to be (negatively) related (-.69) to performance on the Purdue Peg Board (a test of psychomotor dexterity), but positively related (.71) to paired learning ability.

Walker, Neilson and Nicolay (1965b) found a relationship between Taylor Scale scores of Anxiety and performance on Object assembly.

In that some of the tasks of the Object assembly subtest involve presenting the subject with dismembered body (manikin) or body parts (profile), Blatt presumed that this evokes (would be related to) bodily concern. When subjects (children from a guidance clinic) were selected on the basis of reports in their files regarding body concern (and another group that did not reflect this trait), bodily concern was found to covary with performance on the Object assembly task (Blatt, Allison and Baker, 1965). The same positive relationship was found when bodily concern was assessed in adults from their Rorschachs (Blatt, Baker and Weiss, 1970). However, replication of Blatt's studies (e.g. Marsden and Kalter, 1969; Rockwell, 1967; Stewart, Powers and Gouaux, 1973) failed to repeat his results.

Block design

Block design seems to be thought of as a test involving synthesizing ability. Cohen (1952a) confirmed that Block design is a good test of non-verbal organizational ability. But performance on Block design did not seem to be strongly related to measures of originality (.33) or conceptual elaboration (.38) (as assessed by the Torrance Test of Creative Thinking [Torrance, 1966]) (Martin, Blair, Stokes and Armstrong, 1977). Performance on Block design seemed to have little relationship (.28) with performance on the Bender Gestalt Test (Doubros and Mascarenhas, 1969; Simensen, 1974). But performance on Block design was found to be related to problem solving ability (Davis, Hamlett and Reitan, 1966).

Digit symbol

Wechsler thought Digit symbol invloved "mental efficiency"; Rapaport thought that Digit symbol involved visual motor coordination, while Reichard and Schafer and Zimmerman *et al.* think that it has to do with learning ability.

While Cohen (1952a) found that Digit symbol loaded significantly on a factor of ease of distractibility (mental efficiency?), other research did not find any significant relationship between performance on the Digit symbol subtest and Taylor Manifest Anxiety Scale scores (e.g. Boor and Schill, 1967; Goodstein and Farber, 1957; Johnston and Cross, 1962), or Sarason Test Anxiety Scale (Sarason and Minard, 1962); significant differences were found when defensiveness was taken into consideration

(Boor and Schill) and the relationship to anxiety was found to have a U-curve distribution (re Taylor scores) (Matarazzo and Phillips, 1955). Neither frustration (induced by the examiner: Solkoff and Chrisien, 1963) nor depressiveness, *per se* (rather, degree of severity of psychopathology: Beck, Feshbach and Legg, 1962) affected performance on the Digit symbol subtest.

As a test of psychomotor efficiency, Burik (1950) and Murstein and Leipold (1961) found that Digit symbol was more related to motoric efficiency than learning ability, and Johnson and Lyle (1972a, b, 1973; Lyle and Johnson, 1973) found that poor performance on Coding (the notation for the Digit symbol task on the WISC) was related to a variety of other measures of psychomotor efficiency as well as learning. Doubros and Mascarenhas (1965) found a correlation of −.22 of Coding with Bender Gestalt performance.

There is some research to suggest that Digit symbol is related to motivational factors (psychological energy?). Wachtel and Blatt (1965) found performance on Digit symbol to be related to academic achievement (college grades), and Oakland (1969) found a positive (.51) relationship between the quality of performance (motivation) in a rehabilitation clinic, but Vidler and Rawan (1974) found a near zero (.06) relationship between scores on Digit symbol and curiosity (as measured by a Curiosity Scale they constructed).

The most disturbing psychometric evidence regarding the attempt to define the psychological meaning of the subtests (that is, what psychological processes are consistently assessed by each subtest) are the data of Balinsky (1941) who discovered that the subtests could be part of one factor at one age, another, at another. Thus, as for an assessment of the psychological processes assessed by each subtest, these could change from one age to another. A subtest measuring one factor at one age, could not be relied upon to measure the same factor at another age. Such inconstancy in psychological meaning of at least some of the subtests cannot help but influence the outcome of studies which compare the performance of different groups of subjects on the subtests. Perhaps this phenomenon is true for different groups of patients; some subtests might be influenced by (reflect the presence of) one (or more) psychological functions in, for example, the cerebrally impaired, but another psychological function (or functions) in schizophrenia. The influence of such variability in subtest meaning cannot be ignored in trying to explain why pattern (or scatter) analysis failed.

As regards the personality attributes of the Wechsler subtests, Spaner (1950) correlated factors on the Rorschach and Wechsler he assumed had a common psychological *rationale*. For example, from the Rorschach literature Spaner concluded that the number of responses is sometimes thought of as being, in part, a function of the quantity of the associational process, itself a function of the richness of past experience. Spaner hypothesized that the number of Rorschach responses, then, should correlate with scores on Information. Since Form Level (F+%) of the Rorschach was considered to be a measure of judgment (in this instance perceptual as well as conceptual) it should be related to Comprehension, a subtest presumed to involve judgment. Spaner goes through each dimension of the Rorschach (sometimes convincingly, sometimes he seems to be "stretching" in order to make the point of a similar *rationale*), but the result of his correlational study was that very few of the Wechsler– Rorschach intercorrelations were high enough to reach significance. Vocabulary seemed to bear some relationship to the number of difficult percepts given to the Rorschach cards (.339); the relationship of Picture arrangement to the number of human responses was −.328, and .356 to the number of human movement responses (M). The relationship of scores on Comprehension with Form Level was .237, and the scores on Information and number of responses was .219. However, as Spaner concluded, "The most significant finding of the entire study is the generally negative character of the results."

Holzberg and Belmont (1952), in the manner of Spaner, correlated variables on the Rorschach they presumed would relate to variables on the Wechsler. The result of their analysis was the same as Spaner's; viz. nothing related to anything; no correlation (of Rorschach and Wechsler data) was above .30. Of 45 predicted relationships, four sets of Rorschach and Wechsler variables were found to relate in a manner beyond zero, but not much more. Lotsof, Comrey, Bogartz and Arnsfield (1958) factor analyzed a matrix of correlations composed of Wechsler and Rorschach variables. The Rorschach and the Wechsler test data did not factor out together. Either the Rorschach and the Wechsler assess an absolutely different set of psychological functions, or the assumptions regarding the meaning of the Rorschach variables is as much in error as that of the Wechsler or both.

Other studies exploring the personality attributes of the subtests have related Wechsler data to that of the MMPI (e.g. Brower, 1947; Watson, Davis and McDermott, 1976; Winfield, 1953). The problem with this research is that the MMPI variables were related to Full Scale I.Q. only, and even then, inconsistent findings resulted from study to study. Few studies have explored the relationship of personality characteristics to the individual subtests. Table 14 presents the research findings of Turner, Willerman and Horn (1976) correlating the factors from the Cattell 16PF with subtest data.

TABLE 14. *Personality factors (16PF)*

WAIS Variable	Extraversion	Anxiety	Cortetia	Temperamental independence	Combined
Information	.15	−.20	.19	.46	.46
Comprehension	.20	−.13	.25	.42	.42
Arithmetic	.07	−.23	.30	.37	.40
Similarities	.06	−.11	.18	.34	.34
Digit span	.07	.03	.17	.15	.19
Vocabulary	.18	−.09	.17	.47	.47
Picture completion	.08	−.14	.32	.36	.40
Picture arrangement	−.02	−.03	.29	.27	.34
Block design	.01	−.09	.27	.38	.40
Object assembly	−.07	.11	.29	.26	.33
Digit symbol	.08	−.20	.06	.22	.22
Verbal I.Q.	.16	−.17	.27	.48	.49
Performance I.Q.	.03	−.08	.32	.44	.46
Full Scale I.Q.	.11	−.15	.33	.50	.52

From Table 14 we see that extraversion and anxiety seem to bear little relationship to any of the subtests; Cattell's factor of "temperamental independence" (health) does. Gaines and Morris (1978) correlated the F Scale of the MMPI (as a measure of psychopathology) with the subtests; the following significant relationships were found: Arithmetic (−.86), Digit symbol (−.70), Picture arrangement (−.31).

When it comes to exploring the cognitive attributes of the subtests we observe that limited work has been done. For example, of the studies that have attempted to explore the cognitive correlates of Wechsler subtest data, the Progressive Matrices has been the most frequent tool employed (e.g. Barratt, 1956; Corter, 1952; Desai, 1955; Jurjevich, 1967; Levine and Iscoe, 1954; Martin and Wiechers, 1954). Corter (1952) correlated a limited number of Wechsler subtests (Similarities, Comprehension and Block design) with Primary Mental Abilities. The outcome of that study was that Similarities (but not Comprehension) was found to be psycho-metrically infused with the factors of concept formation and deductive responsiveness, while Block design was infused with the factors of spatial relations and mental productiveness.

Stempel (1953) correlated performance on the Verbal and Performance segments of the Wechsler with performance on the SRA Primary Mental Abilities Test. The results were:

PMA	V	P
Space	.49	.34
Number	.15	.38
Reasoning	.63	.55
Perception	.18	.42
Verbal meaning	.68	.40

There are some unexpected relationships (and/or lack of them) in these two sets of data. In the data presented by Lin and Rennick, a test of conceptual ability correlates equally as strongly with performance on Digits (.42 M, .26 F) as Vocabulary (.45 M, .34 F), Comprehension (.41 M, .37 F), or Similarities (.45 M, .37 F). And in the data presented by Stempel, spatial ability correlates less with the tests of spatial ability than those of verbal ability. The meaning of these "anomalies" is unknown at this point, with these data, but certainly reflects the "capricious" nature of the relationship of Wechsler data to data from conceptual and/or more generally cognitive tasks.

Other studies with the Wechsler and the test of Primary Mental Abilities have been more comprehensive in terms of the exploration of the Wechsler subtests. The result of that research is found in Table 15.

From Table 15 it can be seen that the relationship of scores on the Progressive Matrices and Wechsler test data appears substantial, *but* the results do not appear stable (the correlations change substantially from one study to another).

As Jurjevich wrote in conclusion of his study relating performance on

TABLE 15. *Correlation of progressive matrices with Wechsler test data*

Wechsler variable	Study			
	Barratt (1956)	Desai (1955)	Levine and Iscoe (1954)	Martin and Wiechers (1954)
Full Scale I.Q.	.75			.91
Verbal I.Q.	.69			.84
Performance I.Q.	.70			.83
Information	.59	.37		.47
Comprehension	.08	.57	.21	.70
Arithmetic	.54	.65		.66
Similarities	.59	.62		.62
Vocabulary	.56	.38	.48	.73
Digit span	.42	.52		
Picture completion	.42			.62
Picture arrangement	.30			.58
Block design	.60		.63	.71
Object assembly	.39			.73
Coding	.33			.60

the Wechsler with performance on the Progressive Matrices (and the Gorham Proverbs Test [Gorham, 1956]), the results indicate "a barely satisfying degree of congruence . . . on the three tests" (Jurjevich, 1967, p. 1285).

Another multivariate test of cognitive abilities which has been used in Wechsler research has been the Illinois Test of Psycholinguistic Abilities (ITPA). Employing emotionally disturbed children (being seen in a guidance center), Garms (1970a) found the following (statistically significant) relationships between the ITPA and the WISC:

auditory reception: Digits (.87), Vocabulary (.35), Arithmetic (.35) and Picture arrangement (.32)

auditory association: Similarities (.48), Vocabulary (.44) and Information (.37)

auditory learning: Information (.62), Vocabulary (.51), Arithmetic (.36), Comprehension (.34) and Similarities (.30)

auditory sequential memory: Digits (.37) and Block design (.34)

visual reception: Picture completion (.39), Vocabulary (.29), Information (.25), Block design (.24) and Picture arrangement (.15)

visual-motor association: none

visual discrimination: Picture completion (.35), Block design (.25) and Vocabulary (.23)

manual expression: Digits (.47) and Similarities (.33)

visual sequential memory: Similarities (.56), Arithmetic (.50), Block design (.37) and Vocabulary (.35).

Leton (1972), employing learning disabled children (no age grouping given) with modest I.Q.s (in the 80s and 90s), found the following relationship between ITPA and WISC performance through factor analysis:

a factor of verbal association: Vocabulary

a factor of visual analysis and motor association: Block design and Picture arrangement

a factor of comprehension of Similarities and Differences: Similarities (with a negative loading by Object assembly)

a factor of auditory memory: Digits and Picture completion

a factor of visual sequencing: Picture arrangement

a factor of logical reasoning: Arithmetic

a factor of verbal comprehension: Comprehension, Vocabulary and Information

Leton, and Huizinga (1973) also related performance on the ITPA to each individual subtest performance. These data may be found in Table 16.

Huizinga also correlated the factors of the ITPA with the overall I.Q. scores (see Table 16).

There are some similarities and differences between the results of these two studies. Scanning the data from the study by Leton and that by Huizinga suggests that while in both studies the verbal tasks seem more related to the ITPA factors than the non-verbal tasks of the WISC, the strength of these relationships differs; they are stronger in the study by Huizinga than that done by Leton. Perhaps this is because Huizinga used normal children while Leton studied learning disabled children. But what this suggests is that the relationship of Wechsler variables to a given cognitive task may change with groups of different kinds of people (personality-wise, diagnostic-wise, or age-wise). White the overall relationship of WISC variables to ITPA factors is at best modest, results of studies bearing on the relationship of Wechsler variables to other factors feeds the concern of clinicians that they cannot rely on this kind of research to alter their clinical hypotheses one way or another.

TABLE 16. *Correlation of ITPA factors with WISC subtests (Leton, 1972)*

ITPA Factors	I	C	A	S	V	D	PC	PA	BD	OA	DS
Auditory-vocal automatic	23	14	-08	14	40	14	18	06	-08	07	-14
Visual decoding	17	20	-08	45	18	05	24	-01	10	-13	10
Motor encoding	17	14	-11	16	13	00	00	18	29	20	02
Auditory-vocal association	25	21	-12	48	33	17	32	03	-07	01	-15
Visual-motor sequencing	-11	-01	05	00	-02	-12	25	13	10	12	23
Auditory-vocal sequencing	12	23	02	27	23	38	30	08	01	14	07
Visual-motor association	-09	18	07	07	18	07	15	14	16	08	22
Auditory decoding	14	18	-23	11	18	02	13	07	-06	15	-03

Correlation of ITPA factors with WISC subtests (Huizinga, 1973)

	I	C	A	S	V	D	PC	PA	BD	OA	DS
Auditory reception	52	35	31	54	46		17	21	32	16	08
Auditory association	48	42	44	62	57		03	27	24	18	16
Verbal expression	26	33	31	29	49		20	27	12	22	21
Visual reception	25	20	50	46	39		21	39	37	33	10
Visual association	43	29	44	28	48		30	35	36	21	18
Manual expression	28	21	27	30	48		21	15	26	11	01
Auditory sequential memory	20	19	28	32	34		08	19	21	16	12
Visual sequential memory	14	02	16	22	05		08	08	30	26	33
Visual closure	03	23	10	21	20		18	28	16	31	28
Auditory closure	28	20	46	36	39		10	31	20	17	15

These tables have been adapted from the material presented in these studies.
Decimal points have been omitted.

Dickstein (1969) assessed the relationship between cognition and Wechsler data. The assessment of cognitive functions was accomplished by the use of a wide variety of tests of cognitive ability, including the excellent Educational Testing Service's set of tests of cognitive factors (French, Ekstrom and Price, 1963). The disappointing aspect of this study was that she then related this wealth of cognitive functioning to two of the Wechsler subtests: Vocabulary and Information. As one might have predicted from her choice of subtests, performance on Vocabulary and Information showed no particular relationship to the cognitive tasks.

Dudek, Goldberg, Lester and Harris (1969) found no substantial relationship between Piagetian measures of cognition and the Wechsler data. Karp, Silberman and Winters (1969) correlated Wechsler data with performance on the Embedded Figures Test (for individuals of low and upper socio-economic level). There was some noticeable effect of socio-economic level on the correlations with the Wechsler data (on Vocabulary, the correlation for the lower socio-economic group and EFT was .41, .17 for individuals in the upper socio-economic level, and on Picture completion, the correlation for the lower socio-economic group was .32, for the upper group .16). Other correlations for the Embedded Figures Test and Wechsler data (where both socio-economic groups functioned more compatibly) were: Information (around .30), Comprehension (.47), Block design (in the .70s), and Object assembly (.53).

Fuller (1966) correlated performance on the WISC with a test which purports to be able to help determine whether organic factors are involved in reading and learning disorders (the Minnesota Percepto-Diagnostic Test). With emotionally disturbed children, performance on the Minnesota Percepto-Diagnostic Test was found to be negatively related with performance on Arithmetic (-.40), Information (-.33), and Picture completion (-.27). Levine, Spivack, Fuschillo and Tavernier (1959) related performance on the Wechsler test to performance on several tasks of cognitive and motor inhibition. With their sample of emotionally disturbed adolescents, performance on these tasks of cognitive and motor inhibition were positively related to overall I.Q.; the better performance on the Wechsler, the greater the capability to exercise psychological control. Brannigan and Ash (1977) related reflective-impulsive cognitive style (Kagan et al., 1964) to Wechsler data. As compared to those characterized as impulsive, those characterized as reflective were higher on: Information, Comprehension,

Digits, Picture completion, Picture arrangement, Block design, and Object assembly (but not on Similarities, Vocabulary, and Coding). Fogel (1965), whose sample of subjects consisted of brain-damaged and non-brain-damaged patients, assessed abstract ability with the Gorham Proverbs Test. Abstract ability, thus measured, was found to be related to performance on Comprehension (.53), Arithmetic (.50), Similarities (.45), Block design (.45), Picture arrangement (.44) and Digits (.39).

Shore, Shore and Pihl (1971) and Lin and Rennick (1974) correlated performance on the Wechsler and that of the Category Test. Shore *et al.* do not present the correlations, but state that they were "in the acceptable range." Lin and Rennick present the actual correlations (for men and women separately):

	M	F
I	.37	.32
C	.41	.37
A	.52	.39
S	.45	.37
D	.42	.26
V	.45	.34
PC	.54	.44
BD	.62	.51
PA	.38	.39
OA	.56	.49
VIQ	.54	.44
PIQ	.64	.54
FSIQ	.63	.52

In the original presentation, because of the nature of the population sampled (epileptics) the correlations were presented in their negative (minus) form. Ignoring the minuses (all were minus figures) enables us to get a clearer picture of the relationship of the Wechsler variables to this test of conceptual ability. Looking at the array of figures, we would have to say the relationship is, at best, modest.

Millham, Jacobson and Berger (1971) found a .31 relationship between WAIS data and that from the Shipley–Hartford Test of conceptual learning, and Craddick and Stern (1963) found little relationship between WAIS performance and the Kahn Test of Symbol arrangement. Silverstein (1960) related Wechsler test data to data from the Object Sorting Test. He concluded that the Wechsler test does not appear to tap any of an individual's ability to deal with conceptual relations (at least as measured by the Object Sorting Test), as much as an individual's ability to comprehend highly conventional concepts.

In review of this section examining those studies which have attempted to investigate the personality and cognitive attributes of the Wechsler subtests, a number of conclusions may be drawn. In the first place, one is struck with the general dearth of studies done in general, and of truly comprehensive (exploring the personality and cognitive attributes in breadth and depth) studies in particular. Second, one can be impressed with the modest level of the relationship between the personality and cognitive variables which have been explored. Such findings do not cause one to have a great deal of confidence in statements which have attempted to identify the personality and/or cognitive attributes of the subtests born out of clinical experience and/or supposition or inference. This only highlights how speculative these statements are. As we look at the large number of variables which *have* been found to influence performance on the Wechsler subtests, such as: gender, level of intelligence, age, socio-economic and cultural background, to unknown degrees for each person or even groups of people in addition to (and/or in interaction with) factors of personality and/or psychopathology, we begin to get a glimpse of how difficult it is to assess the impact of these various factors on the performance of individuals on the Wechsler subtests. If we add to this the problems caused by the "static" due to the psychometric weaknesses of the test (the factors inherent in the test which eventuate in scatter and variability such as the fact that the subtests are not "pure," that is, unidimensional subtests of intellective factors, e.g. Cohen (1952a), Dinning (1976), Jastak (1949), Marks (1953), and McNemar (1964)), the situation becomes virtually impossible. To expect that one would be able to "listen" to the "sound" of unique subtest patterning through the "static" caused by subject factors (demographic) and test factors is to, perhaps, expect the improbable.

CHAPTER 8

The Use of the Wechsler
in Scholastic Assessment

THUS far we have seen that the clinical utility of the Wechsler tests, for a variety of reasons, falls short of acceptability. We can, at this point, question whether the data from the Wechsler tests can be helpful in assisting with the task of making an accurate diagnosis, certainly in any objective (i.e. pattern analysis, scatter analysis, ratios) way. And as regards the prediction of behavior, Wechsler tests have been useless in trying to predict, for example, violent behavior (Shawver and Jew, 1978), hospital treatment outcome (Glick and Sternberg, 1969), posthospital adjustment (Lowe, 1967), continuation of psychotherapy (Hiler, 1958), and while Kaufman (1970) found that employed mentally retarded have a somewhat higher I.Q. (on the WAIS) than unemployed retardates, Wechsler test data could not predict how much individuals would benefit from vocational training (e.g. McKerracher and Orritt, 1972; Tseng, 1972; Webster, 1974). There was also very little correlation between performance rating (of management-level employees) and Wechsler data (e.g. Balinsky and Shaw, 1956). The question now becomes: of what use *are* Wechsler test data?

By definition, the Wechsler tests are tests of intelligence. We should expect, therefore, that if they do *anything* well, the Wechsler should perform best where intelligence is a primary variable, viz., school. We will, now, examine the relationship of Wechsler test data to a variety of scholastic measures.

Grade Point Average

A number of studies have related Wechsler I.Q. to grade point average (e.g. Conry and Plant, 1965; Dudek, Goldberg, Lester and Harris, 1969a; Frandsen, 1950; Gerboth, 1950; Goldman and Hasting, 1976; Kimbrell,

1960; Plant and Lynd, 1959; Quereshi and Miller, 1970; Sartain, 1946; Sewell and Severson, 1975; Wall, Marks, Ford and Zeigler, 1962; Zung and Gianturco, 1968). Table 17 presents an overview of the findings of these studies.

From Table 17 we can see that in all but one study, the Verbal I.Q. demonstrated a better relationship to scholastic grades than the Performance I.Q., and the Verbal I.Q. has as good a relationship with grade point average as does Full Scale I.Q. Thus we can say that the Verbal I.Q. has been shown to relate strongly enough to grade point average to be able to predict it. The data also demonstrate that the individual subtests maintain a variable relationship to grade point average. These studies (by Conry and Plant, 1965; Dudek *et al.*, 1969a; Frandsen, 1950, and Quereshi and Miller, 1970) are presented in Table 18.

TABLE 17. *Correlation of I.Q. scores and grade point average*

Study	Test	Target	I.Q. Score		
			Verbal	Performance	Full Scale
Anderson *et al* (1942)	I	college, 1st semester	.50	.19	.41
	I	college, 1st year	.52	.23	.45
Conry and Plant (1965)	WAIS	high school	.63	.43	.62
	WAIS	college	.47	.24	.44
Dudek *et al* (1969)	WISC	kindergarten	.34	.47	.47
Frandsen (1950)	I	high school	.69	.48	.69
Gerboth (1950)	I	college			.29
Goldman and Hasting (1976)	WISC	minority students: 1st grade			.27
Kimbrell (1960)	WISC	educable defectives			.40
Merrill and Heathers (1953)	I	college	.58	.17	.46
Plant and Lynd (1959)	WAIS	freshman grades	.58	.31	.53
Quereshi and Miller (1970)	WAIS	high school	.69	.57	.72
	II	high school	.64	.52	.65
	WISC	high school	.62	.58	.68
Sartain (1946)	I	college	.58	.35	.53
Wall *et al* (1962)	WAIS	college	.30	.22	.30
Zung and Gianturco (1968)	WAIS	college	.60	.45	.62

Inspection of Table 18 shows that generally the highest correlations with grade point average is Vocabulary, followed by Information, and, to some extent, Similarities and Arithmetic.

Weisgerber (1955) grouped the subtests in terms of whatever cognitive functions he presumed common to the grouping he constructed. Weisgerber then examined the relationship of these cognitive skills and grade point average. Linguistic abilities (Information, Comprehension, Similarities) correlated with grade point average: .213; clerical skills (Digits, Arithmetic, Digit symbol) correlated with grade point average .373; and spatial skills (Picture completion, Object assembly, Block design) correlated with grade point average .050.

Simpson (1970b) used Wechsler data to predict graduation from high school; the correlations were: Full Scale I.Q. .223; Verbal I.Q. .349; Performance I.Q. .031.

Scholastic Aptitudes

Here, we will examine the relationship of Wechsler data to specific scholastic abilities: reading, arithmetic and vocabulary.

Reading ability

Sometimes the correlations of the Wechsler data with test assessment of reading ability have been shown to be high (e.g. Altus, 1952 (Full Scale I.Q.: .84), Ames and Walker, 1964 (Full Scale I.Q.: .57), Barratt and Baumgarten, 1957 (for achievers: Full Scale I.Q.: .56, Verbal I.Q.: .61, Performance I.Q.: .29; for underachievers: Full Scale I.Q.: .63, Verbal I.Q.: .51, Performance I.Q.: .30); Hartlage and Boone, 1977 (Full Scale I.Q., WISC: .72, WISC-R: .70), Henderson, Butler and Goffeney, 1969 (whites: .38, non-whites: .54)); sometimes they have proven to be rather low (e.g. Duffy, Clair, Egeland and DiNello, 1972 (3rd grade: .26, 4th grade: .38, 5th grade: .38); Egeland, 1970 (.20); Henderson and Rankin, 1973 (Mexican-American children: .27); Kaufman, 1973 (Full Scale I.Q.: .36, Verbal I.Q.: .35, Performance I.Q.: .28)). Confusingly, the variation in correlations do not seem to relate to anything "palpable," e.g. kinds of subjects sampled.

TABLE 18. *Correlation of subtest score with grade point average*

Study	Test	Target	I	C	S	A	D	V	PA	PC	BD	OA	DS
Conry and Plant (1965)	WAIS	high school	.54	.55	.50	.45	.37	.65	.22	.33	.29	.17	.34
	WAIS	college	.48	.33	.39	.19	.04	.46	.07	.20	.19	.12	.15
Dudek et al (1969)	WISC	kindergarten	.36	–	.38	.29	.45	–	.54	–	.37	.24	.25
Drandsen (1950)	I	high school	.56	.51	.54	.55	.45	–	.15	.25	.44	.11	.36
Quereshi and Miller (1970)	WAIS	high school	.52	.25	.45	.53	.41	.61	.28	.39	.36	.40	.55
	WISC	high school	.44	.07	.41	.52	.46	.50	.26	.43	.46	.41	.43
	II	high school	.41	.24	.42	.55	.34	.40	.29	.34	.41	.45	.35

Robeck (1960) found that reading disability was associated with poor performance on Digits, Arithmetic, Information and Coding.

Arithmetical ability

In the same way as reading ability, correlations of the Wechsler data with test assessment of mathematical ability have been shown to be relatively high sometimes (e.g. Duffy *et al.*, 1972 (WISC: Full Scale I.Q., 3rd grade: .35, 4th grade: .31, 5th grade: .49); Henderson *et al.*, 1969 (WISC Full Scale I.Q.: whites: .62, non-whites: .61); Kaufman, 1973 (WPPSI Full Scale I.Q.: .30, Verbal I.Q.: .26, Performance I.Q.: .27); Mussen, Dean and Rosenberg, 1952 (WISC Full Scale I.Q.: .81, Verbal I.Q.: .74, Performance I.Q.: .74)), other times, low (e.g. Engin, 1975 (WISC Verbal I.Q.: arithmetic computation: .22, arithmetic concepts: .480)). Where one sees a real difference in the relationship of Wechsler data to arithmetical ability due to the subjects being sampled is with regard to achievers versus non-achievers; achievers achieved a correlation with arithmetical ability of: Full Scale I.Q.: .14, Verbal I.Q.: .09, Performance I.Q.: .14, while non-achievers achieved correlations of: Full Scale I.Q.: .79, Verbal I.Q.: .73, Performance I.Q.: .33 (Barratt and Baumgarten, 1957).

Vocabulary (word knowledge)

In light of the generally high correlation between Vocabulary and Full Scale I.Q., surprisingly, the correlation between Wechsler data and word knowledge, as assessed by the achievement tests, is, at best, modest (e.g. Duffy *et al.*, 1972 (WISC Full Scale I.Q., 3rd grade: .28, 4th grade: .48, 5th grade: .39), Egeland, DiNello and Carr, 1970 (WISC Full Scale I.Q.: .25), Engin, 1975 (WISC Verbal I.Q.: .35), Kaufman, 1973 (WPPSI Full Scale I.Q.: .35, Verbal I.Q.: .29, Performance I.Q.: .31)).

I.Q. did not seem to be related to learning ability (e.g. Baumeister and Hawkins, 1966; McLean, 1954). But Nalven and Bierbryer (1969) found Wechsler data to demonstrate satisfactory correlations with teacher rating of the students' ability to comprehend (Full Scale I.Q.: .74, Verbal I.Q.: .79, Performance I.Q.: .56, Information: .81, Vocabulary: .81, Similarities: .68, Comprehension: .56, Coding: .56, Arithmetic: .53,

Picture arrangement: .53, Block design: .40, Picture completion: .37, and Object assembly: .35).

No particular subtest pattern was found to correlate with underachieving (e.g. Bush and Mattson, 1973; Dudek and Lester, 1968; Jenkin, Spivack, Levine and Savage, 1964), except that underachievers tended to do poorly on tests that assessed attention and concentration (for example, Digits, Arithmetic and Digit symbol).

As we look over the obtained relationship of Wechsler data to a variety of assessments of scholastic ability (grade point average, performance on achievement tests, teacher ratings), one cannot help but conclude how modest, at best, that relationship is. Undoubtedly performance in school or with regard to scholastic material is a function of more than just level of intelligence. However, the rather modest relationship of Wechsler data to scholastic achievement would seem to rule it out as a method of trying to predict how an individual will do in school. At the same time, because of the many variables involved in scholastic behavior, assessing I.Q. will not enable the clinician to know whether the factor of intelligence is the factor causing the person to have trouble in school. Obviously, with the low correlations between Wechsler data and scholastic achievement, that means some individuals with low I.Q.s are doing well in school, not just vice versa. The overall conclusion would seem to be that Wechsler test data do not seem to be helpful as regards the assessment of potential scholastic achievement.

CHAPTER 9

Summary and Conclusions

IT IS time, now, for us to review what we have found with regard to the test(s)* Wechsler developed and its (their) value for the clinical enterprise.

In the first place it must be acknowledged that the question of what intelligence is, and whether or not the test Wechsler developed conforms to the most meaningful definition of intelligence is not of concern for us. An exploration of the issue of *the* definition of intelligence has been explored elsewhere (e.g. Frank, 1976; Matarazzo, 1976); it turns out, as one might expect, there are a multitude of definitions of intelligence. Wechsler's definition of intelligence is:

> Intelligence is the aggregate or global capacity of the individual to act purposefully, to think rationally and to deal effectively with his environment. (Wechsler, 1939, p. 3)

There is no basic quarrel with Wechsler's definition. Wechsler's definition echoes Spearman's (1904, 1923), who spoke of *g*, a global capacity, and an aggregate of *s*, that is, special attributes or abilities, and William Stern (1914) whose definition of intelligence was the capacity for adaptation. In that regard, Wechsler's test is consonant with his definition of intelligence. It is not Wechsler's definition of intelligence which is in question; it is the nature of the structure of his test and the use to which it has been put by him and others which is.

When Wechsler entered the field of psychology,† applied psychology and testing of intelligence were synonymous. Thus, from the very beginning of his career Wechsler was embodied in the psychological culture of Binet,

---

*For the sake of ease of reading, the word "test" shall be utilized to refer to all of the tests that Wechsler developed.

†Matarazzo (1976) has a brief description of Wechsler's life and career (in the chapter, "The Definition of Intelligence"). Therein, we are informed that Wechsler graduated from Columbia University in 1917 with a master's in psychology and was inducted into military service as a consequence of the First World War.

Spearman, Thorndike, and Yerkes. Essentially, the field of intelligence testing was dominated by the test Binet had developed and Binet's ideas about intelligence. Binet subscribed to the notion that a test of intelligence was, basically, a test of cognitive functions and their use by the individual, e.g. problem-solving and adaptation, that intelligence was influenced by non-intellectual factors, and that the notion that different forms of psychopathology eventuated in differential disturbances is one or another area of cognition (à la Kraepelin) and, hence, different forms of psychopathology would be expected to produce different (and unique) patterns of subtests.

Factor analytic studies have demonstrated that the Binet does, in fact, assess a variety of cognitive/intellective factors, and research in psychology has certainly supported the Kantian notion of the subjective nature of cognition. And the psychologists of Wechsler's early days in his career were using the Binet to explore the nature of the intellective/cognitive disorders in psychiatric patients. The problem with the Binet was its structure. While the test did explore a variety of cognitive/intellective functions, it did so inefficiently; viz., all the cognitive/intellective functions were not assessed at each age level, the subtests which did explore the same cognitive/intellective functions at different age levels were not all the same length or difficulty, while verbal and non-verbal functions were assessed, they were not assessed equally, and there was no psychometric way of comparing performance on one subtest with another, either in terms of an individual with regard to his own intellectual performance or in terms of comparing the intellectual performance of one individual with another. In the two years Wechsler spent in military service he was a psychometrician, and, as such, not only utilized the Binet but also the Army Alpha and Beta tests (the latter being developed under the general tutelage of Yerkes). These tests consisted of tasks of verbal functions (the Army Alpha, composed of the following subtests: Information, Comprehension, Similarities, Arithmetic and Vocabulary) and non-verbal tests of intellectual ability (the Army Beta test which was composed of the following subtests: Picture arrangement, Picture completion, Object assembly, Block design and Digit symbol). What Wechsler did was to add Digits to these verbal tasks (as Terman and Chamberlain (1918) and Whipple (1921) had done before him), combine the verbal and non-verbal subtests into one scale (instead of considering them separately as in the

Army tests), employ Thurstone's (1925) notion to convert the raw scores of each subtest into standard scores (so as to facilitate inter-subtest/inter-function comparisons), and employ Yerkes' (1917) concept of a point scale assessment of intelligence rather than Binet's concept of mental age.

As Matarazzo (1976) points out, after discharge from military service (in 1919), Wechsler did a variety of things, amongst them, holding a position of psychologist at the Bureau of Child Guidance in New York (1922–1924) while attending Columbia University to complete his doctorate (which he did in 1925). From that time (1925) until 1932, Wechsler was in private practice in New York but in 1933 he became Chief Psychologist at Bellevue. It was at Bellevue that Wechsler began employing and refining the Bellevue Scales, his modification of the Army tests of intelligence which, ultimately, became known as the Wechsler–Bellevue Scale of Intelligence. Over the years, Wechsler developed other forms of the Scale: the first form of the test appeared in 1939, Form II (an alternative form of Form I developed so as to facilitate re-testing) appeared in 1946; Form I was modified (structurally and better standardized) and appeared in 1955 as the WAIS; in 1949, Wechsler revised Form II and adapted it for use with children (the WISC); the WISC was further revised for use with even lower ages in 1963 (the WPPSI).

Essentially, however, all these tests are of one mold structurally, and, since they are all outgrowths of the original Wechsler Scale, share similar content. In that regard, comments which are made about the form (i.e. structure) of Wechsler's test can refer to all of them. Any number of individuals have criticized the form of the Wechsler (e.g. Gurvitz, 1952). But when Wechsler presented his Scale to the (professional) world, it was greeted as the great intellectual hope; all of the psychometric inadequacies of the Binet were supposed to be corrected by this instrument so that psychologists could better do what they felt could be done with a test of intelligence in terms of an assessment of psychopathology. As we have seen, that hope was not fulfilled. The use of the Wechsler Scale to assess the differential cognitive/intellective performance of various types of psychiatric patients revealed no greater success than that of the Binet (the research with the Binet was reviewed by Harris and Shakow, 1937). It is our task to try to understand why, although it was structurally more refined than the Binet for the task of pattern and scatter analysis, that effort has come to no better end than the efforts with the Binet.

To answer the question why the research yields such weak support for the clinical use of the Wechsler we must examine some of the assumptions that are inherent in the clinical use of Wechsler data.

The overall assumption is that psychopathology influences cognitive functions and that specific forms of psychopathology would, thus, yield different patterns of cognitive functioning. These are the assumptions we have inherited from Kraepelin and Binet. In order to be used to assess the validity and/or consequence of the Kraepelinian/Binetian assumptions, the Wechsler test would have to:

(1) constitute an assessment of cognitive functions,

(2) constitute an assessment of a wide variety of cognitive functions, and

(3) permit these cognitive/intellective functions to be measured relatively autonomously from each other.

Let us address these assumptions.

Cognition, the meaning-making function, and cognitive functions, those psychological processes which enable humans to make meaning out of their world (e.g. selective, organized and synthesized: attention, memory, perception and thinking) do seem to be assessed by the Wechsler Scale, but the factor analytic research indicates that:

(a) The subtests do not constitute subsets of unique functions; the subtests are factorially complex with the same cognitive/intellective functions being measured by several subtests and one subtest measuring several cognitive/intellective functions simultaneously. In short, the subtests are not "pure." Thus, even if specific forms of psychopathology do eventuate in unique patterns of cognitive/intellective functions, that assessment could not be clearly picked up, and any unique patterning of cognitive/intellective abilities would be made difficult by the complex nature of the subtests.*

(b) While the Wechsler subtests do seem, even in their fashion, to assess cognitive/intellective functions, the question remains as to how many. There is a dearth of studies exploring the cognitive construction of the subtests (which leaves us to have to speculate about the cognitive functions

---

*An insight that seems to have been known to psychologists about tests for a long time (e.g. Oates, 1928), including the fact that different factors are measured by the same test at different ages (Burks, 1930).

each subtest assesses as did Rapaport). The research seems to point to the fact that the Wechsler subtests tap only three cognitive factors, viz., a verbal factor, spatial relations, and attention-concentration (or numerical ability). These constitute a poor sampling of the (at least) nine primary mental abilities (Thurstone, 1938). Thus, the limited range of cognitive/intellective abilities tapped by the Wechsler limits the range of cognitive/intellective abilities which can be explored by the Wechsler in relation to psychopathology.

(c) Factor analytic studies fail to yield factors defined by individual subtests. As we have already noted, the subtests were seen to cluster into three major factors: verbal, spatial and numerical. Thus, we can assume that the subtests tend not to be able to vary independently and freely in psychometric space, but tend to assess similar functions, hence, are more related than independent. Pattern analysis and unique patterning would, therefore, be made difficult.

(d) Clinicians assumed that scatter (the degree to which the subtests vary around some fixed point of measurement such as a mean subtest score, Verbal, Performance or Full Scale I.Q., the individual's own Vocabulary score) was, itself, a function of psychopathology (the assumption was that in normal, healthy people, there would be homogeneity of performance on the subtest, or no scatter). However, that is not what the research revealed. For a variety of reasons, scatter (that is, heterogeneity of subtest performance) is inherent in the Wechsler. For example, if we think of the overall I.Q. measure (i.e. Full Scale I.Q.) as a referent point around which subtests may vary, we have seen (Table 13) that the subtests not only have a modest relationship to the Full Scale I.Q., but also a differential one. This variable relationship to the Full Scale I.Q. not only means a variable relationship to "g" but, also, that variability is inherent in the subtests from the start. Any assessment of scatter, then, would have to factor out the degree of scatter ordinarily expected from the amount of scatter found in specific groups of subjects (research has not done this).

(e) Then there is the fact that the subtests are not of equal difficulty (Jastak, 1950; Mech, 1953; Nickols, 1963; Rabin, Davis and Sanderson, 1946; Rubin-Raskin, 1956).

But it should seem clear that if the psychologist should attempt to explore the amount of scatter produced by specific groups of patients, the amount of scatter inherent in the test would have to be parcelled out.

The clinical research did not do this. Indeed, the research demonstrates that the higher the intelligence, the greater the scatter; scatter-less performance seems characteristic of the retarded, the depressed or the chronically psychiatric ill. Wechsler also made assumptions about what was a significant difference in, for example, a subtest score from its mean or of the Verbal I.Q. from the Performance I.Q., which have not been substantiated by the research (e.g. Jones, 1956).

However, there is still the question of the validity of the Kraepelinian hypothesis to which most subsequent investigators have subscribed. There does not seem to be reason to quarrel with the notion that cognition can be subjective. Kraepelin (and the Binet) assumed that particular forms of psychopathology would reflect specific (and unique) patterns of cognitive functions. Translating that into test language, the assumption was made (by e.g. Binet, Wechsler, Rapaport) that specific forms of psychopathology would be reflected in unique patterns of subtests. The research did not support this assumption. Difficulties in, for example, thinking may be found in a variety of disorders (as might difficulties in attention, memory or perception). What differentiates the cognitive performance of different psychiatric types is a qualitative analysis. Thus, while schizophrenics, organics and obsessives all show impairment in thinking, it is only through an analysis of the content of their thought that the thinking of each kind of patient can be differentiated. Low scores in the subtests *per se* did not differentiate, for example, the schizophrenic from the cerebrally impaired, and, thus, the search for unique subtest patterns turned out to be fruitless.

There is no quarrel with the notion that personality (and, hence, psychopathology) influences cognition. But clinicians have made the assumption that personality is the *only* factor which affects cognitive/intellective functioning. The research, on the other hand, reveals that a multitude of factors influence cognitive/intellective performance* (hence, subtest patterning or scatter) such as: age, gender, socio-economic level and level of education. The research has even demonstrated that subtest patterning is affected by cerebral dominance (which hemisphere is dominant), level of intelligence, and mood.

Finally, testing is an interpersonal event and the test performance of individuals is influenced by this factor, too. First, there is the clinician's

---

*See a similar conclusion made by Blatt and Allison (1968).

perception of the patient which influences his scoring where scoring is based on the judgment of the clinician (see the research on this by, e.g. Arnhoff, 1954; Johnson, 1949; Kaspar, Throne and Schulman, 1968; Sattler, Winget and Roth, 1969; Walker, Hunt and Schwartz, 1965a), the personality of the clinician (e.g. Back and Dana, 1977; Berger *et al.*, 1971; Brigham, 1917; Cohen, 1965; Davis, Peacock, Fitzpatrick and Mulhern, 1969; Dickstein and Kephart, 1972; Donahue and Sattler, 1971; Egeland, 1967; Exner, 1966; Masling, 1959, 1960; Sattler and Theye, 1967; Schroeder and Kleinsasser, 1972) and mood of the subject (e.g. Bergan, McManis and Melchert, 1971; Dickstein and Ayres, 1973; Downey, 1918; Nichols, 1959; Wiener, 1957). The expectation that personality traits would be the *only* subjective factors (that is, factors of the individual) which would influence cognition, was naïve.

For a number of reasons having to do with factors inherent in the test and factors inherent in individuals, the search for objective (unique, discriminating) patterns of subtests was doomed to failure from the start, regardless of the several transformations of the data (e.g. Barnett, 1950; Jastak, 1953), mathematical ratios (for example, as was constructed with the performance of schizophrenics and the cerebrally impaired), or sophisticated mathematical analyses of the data (e.g. Harper, 1950b; Klein, 1948) recommended.

Another issue regarding the simplistic ways the personality-intelligence relationship has been formulated has been pointed out by Eysenck (Eysenck, 1967; Eysenck and White, 1964). Eysenck comments that the search for the relationship between personality traits and intelligence has been done using tests of that relationship which ensure linearity (e.g. Pearson *r*'s). Eysenck presents data to demonstrate that, in fact, the relationship between personality and intelligence is *curvi*linear. The relationship of personality traits is not the same at different intellectual levels, and different degrees of a personality trait eventuate in different configurations of intellectual abilities. Most research in the area of the exploration of personality and intelligence do not take this into consideration. Furthermore, Eysenck points out that most researchers examine the relationship of personality traits to only one facet of intelligence, viz., outcome of effort (that is, success or failure in solving the task at hand). However, other facets of the intellective process (such as: speed, persistence and errorchecking behavior, to name a few) are ignored in this research.

It is not, however, that the Wechsler test(s) only fail to enable the clinician to draw meaningful conclusions about psychopathology; the research also demonstrated that the Wechsler test fails to provide the psychologist sufficient information regarding the prediction of scholastic performance, a place where one might expect a test of intelligence to perform at its best. The research indicates a modest, at best, relationship between performance on the Wechsler and prediction of academic performance. However, that is no particular criticism of the Wechsler test since the research has always demonstrated that tests of intelligence in general bear a modest relationship to academic performance. Better predictors of academic performance have been such factors as: tests of scholastic abilities and teacher ratings (e.g. Coleman and Cureton, 1954). However, the best predictor of academic performance turns out to be grades; grades from lower levels of schooling (e.g. high school) predict to more advanced levels of schooling (e.g. college) to a considerably high degree (e.g. Harris, 1940; Humphreys, 1968). And the Wechsler test is not very helpful in predicting vocational success (Webster, 1979). Moreover, for all of the revisions, the Wechsler remains a test which is not culture fair (e.g. Dean, 1979, Munford and Meyerowitz, 1980; Munford and Munoz, 1980). However, what this *does* reflect is that clinicians do not seem to pay attention to research; the data were there for them to know that intelligence test data relate poorly to academic performance. Once again the Wechsler test failed to live up to the hope that it would do better what other tests of intelligence fail to do.

What, then, is the implication of this review of research as an attempt to assess the heuristic value of the tests Wechsler developed? My personal reading of this research is that the test(s) Wechsler developed have failed to live up to their promise. We have seen that the psychometric inadequacies of the Binet prompted Wechsler to develop his test. The Binet was not a good test for adults, the standardization left a lot to be desired, while assessing a number of intellective/cognitive functions, it did so inefficiently (e.g. not all intellective functions were assessed at each age level, those functions which were assessed at several age levels were done so unequally, non-verbal as well as verbal factors were not represented equally (the Binet was weighted with non-verbal tasks at the lower levels, verbal at the upper), the subtests were not of equal difficulty, and the scoring of the Binet did not allow for a comparative analysis of individuals' performance on different subtests, etc.). Following the trend in the field of intelligence testing to assess intelligence via verbal and non-verbal tasks at the same time, Wechsler adapted the verbal and non-verbal tasks of the Army tests to such a use by combining them into one scale. Then, Wechsler followed the recommendations made by psychometricians to convert the individual subtest scores into standard scores (a suggestion made by, for example, Thurstone) and to score the test as a point scale not an age scale (a suggestion as made, for example, by Yerkes and Thurstone).

It is not the lack of creativity Wechsler displayed in developing his Scale that is in question; as we have seen, it was standard operating procedure for psychologists to develop new scales by borrowing from other tests tests which seemed to fit the needs of the developer of the new Scale. What can be criticized is the fact that Wechsler did not employ the advanced statistical and psychological methods available to him in developing his tests at the time he was developing his test. Wechsler never analyzed his tests to determine the internal consistency of the individual subtests, or the degree to which the subtests constituted assessments of separate functions, nor the degree to which the subtests measured what he said they measured. While he was conservative in the clinical use of his test (Rapaport is really the most radical thinker in this regard, and it was following *his* lead which led so many clinicians into the heights of clinical theorizing), Wechsler nonetheless gave impetus to the expectation that different forms of psychopathology would produce different (and unique) subtest patterns, an assumption the research has failed to support. Not only does the Wechsler test show itself to be unable to assess psychopathology any better than the Binet,* but, as with the Binet, it proves to be no better a predictor of academic performance (the very task which prompted Binet to develop his test in the first place). As a test, therefore, the worth of the Wechsler seems questionable.

In the face of such a conclusion, I believe clinical psychology has several options available to it with regard to the Wechsler test:

(1) continue to use the test exactly as it has been used in the past (in the face of the research which suggests this is inappropriate, for as we know, beliefs of clinicians are slow to change [e.g. Meehl, 1973]);

(2) continue to use the test but rely on a qualitative analysis of an

*See a similar conclusion made by Rabin (1965).

individual's performance on the subtests for clinical insights and give up the search for the elusive, so-called "objective," unique subtest patterns;

(3) if a more "objective" use of the tests is wanted, then I recommend that we stop using the test until it is refined, which would entail:

(a) making the subtests internally consistent,

(b) ensuring a more homogenous relationship of the subtests to the overall measures (e.g. Verbal, Performance and Full Scale I.Q.s),

(c) determining, more precisely, what cognitive functions *are* being assessed by each subtest;

(d) purifying the subtests so that they are not so factorially (with regard to intellective—cognitive functions) complex,

(e) standardizing the test better (particularly with regard to minority groups) and to develop separate norms for each minority group, or

(4) stop trying to assess cognitive functions in this indirect and inefficient way and develop an omnibus test of cognitive functions, one which assesses the breadth of primary mental abilities, or

(5) stop trying to assess academic potential and performance in an indirect way, and utilize those instruments better suited to do a more direct and efficient job,

(6) in light of the many factors seen to influence cognition over and above personality (and/or psychopathology), stop trying to assess personality and/or psychopathology indirectly, that is, through an analysis of cognitive factors, and utilize (and/or develop) instruments which assess the various facets of psychopathology directly.

My own personal overall conclusion from these data is that we can no longer justify using indirect, inefficient or ineffective methods to assess whatever it is we wish to assess in psychology. Personality, psychopathology, scholastic abilities, etc., can all be assessed directly with instruments much better suited to do so than an omnibus assessment of intellective functions which, by its very complexity, means that so many factors (psychometric *and* psychological (e.g. personality, cognitive, etc.)) are involved in the subtests. In the absence of knowing how much of what *is* assessed by each subtest (alone and/or in combination with other subtests) that certainly the Wechsler test(s) in its (their) present psychometric condition argues against its use in clinical endeavours in any objective way. From the research we have covered the results leave little which would allow us to rationalize the continued use of the Wechsler tests in clinical work.

We could develop a program of research to correct the psychometric inadequacies of the test and, then, we could develop a program of research to assess what cognitive and personality factors *are* assessed by the subtest, but why bother? In this age of sophisticated tests (of which there are many) assessment of psychological attributes can be done better directly. The Wechsler tests are like the dinosaur, too large, cumbersome and ill-fitted and awkward in the age in which they developed, unable to remain viable in a psychometric age which has passed it by in conceptualization. As with the dinosaur it is time for the Wechsler test to become extinct.

References

ADAMS, R. L., KOBOS, J. C. and PRESTON, J. (1977) Effect of racial-ethnic grouping, age, and IQ range on the validity of the Satz–Mogel short form of the Wechsler Adult Intelligence Scale. *J. Consult. Clin. Psychol.*, 45, 498–499.

ALEXANDER, W. P. (1935) Intelligence, concrete and abstract. *Br. J. Psychol. Monogr. Suppl.*, No. 19.

ALIMENA, B. (1951) Norms for scatter analysis on the Wechsler Intelligence Scales. *J. Clin. Psychol.*, 7, 289–290.

ALIMENA, B. (1961) A note on norms for scatter analysis on the Wechsler Intelligence Scales. *J. Clin. Psychol.*, 17, 61.

ALLEN, R. M. (1947) The test performance of the brain injured. *J. Clin. Psychol.*, 3, 225–230.

ALLEN, R. M. (1948a) A note on the use of the Bellevue–Wechsler Scale Mental Deterioration Index with brain injured patients. *J. Clin. Psychol.*, 4, 88–89.

ALLEN, R. M. (1948b) The test performance of the brain diseased. *J. Clin. Psychol.*, 4, 281–284.

ALLEN, R. M. (1949) A comparison of the test performance of the brain-injured and the brain-diseased. *Am. J. Psychiat.*, 106, 195–198.

ALLPORT, G. W. (1937) *Personality*. New York: Holt.

ALLPORT, G. and VERNON, P. E. (1933) *Studies in Expressive Movement*. New York: Macmillan.

ALPER, A. E. (1967) An analysis of the Wechsler Intelligence Scale for Children with institutionalized mental retardates. *Am. J. Ment. Defic.*, 71, 624–630.

ALTUS, G. T. (1952) A note on the validity of the Wechsler Intelligence Scale for Children. *J. Consult. Psychol.*, 16, 231.

ALTUS, G. T. (1956) A WISC profile for retarded readers. *J. Consult. Psychol.*, 20, 155–156.

ALTUS, W. D. (1945) The differential validity and difficulty of subtests of the Wechsler Mental Ability Scale. *Psychol. Bull.*, 42, 238–249.

ALTUS. W. D. and CLARK, J. H. (1949) Subtest variation on the Wechsler–Bellevue for two institutionalized behavior problem groups. *J. Consult. Psychol.*, 13, 444–447.

AMES, L. B. and WALKER, R. N. (1964) Prediction of later reading ability from Kindergarten Rorschach and IQ scores. *J. Educ. Psychol.*, 55, 309–313.

ANDERSEN, A. L. (1950) The effect of laterality localization of brain damage on Wechsler–Bellevue indices of deterioration. *J. Clin. Psychol.*, 6, 191–194.

ANDERSEN, A. L. (1951) The effect of laterality of localization of focal brain lesions on the Wechsler–Bellevue subtests. *J. Clin. Psychol.*, 7, 149–153.

ANDREW, J. M. (1974) Delinquency, the Wechsler P > V sign, and the I-level system. *J. Clin. Psychol.*, **30**, 331–335.

ANGERS, W. P. (1958) A psychometric study of institutionalized epileptics on the Wechsler–Bellevue. *J. Gen. Psychol.*, **58**, 225–247.

ANSBACHER, H. (1937) Perception of number as affected by the monetary value of the objects: A critical study of the method used in the extended constancy phenomenon. *Arch. Psychol.*, No. 215.

APPELBAUM, A. S. and TUMA, J. M. (1977) Social class and test performance: Comparative validity of the Peabody with the WISC and WISC-R for two socio-economic groups. *Psychol. Rep.*, **40**, 139–145.

ARMSTRONG, R. G. (1955) A reliability study of a short form of the WISC vocabulary subtest. *J. Clin. Psychol.*, **11**, 413–414.

ARNHOFF, F. N. (1954) Some factors influencing the unreliability of clinical judgments. *J. Clin. Psychol.*, **10**, 272–275.

ARTHUR, G. (1925) A new point performance scale. *J. Appl. Psychol.*, **9**, 390–416.

ARTHUR, G. (1930) *A Point Scale of Performance Tests.* New York: Commonwealth Fund.

ASCH, S. E. (1936) A study of change in mental organization. *Arch. Psychol.*, No. 195.

ATCHISON, C. O. (1955) Use of the Wechsler Intelligence Scale for Children with eighty mentally defective Negro children. *Am. J. Ment. Defic.*, **60**, 378–379.

AYRES, L. P. (1911) The Binet–Simon measuring scale for intelligence: Some criticisms and suggestions. *Psychol. Clin.*, **5**, 187–196.

BABCOCK, H. (1930) An experiment in the measurement of mental deterioration. *Arch. Psychol.*, No. 117.

BACK, R. and DANA, R. H. (1977) Examiner sex bias and Wechsler Intelligence Scale for Children scores. *J. Consult. Clin. Psychol.*, **45**, 500.

BAILEY, K. G. and GIBBY, R. G. (1971) Developmental differences in self-ratings on intelligence. *J. Clin. Psychol.*, **27**, 51–54.

BALDWIN, J. M. (1894) Psychology past and present. *Psychol. Rev.*, **1**, 363–391.

BALINSKY, B. (1941) An analysis of the mental factors of various age groups from nine to sixty. *Genet. Psychol. Monog.*, **23**, 191–234.

BALINSKY, B. and SHAW, H. W. (1956) The contribution of the WAIS to a management appraisal program. *Personnel Psychol.*, **9**, 207–209.

BALINSKY, B., ISRAEL, H. and WECHSLER, D. (1939) The relative effectiveness of the Stanford–Binet and the Bellevue Intelligence Scale in diagnosing mental deficiency. *Am. J. Orthopsychiat.*, **9**, 798–801.

BALTHAZAR, E. E. (1963) Cerebral unilateralization in chronic epileptic cases: The Wechsler Object Assembly subtests. *J. Clin. Psychol.*, **19**, 169–171.

BALTHAZAR, E. E. and MORRISON, D. J. (1961) The use of Wechsler Intelligence Scales as diagnostic indicators of left–right and indeterminate unilateral brain damage. *J. Clin. Psychol.*, **17**, 161–165.

BALTHAZAR, E. E., TODD, R. E., MORRISON, D. H. and ZIEBELL, P. W. (1961) Visuo-constructive and verbal responses in chronic brain-damaged patients and familial retardates. *J. Clin. Psychol.*, **17**, 293–296.

BARCLAY, A., FRIEDMAN, E. D. and FIDEL, Y. (1969) A comparative study of WISC and WAIS performance and score patterns among institutionalized retardates. *J. Ment. Defic. Res.*, **13**, 99–105.

BARKER, R. G. (1938) The effect of frustration upon cognitive ability. *Character Personal.*, **7**, 145–150.

BARNETT, I. (1950) The Use of Z scores in equating the Wechsler–Bellevue subtests. *J. Clin. Psychol.*, 6, 184–188.

BAROFF, G. S. (1959) WISC patterning in endogenous mental deficiency. *Am. J. Ment. Defic.*, 64, 482–485.

BARRATT, E. S. (1956) The relationship of the Progressive Matrices (1938) and the Columbia Mental Maturity to the WISC. *J. Consult. Psychol.*, 20, 294–296.

BARRATT, E. S. and BAUMGARTEN, D. L. (1957) The relationship of WISC and Stanford–Binet to school achievement. *J. Consult. Psychol.*, 21, 144.

BARRY, J. R., FULKERSON, S. C., KUBALA, A. L. and SEAQUIST, M. P. (1956) Score equivalence of the Wechsler–Bellevue Intelligence Scales, Forms I and II. *J. Clin. Psychol.*, 12, 57–60.

BASSETT, J. E. and GAYTON, W. F. (1969) The use of Doppelt's abbreviated form of the WAIS with mental retardates. *J. Clin. Psychol.*, 25, 276–277.

BAUMEISTER, A. A. (1964) Use of the WISC with mental retardates: A review. *Am. J. Ment. Defic.*, 69, 183–194.

BAUMEISTER, A. A. and BARTLETT, C. J. (1962a) A comparison of the factor structure of normals and retardates on the WISC. *Am. J. Ment. Defic.*, 66, 641–646.

BAUMEISTER, A. A. and BARTLETT, C. J. (1962b) Further factorial investigations of WISC performance of mental defectives. *Am. J. Ment. Defic.*, 67, 257–261.

BAUMEISTER, A. A. and HAWKINS, W. F. (1966) WISC scores of retardates in relation to learning ability. *J. Clin. Psychol.*, 22, 75–76.

BAY, M. S. and BERKS, M. D. (1948) Comprehension, similarities, and digit symbols of the Wechsler–Bellevue Scale used in a court clinic. *Am. Psychol.*, 3, 365. (Abstract).

BAYLEY, N. (1933) Mental growth during the first three years: A developmental study of sixty-one children by repeated tests. *Genet. Psychol. Monogr.*, 14, No. 1.

BAYLEY, N. (1955) On the growth of intelligence. *Am. Psychol.*, 10, 805–818.

BECK, A. T., FESHBACH, S. and LEGG, D. (1962) The clinical utility of the Digit Symbol test. *J. Consult. Psychol.*, 26, 263–268.

BECK, H. S. and LAM, R. L. (1955) Use of the WISC in predicting organicity. *J. Clin. Psychol.*, 11, 154–158.

BECKER, B. (1975) Intellectual changes after closed head injury. *J. Clin. Psychol.*, 31, 307–309.

BELMONT, L. and BIRCH, H. G. (1966) The intellectual profile of retarded readers. *Percept. Motor Skills*, 22, 787–816.

BELMONT, I., BIRCH, H. G. and BELMONT, L. (1967) The organization of intelligence test performance in educable mentally sub-normal children. *Am. J. Ment. Defic.*, 71, 969–976.

BENSBERG, G. J. and SLOAN, W. (1950) A study of Wechsler's concept of "normal deterioration" in older mental defectives. *J. Clin. Psychol.*, 6, 359–362.

BEN-YISHEY, Y., DILLER, L., MANDELBERG, I., GORDON, W. and GERSTMAN, L. J. (1971) Similarities and differences in Block Design performance between older normal and brain-injured persons. *J. Abnorm. Psychol.*, 78, 17–25.

BERGAN, A., McMANIS, D. L. and MELCHERT, P. A. (1971) Effects of social and token reinforcement on WISC Block Design performance. *Percept. Motor Skills.*, 32, 871–880.

BERGER, L., BERNSTEIN, A., KLEIN, E., COHEN, J. and LUCAS, G. (1964) Effects of aging and pathology on the factorial structure of intelligence. *J. Consult. Psychol.*, 28, 199–207.

BERKOWITZ, B. (1953) The Wechsler–Bellevue performance of white males past age 50. *J. Gerontol.*, 8, 76–80.

BERKOWITZ, B. and GREEN, R. F. (1963) Changes in intellect with age: I. Longitudinal study of Wechsler–Bellevue scores. *J. Genet. Psychol.*, 103, 3–21.

BERNSTEIN, A. S., KLEIN, E. B., BERGER, L. and COHEN, J. (1965) Relationship between institutionalization, other demographic variables, and the structure of intelligence in chronic schizophrenics. *J. Consult. Psychol.*, 29, 320–324.

BERNSTEIN, R. and CORSINI, R. J. (1953) Wechsler–Bellevue patterns of female delinquents. *J. Clin. Psychol.*, 9, 176–179.

BERSOFF, D. N. (1970) The revised deterioration formula for the Wechsler Adult Intelligence Scale: A test of validity. *J. Clin. Psychol.*, 26, 71–73.

BERSOFF, D. N. (1971) Short forms of individual intelligence tests for children: Review and critique. *J. Sch. Psychol.*, 9, 310–320.

BIJOU, S. W. (1947a) The psychometric pattern approach as an aid to clinical analysis – A review. *Am. J. Ment. Defic.*, 46, 354–362.

BIJOU, S. W. (1942b) A genetic study of the diagnostic significance of psychometric patterns. *Am. J. Ment. Defic.*, 47, 171–177.

BINET, A. (1905) A propos la mesure de l'intelligence. *L'Année Psychol.*, 11, 69–82.

BINET, A. and HENRI, V. (1895) La psychologie individuelle. *L'Année Psychol.*, 2, 411–465.

BINET, A. and SIMON, T. (1905) Methodes nouvelles pour le diagnostic du niveau intellectual des anormaux. *L'Année Psychol.*, 11, 193–244.

BINET, A. and SIMON, T. (1905) Le développement de l'intelligence chez les enfants. *L'Année Psychol.*, 14, 1–94.

BINET, A. and SIMON, T. (1916) *The Development of Intelligence in Children.* Baltimore: Williams & Wilkins.

BIRCH, H. G., BELMONT, L. and BELMONT, I. (1967) Brain damage and intelligence in educable mentally subnormal children. *J. Nerv. Ment. Dis.*, 144, 247–257.

BIRREN, J. E. (1951) A factorial analysis of the Wechsler–Bellevue Adult Intelligence Scale given to an elderly population. *Am. Psychol.*, 6, 398–399. (Abstract)

BIRREN, J. E. (1952) A factorial analysis of the Wechsler–Bellevue Scale given to an elderly population. *J. Consult. Psychol.*, 16, 399–405.

BIRREN, J. E. and MORRISON, D. F. (1961) Analysis of the WAIS subtests in relation to age and education. *J. Gerontol.*, 16, 363–369.

BLACK, F. W. (1974a) WISC verbal-performance discrepancies as indicators of neurological dysfunction in pediatric patients. *J. Clin. Psychol.*, 30, 165–167.

BLACK, F. W. (1974b) Patterns of cognitive impairment in children with suspected and documented neurological dysfunction. *Percept. Motor Skills*, 39, 115–120.

BLACK, F. W. (1976) Cognitive deficits in patients with unilateral war-related frontal lobe lesions. *J. Clin. Psychol.*, 32, 366–372.

BLAKE, R. R. and McCARTY, B. S. (1948) A comparative evaluation of the Bellevue–Wechsler Mental Deterioration Index distribution of Allen's brain injured patients and of normal subjects. *J. Clin. Psychol.*, 4, 415–418.

BLAKEMORE, C. B., ETTINGER, G. and FALCONER, M. A. (1966) Cognitive abilities in relation to frequency of seizures and neuropathology of the temporal lobes in man. *J. Neurol. Neurosurg. Psychiat.*, 29, 268–272.

BLATT, S. J. (1959) Recall and recognition vocabulary: Implications for intellectual deterioration. *Arch. Gen. Psychiat.*, 1, 473–476.

BLATT, S. J. and ALLISON, J. (1968) The intelligence test in personality assessment. In, A. I. Rabin (Ed.), *Projective Techniques in Personality Assessment*, pp. 421–460. New York: Springer.

BLATT, S. J. and QUINLAN, P. (1967) Punctual and procrastinating students: A study of temporal parameters. *J. Consult. Psychol.*, 31, 169–174.

BLATT, S. J., ALLISON, J. and BAKER, B. L. (1965) The Wechsler Object Assembly subtest and bodily concerns. *J. Consult. Psychol.*, 29, 223–230.

BLATT, S. J., BAKER, B. L. and WEISS, J. (1970) Wechsler Object Assembly subtest and bodily concerns: A review and replication. *J. Consult. Clin. Psychol.*, 34, 269–274.

BLOOM, A. S. and RASKIN, L. M. (1980) WISC-R verbal-performance IQ discrepancies: A comparison of learning disabled children to the normative sample. *J. Clin. Psychol.*, 36, 322–323.

BLOOM, R. B. and ENTIN, A. D. (1975) Intellectual functioning and psychopathology: A canonical analysis of WAIS and MMPI relationships. *J. Clin. Psychol.*, 31, 697–698.

BLUM, J. E., FOSSHAGE, J. L. and JARVIX, L. F. (1972) Intellectual changes and sex differences in octogenarians: A twenty-year longitudinal study of aging. *Devel. Psychol.*, 7, 178–187.

BOEHM, A. E. and SARASON, S. B. (1947) Does Wechsler's formula distinguish intellectual deterioration from mental deficiency? *J. Abnorm. Soc. Psychol.*, 42, 356–358.

BOLLES, M. M. (1937) The basis of pertinence: A study of the test performance of aments, dements and normal children of the same age. *Arch. Psychol.*, No. 212.

BOLLES, M. and GOLDSTEIN, K. (1938) A study of the impairment of "abstract behavior" in schizophrenic patients. *Psychiat. Q.*, 12, 42–65.

BOLTER, J., VENEKLASEN, J. and LONG, C. J. (1981) Investigation of WAIS effectiveness in discriminating between temporal and generalized seizure patients. *J. Consult. Clin. Psychol.*, 49, 549–553.

BOLTON, N., BRITTON, P. G. and SAVAGE, R. D. (1966) Some normative data on the WAIS and its indices in an aged population. *J. Clin. Psychol.*, 22, 184–188.

BOLTON, T. L. (1892) The growth of memory in school children. *Am. J. Psychol.*, 4, 362–380.

BOOR, M. (1975) WAIS performance differences of male and female psychiatric patients. *J. Clin. Psychol.*, 31, 468–470.

BOOR, M. and SCHILL, T. (1967) Digit Symbol performance of subjects varying in anxiety and defensiveness. *J. Consult. Psychol.*, 31, 600–603.

BOOR, M. and SCHILL, T. (1968) Subtest performance on the Wechsler Adult Intelligence Scale as a function of anxiety and defensiveness. *Percept. Motor Skills*, 27, 33–34.

BORTNER, M. and BIRCH, G. (1969) Patterns of intellectual ability in emotionally disturbed and brain-damaged children. *J. Spec. Educ.*, 3, 351–369.

BOTWINICK, J. and BIRREN, J. E. (1951a) The measurement of intellectual decline in the senile psychoses. *J. Consult. Psychol.*, 15, 145–150.

BOTWINICK, J. and BIRREN, J. E. (1951b) Differential decline in the Wechsler–Bellevue subtests in the senile psychoses. *J. Gerontol.*, 6, 365–368.

BRADWAY, K. and BENSON, S. (1955) The application of extreme deviation to Rapaport's Wechsler–Bellevue data. *J. Clin. Psychol.*, 11, 285–291.

BRADY, K. W. (1933) The influence of past experience in visual perception. *J. Exp. Psychol.*, 16, 613–643.

BRANNIGAN, G. G. (1975) Wechsler Picture Arrangement and Comprehension scores as measures of social maturity. *J. Psychol.*, 89, 133–135.

BRANNIGAN, G. G. (1976) Children's social desirability response tendencies and Wechsler Comprehension and Picture Arrangement performance. *Psychol. Rep.*, 38, 1194.

BRANNIGAN, G. G. and ASH, T. (1977) Cognitive tempo and WISC-R performance. *J. Clin. Psychol.*, 33, 212.

BRECHER, S. (1946) The value of diagnostic signs for schizophrenia on the Wechsler–Bellevue Adult Intelligence Test. *Psychiat. Q., Suppl.*, 20, 58–64.

BREIGER, B. (1956) The use of the W–B Picture Arrangement subtest as a projective technique. *J. Consult. Psychol.*, 20, 132.

BRIGHAM, C. C. (1917) Two studies in mental tests. *Psychol. Monogr.*, 24, No. 102.

BRITTON, P. G. and SAVAGE, R. D. (1966) A short form of the WAIS for the aged. *Br. J. Psychiat.*, 112, 417–418.

BROWER, D. (1947) The relation between intelligence and Minnesota Multi-phasic Personality Inventory scores. *J. Soc. Psychol.*, 25, 243–245.

BROWN, F. (1960) Intelligence test patterns of Puerto Rican psychiatric patients. *J. Soc. Psychol.*, 52, 225–230.

BROWN, F. (1968) Applicability of the Jastak short form revision of the WAIS Vocabulary subtest to psychiatric patients. *J. Clin. Psychol.*, 24, 454–455.

BROWN, M. (1942) A simple method for rapid estimation of intelligence in adults. *Am. J. Orthopsychiat.*, 12, 411–413.

BROWN, M. H. and BRYAN, E. (1955) Sex differences in intelligence. *J. Clin. Psychol.*, 11, 303–304.

BROWN, M. N. (1949) A critique of the Wechsler–Bellevue system of weighted scores. *J. Clin. Psychol.*, 5, 170–173.

BROWN, O. (1967) Relation of WAIS verbal and performance IQs for four psychiatric conditions. *Psychol. Rep.*, 20, 1015–1020.

BROWN, R. R. and PARTINGTON, J. E. (1942) The intelligence of the narcotic drug addict. *J. Gen. Psychol.*, 26, 175–179.

BROWN, W. M. (1923) Character traits as factors in intelligence test performance. *Arch. Psychol.*, No. 65.

BROWN, W. M. (1924) A study of the "caution" factor and its importance in intelligence test performance. *Am. J. Psychol.*, 35, 368–386.

BURGESS, M. M., KODANAZ, A., ZIEGLER, D. and GREENBURG, H. (1970) Prediction of brain damage in two clinical populations. *Percept. Motor Skills*, 30, 523–532.

BURIK, T. E. (1950) Relative role of the learning and motor factors involved in the digit symbol test. *J. Psychol.*, 30, 33–42.

BURKS, B. S. (1930) When does a test measure the same functions at all levels? *J. Educ. Psychol.*, 21, 616–620.

BURKS, H. F. and BRUCE, P. (1955) The characteristics of poor and good readers as disclosed by the Wechsler Intelligence Scale for Children. *J. Educ. Psychol.*, 46, 488–493.

BURNES, K. (1970) Patterns of WISC scores for children of two socioeconomic classes and races. *Child Dev.*, 41, 493–499.

BURNHAM, C. A. (1949) A study of the degree of relationship between Rorschach

H% and Wechsler–Bellevue Picture Arrangement. *J. Projective Tech.*, 13, 206–209.

BURT, C. (1911) Experimental tests of higher mental processes and their relation to general intelligence. *J. Exp. Pedagogy*, 1, 93–112.

BURTON, D. A. (1968) The Jastak short form WAIS Vocabulary applied to a British psychiatric population. *J. Clin. Psychol.*, 24, 345–347.

BUSH, W. J. and MATTSON, B. D. (1973) WISC test patterns and underachievers. *J. Learning Disorders*, 6, 251–256.

BYCHOWSKI, G. (1935) Certain problems of schizophrenia in light of cerebral pathology. *J. Nerv. Ment. Dis.*, 81, 280–298.

CALDWELL, M. B. and DAVIS, J. C. (1956) A short form of the Wechsler–Bellevue Intelligence Scale Form II for a psychotic population. *J. Clin. Psychol.*, 12, 402–403.

CALDWELL, M. B. and SMITH, T. A. (1968) Intellectual structure of Southern Negro children. *Psychol. Rep.*, 23, 63–71.

CALLENS, C. J. and MELTZER, M. L. (1969) Effect of intelligence, anxiety and diagnosis on Arithmetic and Digit Span performance on the WAIS. *J. Consult. Clin. Psychol.*, 33, 630.

CALVIN, A. D., KOONS, P. B., BINGHAM, J. L. and FINK, H. H. (1955) A further investigation of the relationship between manifest anxiety and intelligence. *J. Consult. Psychol.*, 19, 280–282.

CAMERON, N. (1938a) Reasoning, regression and communication in schizophrenia. *Psychol. Monogr.*, 50, Whole No. 221.

CAMERON, N. (1938b) A study of thinking in senile deterioration and schizophrenic disorganization. *Am. J. Psychol.*, 51, 650–664.

CAMERON, N. (1939) Deterioration and regression in shizophrenic thinking. *J. Abnorm. Soc. Psychol.*, 34, 265–270.

CAMP, B. W. (1966) WISC performance in acting-out and delinquent children with and without EEG abnormality. *J. Consult. Psychol.*, 30, 350–353.

CAPPS, H. M. (1939) Vocabulary changes in deterioration. *Arch. Psychol.*, No. 242.

CAPRETTA, P. J. and BERKUN, M. M. (1962) Validity and reliability of certain measures of psychological stress. *Psychol. Rep.*, 10, 875–878.

CARLETON, F. O. and STACEY, C. L. (1954) Evaluation of selected short forms of the Wechsler Intelligence Scale for Children (WISC). *J. Clin. Psychol.*, 10, 258–261.

CARSON, A. S. and RABIN, A. I. (1960) Verbal comprehension and communication in Negro and white children. *J. Educ. Psychol.*, 51, 47–51.

CATTELL, R. B. (1930) The subjective character of cognition. *Br. J. Psychol., Monogr. Suppl.*, No. 14.

CATTELL, R. B. (1937) Measurement versus intuition in applied psychology. *Character Personal.*, 6, 114–131.

CATTELL, R. B. (1949) r_p and other coefficients of pattern similarity. *Psychometrika*, 14, 279–298.

CATTELL, R. B. (1957) *Handbook for the IPAT Anxiety Scale*. Melbourne: A. C. E. R.

CHODORKOFF, B. and MUSSEN, P. (1952) Qualitative aspects of the Vocabulary responses of normals and schizophrenics. *J. Consult. Psychol.*, 16, 43–48.

CLARK, J. H. and MOORE, J. H. (1950) The relationship of Wechsler–Bellevue patterns to psychiatric diagnosis of Army and Air Force prisoners. *J. Consult. Psychol.*, 14, 493–495.

CLAYTON, H. and PAYNE, D. (1959) Validation of Doppelt's WAIS short form with a clinical population. *J. Consult. Psychol.*, 23, 467.

CLEMENTS, G. R. (1965) An abbreviated form of the Wechsler Intelligence Scale for Children. *J. Consult. Psychol.*, 29, 92.

CLEVELAND, S. E. and DYSINGER, D. W. (1944) Mental deterioration in senile psychosis. *J. Abnorm. Social Psychol.*, 39, 368–372.

COATES, S. and BROMBERG, P. M. (1973) Factorial structure of the Wechsler Preschool and Primary Scale of Intelligence between the ages of 4 and 6½. *J. Consult. Clin. Psychol.*, 40, 365–370.

COHEN, E. (1965) Examiner differences with individual intelligence tests. *Percept. Motor Skills*, 20, 1324.

COHEN, J. (1950) A comparative analysis of the factors underlying intelligence test performance of different neuropsychiatric groups; multiple factor analysis of the Wechsler Bellevue Intelligence Scale performance of schizophrenic, psychoneurotic and brain damaged groups. Unpublished doctoral dissertation, New York University.

COHEN, J. (1951) A factor-anayltic comparison of intelligence test performance of different neuropsychiatric groups. *Am. Psychol.*, 6, 334–335. (Abs.)

COHEN, J. (1952a) Factors underlying Wechsler–Bellevue performance of three neuropsychiatric groups. *J. Abnorm. Soc. Psychol.*, 47, 359–365.

COHEN, J. (1952b) A factor-analytically based rationale for the Wechsler–Bellevue. *J. Consult. Psychol.*, 16, 272–277.

COHEN, J. (1955) The efficacy of diagnostic pattern analysis with the Wechsler–Bellevue. *J. Consult. Psychol.*, 19, 303–306.

COHEN, J. (1957a) The factorial structure of the WAIS between early adulthood and old age. *J. Consult. Psychol.*, 21, 283–290.

COHEN, J. (1957b) A factor-analytically based rationale for the Wechsler Adult Intelligence Scale. *J. Consult. Psychol.*, 21, 451–457.

COHEN, J. (1959) The factorial structure of the WISC at ages 7–6, 10–6, and 13–6. *J. Consult. Psychol.*, 23, 285–299.

COLE, D. and WELEBA, L. (1956) Comparison data on the Wechsler–Bellevue and the WAIS. *J. Clin. Psychol.*, 12, 198–199.

COLE, N. S. and FOWLER, W. R. (1974) Pattern analysis of WISC scores achieved by culturally disadvantaged Southern blacks. *Psychol. Rep.*, 35, 305–306.

COLE, S. and HUNTER, M. (1971) Pattern analysis of WISC scores achieved by culturally disadvantaged children. *Psychol. Rep.*, 29, 191–194.

COLE, S. N., WILLIAMS, R. L., NIX, A. P. and LITAKER, R. G. (1967) Validity of an abbreviated WISC scale for retarded and borderline children. *Psychol. Rep.*, 21, 571–572.

COLEMAN, J. C. and RASOF, B. (1963) Intellectual factors in learning disorders. *Percept. Motor Skills*, 16, 139–152.

COLEMAN, W. and CURETON, E. E. (1954) Intelligence and achievement: The "jangle fallacy" again. *Educ. Psychol. Measure.*, 14, 347–351.

CONRAD, H. S. (1931) The measurement of adult intelligence, and the requisites of a general intelligence test. *J. Soc. Psychol.*, 2, 72–85.

CONRY, R. and PLANT, W. T. (1965) WAIS and group test predictions of an academic success. *Educ. Psychol. Measure.*, 25, 493–500.

COOK, T. H. and SOLWAY, K. S. (1974) WISC subtest patterns of delinquent male retardates. *Psychol. Rep.*, 35, 22.

CORNELL, E. L. and COXE, W. C. (1934) *A Performance Ability Scale.* New York: World Book.

COROTTO, L. V. (1961) The relation of Performance to Verbal IQ in acting out juveniles. *J. Psychol. Stud.*, 12, 162–166.

CORSINI, R. J. and FASSETT, K. K. (1952) The validity of Wechsler's Mental Deterioration Index. *J. Consult. Psychol.*, 16, 462–468.

CORTER, H. M. (1952) Factor analysis of some reasoning tests. *Psychol. Monogr.*, 66, Whole No. 340.

CORWIN, B. J. (1967) The relationship between reading achievement and performance on individual ability tests. *J. Sch. Psychol.*, 5, 156–157.

COTZIN, M. and GALLAGHER, J. J. (1949) Validity of short forms of the Wechsler–Bellevue Scale for mental defectives. *J. Consult. Psychol.*, 13, 357–365.

COTZIN, M. and GALLAGHER, J. J. (1950) The Southbury Scale: A valid abbreviated Wechsler–Bellevue for mental defectives. *J. Consult. Psychol.*, 14, 358–364.

COVIN, T. M. (1977a) Comparability of WISC and WISC-R scores for 30 8- and 9-year-old institutionalized Caucasian children. *Psychol. Rep.*, 40, 382.

COVIN, T. M. (1977b) Comparison of WISC and WISC-R Full Scale IQs for a sample of children in special education. *Psychol. Rep.*, 41, 237–238.

COVIN, T. M. and COVIN, J. N. (1976) Comparability of Peabody and WAIS scores among adolescents suspected of being mentally retarded. *Psychol. Rep.*, 39, 33–34.

COVIN, T. M. and HATCH, G. L. (1976) Intellectual differences in Black and White Southern low achievers. *Psychol. Rep.*, 39, 1269–1270.

COVIN, T. M. and HATCH, G. L. (1977) WISC Full Scale IQ mean differences of Black children and White children aged 6 through 15 and having problems in school. *Psychol. Rep.*, 40, 281–282.

COYLE, F. A. and BELLAMY, E. E. (1970) Use of the California abbreviated WISC with institutionalized retardates. *Am. J. Ment. Defic.*, 74, 578.

CRADDICK, R. A. (1961) Wechsler–Bellevue IQ scores of psychopathic and non-psychopathic prisoners. *J. Psychol. Stud.*, 12, 167–172.

CRADDICK, R. A. and GROSSMAN, K. (1962) Effects of visual distraction upon performance on the WAIS Digit Span. *Psychol. Rep.*, 10, 642.

CRADDICK, R. A. and STERN, M. R. (1963) Relation between the WAIS and the Kahn Test of Symbol Arrangement. *Percept. Motor Skills*, 17, 583–585.

CRAIG, R. J. (1969) An illustration of the Wechsler Picture Arrangement Subtest as a thematic technique. *J. Projective Techniq. Personal. Assess.* 38, 286–289.

CROCKETT, B. K., RARDIN, M. W. and PASEWARK, R. A. (1975) Relationship between WPPSI and Stanford–Binet IQs and subsequent WISC IQs in Headstart children. *J. Consult. Clin. Psychol.*, 43, 922.

CRONBACH, L. J. (1949) *Essentials of Psychological Testing*. New York: Harper.

CRONBACH, L. J. and GLESSER, G. C. (1953) Assessing similarity between profiles. *Psychol. Bull.*, 50, 456–473.

CROOKES, T. G. (1974) Indices of early dementia on WAIS. *Psychol. Rep.*, 34, 734.

CROPLEY, A. J. (1964) Differentiation of abilities, socioeconomic status, and the WISC. *J. Consult. Psychol.*, 28, 512–517.

CUMMINGS, S. B., MacPHEE, H. M. and WRIGHT, H. F. (1946) A rapid method of estimating the IQs of subnormal white adults. *J. Psychol.*, 21, 81–89.

CUMMINS, J. P. and DAS, J. P. (1980) Cognitive processing, academic achievement, and WISC-R performance in EMR children. *J. Consult. Clin. Psychol.*, 48, 777–779.

136   THE WECHSLER ENTERPRISE

CURTIS, J. N. (1918) Point scale examinations on the high-grade feeble-minded and the insane. *J. Abnorm. Psychol.*, **13**, 77–118.
CUTTS, R. A. and SLOAN, W. (1945) Test patterns of adjusted defectives on the Wechsler–Bellevue Test. *Am. J. Ment. Defic.*, **50**, 98–101.
DANA, R. H. (1957a) A comparison of four verbal subtests on the Wechsler–Bellevue, Form I, and the WAIS. *J. Clin. Psychol.*, **13**, 70–71.
DANA, R. H. (1957b) Manifest anxiety, intelligence, and psychopathology. *J. Consult. Psychol.*, **21**, 38–40.
DAVEY, C. M. (1926) A comparison of group verbal and pictorial tests of intelligence. *Br. J. Psychol.*, **17**, 27–48.
DAVIDSON, K. S., GIBBY, R. G., McNEIL, E. B., SEGAL, S. J. and SILVERMAN, H. (1950) A preliminary study of Negro and White differences on Form I of the Wechsler–Bellevue Scales. *J. Consult. Psychol.*, **14**, 489–492.
DAVIS, J. C. (1957) The scatter pattern of a Southern Negro group on the Wechsler–Bellevue Intelligence Scale. *J. Clin. Psychol.*, **13**, 298–300.
DAVIS, L. J., HAMLETT, I. C. and REITAN, R. M. (1966) Relationship of conceptual ability and academic achievement to problem-solving and experiential backgrounds of retardates. *Percept. Motor Skills*, **22**, 499–505.
DAVIS, P. C. (1956) A factor analysis of the Wechsler–Bellevue Scale. *Educ. Psychol. Measure.*, **16**, 127–146.
DAVIS, W. E. (1969) Effect of prior failure on subjects' WAIS Arithmetic subtest scores. *J. Clin. Psychol.*, **25**, 72–73.
DAVIS, W. E., PEACOCK, W., FITZPATRICK, P. and MULHERN, M. (1969) Examiner differences, prior failure, and subjects' WAIS Arithmetic scores. *J. Clin. Psychol.*, **25**, 178–180.
DAVIS, W. E., BECKER, B. C. and DEWOLFE, A. S. (1971a) Categorization of patients with personality disorders and acute brain trauma through WAIS subtest variations. *J. Clin. Psychol.*, **27**, 358–360.
DAVIS, W. E., DIZZONNE, M. F. and DEWOLFE, A. S. (1971b) Relationships among WAIS subtest scores, patient's premorbid history, and institutionalization. *J. Consult. Clin. Psychol.*, **36**, 400–403.
DAVIS, W. E., DEWOLFE, A. S. and GUSTAFSON, R. C. (1972) Intellectual deficit in process and reactive schizophrenia and brain injury. *J. Consult. Clin. Psychol.*, **38**, 146.
DEAN, R. S. (1977) Patterns of emotional disturbance on the WISC-R. *J. Clin. Psychol.*, **33**, 486–490.
DEAN, R. S. (1979) Distinguishing patterns for Mexican-American children on the WISC-R. *J. Clin. Psychol.*, **35**, 790–794.
DEHORN, A. and KLINGE, V. (1978) Correlations and factor analysis of the WISC-R and the Peabody Picture Vocabulary Test for an adolescent psychiatric sample. *J. Consult. Clin. Psychol.*, **46**, 1160–1161.
DEIKER, T. E. (1973) WAIS characteristics of indicted male murderers. *Psychol. Rep.*, **32**, 1066.
DELATTRE, L. and COLE, D. (1952) A comparison of the WISC and the Wechsler–Bellevue. *J. Consult. Psychol.*, **16**, 228–230.
DELUCA, J. (1968) Predicting the Full Scale WAIS IQ of Army basic trainees. *J. Psychol.*, **68**, 83–86.
DENNERLL, R. D. (1964) Prediction of unilateral brain dysfunction using Wechsler test scores. *J. Consult. Psychol.*, **28**, 278–284.

DENNERLL, R. D., JEN, B. J. and SOKOLOV, S. L. (1964) WISC and WAIS in children and adults with epilepsy. *J. Clin. Psychol.*, **20**, 236–240.

DERSHOWITZ, Z. and FRANKEL, Y. (1975) Jewish culture and the WISC and WAIS patterns. *J. Consult. Clin. Psychol.*, **43**, 126–134.

DESAI, M. M. (1955) The relationship of the Wechsler–Bellevue Verbal Scale and the Progressive Matrices Test. *J. Consult. Psychol.*, **19**, 60.

DEWOLFE, A. S. (1971) Differentiation of schizophrenia and brain damage with the WAIS. *J. Clin. Psychol.*, **27**, 209–211.

DEWOLFE, A. S., BARRELL, R. P., BECKER, B. C. and SPANER, F. (1971) Intellectual deficit in chronic schizophrenia and brain damage. *J. Consult. Clin. Psychol.*, **36**, 197–204.

DIAMOND, S. (1947) The Wechsler–Bellevue Intelligences Scales and certain vocational aptitude tests. *J. Psychol.*, **24**, 279–282.

DIBNER, A. S. and CUMMINS, J. F. (1961) Intellectual functioning in a group of normal octogenarians. *J. Consult. Psychol.*, **25**, 137–141.

DICKSTEIN, L. S. (1969) Prospective span as a cognitive ability. *J. Consult. Clin. Psychol.*, **33**, 757–760.

DICKSTEIN, L. S. and AYRES, J. (1973) Effect of an incentive upon intelligence test performance. *Psychol. Rep.*, **33**, 127–130.

DICKSTEIN, L. S. and BLATT, S. J. (1967) The WAIS Picture Arrangement subtest as a measure of anticipation. *J. Projective Techniq.*, **31** (3), 32–38.

DICKSTEIN, L. S. and BLATT, S. J. (1966) Death concern, futurity, and anticipation. *J. Consult. Psychol.*, **30**, 11–17.

DICKSTEIN, L. S. and KEPHART, J. L. (1972) Effect of explicit examiner expectancy upon WAIS performance. *Psychol. Rep.*, **30**, 207–212.

DICKSTEIN, L. S. and MACEVITT, M. (1971) Comprehension subtest of the WAIS and need for approval. *Psychol. Rep.*, **28**, 482.

DICKSTEIN, L. S. and WEISS, V. A. (1972) Effect of failure upon WAIS arithmetic, digit span, and object assembly subtests. *Psychol. Rep.*, **30**, 23–26.

DINNING, W. D. (1976) Variance components of the WISC-R in eleven age groups. *Psychol. Rep.*, **38**, 1001–1002.

DOEHRING, D. G. and REITAN, R. M. (1962) Concept attainment of human adults with lateralized cerebral lesions. *Percept. Motor Skills*, **14**, 27–33.

DOEHRING, D. G., REITAN, R. M. and KLØVE, H. (1961) Changes in patterns of intelligence test performance associated with homonymous visual field defects. *J. Nerv. Ment. Dis.*, **132**, 227–233.

DOLL, E. A. (1917) A brief Binet–Simon Scale. *Psychol. Clin.*, **11**, 197–211, 254–261.

DOLL, E. A. (1920) Intelligence and industrial tests in institutional management. *J. Delinq.*, **5**, 215–223.

DONAHUE, D. and SATTLER, J. M. (1971) Personality variables affecting WAIS scores. *J. Consult. Clin. Psychol.*, **36**, 441.

DOPPELT, J. E. (1956) Estimating the Full Scale score on the Wechsler Adult Intelligence Scale from scores on four subtests. *J. Consult. Psychol.*, **20**, 63–66.

DOPPELT, J. E. and KAUFMAN, A. S. (1977) Estimation of the difference between WISC-R and WISC IQs. *Educ. Psychol. Measure.*, **37**, 417–424.

DOPPELT, J. E. and WALLACE, W. L. (1955) Standardization of the Wechsler Adult Intelligence Scale for older persons. *J. Abnorm. Soc. Psychol.*, **51**, 312–330.

DORKEN, H. and GREENBLOOM, G. C. (1953) Psychological investigation of senile

dementia: II. The Wechsler–Bellevue adult intelligence scale. *Geriatrics*, 8, 324–333.
DOUBROS, S. G. and MASCARENHAS, J. (1969) Relations among Wechsler Full-Scale scores, organicity-sensitive subtest scores and Bender-Gestalt error scores. *Percept. Motor Skills*, 29, 719–722.
DOWNEY, J. E. (1917) The Stanford Adult Intelligence Tests. *J. Delinq.*, 2, 144–155.
DOWNEY, J. E. (1918) The constancy of the IQ. *J. Delinq.*, 3, 122–131.
DREGER, R. M. and MILLER, K. S. (1960) Comparative psychological studies of Negroes and Whites in the United States. *Psychol. Bull.*, 57, 361–402.
DUDEK, S. Z. and LESTER, E. P. (1968) The good child facade in chronic under-achievers. *Am. J. Orthopsychiat.*, 38, 153–160.
DUDEK, S. Z., LESTER, E. P. and GOLDBERG, J. S. (1969b) Relationship of Piaget measures to standard intelligence and motor scales. *Percept. Motor Skills*, 28, 351–362.
DUDEK, S. Z., GOLDBERG, J. S., LESTER, E. P. and HARRIS, B. R. (1969a) The validity of cognitive, perceptuo-motor and personality variables for the prediction of achievement in Grade I and Grade II. *J. Clin. Psychol.*, 25, 165–170.
DUFFY, O. B., CLAIR, T. N., EGELAND, B. and DINELLO, B. (1972) Relationship of intelligence, visual-motor skills, and psycholinguistic abilities with achievement in the third, fourth, and fifth grades: A follow-up study. *J. Educ. Psychol.*, 63, 358–362.
DUKE, R. B. (1967) Intellectual evaluation of brain-damaged patients with a WAIS short form. *Psychol. Rep.*, 20, 858.
DUMAS, F. M. (1949) The coefficient of profile similarity. *J. Clin. Psychol.*, 5, 123–131.
DUNCAN, D. R. and BARRETT, A. M. (1961) A longitudinal comparison of intelligence involving the Wechsler–Bellevue I and WAIS. *J. Clin. Psychol.*, 17, 318–319.
DUNN, J. A. (1968) Anxiety, stress, and the performance of complex intellectual tasks: A new look at an old question. *J. Consult. Clin. Psychol.*, 32, 669–673.
DUTOIT, J. M. (1954) A modification of the index of profile similarity. *J. Clin. Psychol.*, 10, 384–386.
EDWARDS, G. A. (1966) Anxiety correlates of the Wechsler Adult Intelligence Scale. *Cal. J. Educ. Res.*, 17, 144–147.
EGELAND, B. (1967) Influence of examiner and examinee anxiety on WISC performance. *Psychol. Rep.*, 21, 409–414.
EGELAND, B., DINELLO, M. and CARR, D. (1970) The relationship of intelligence, visual-motor, psycholinguistic and reading readiness skills with achievement. *Educ. Psychol. Measure.*, 30, 451–458.
EISDORFER, C. and COHEN, L. D. (1961) The generality of the WAIS standardization for the aged: A regional comparison. *J. Abnorm. Social Psychol.*, 62, 520–527.
EISDORFER, C., BUSSE, E. W. and COHEN, L. D. (1959) The WAIS performance of an aged sample: The relationship between verbal and performance IQs. *J. Gerontol.*, 14, 197–201.
EKSTROM, R., FRENCH, J. W., HARMAN, H. and DERMEN, D. (1976) *Manual for Kit of Factor-Reference Cognitive Tests*. Princeton, N.J.: Educational Testing Service.
ELWOOD, D. L. (1969) Automation of psychological testing. *Am. Psychol.*, 24, 287–289.
ELWOOD, D. L. (1972a) Validity of an automated measure of intelligence in borderline retarded subjects. *Am. J. Ment. Defic.*, 77, 90–94.

ELWOOD, D. L. and GRIFFIN, H. R. (1972) Individual intelligence testing without the examiner: Reliability of an automated method. *J. Consult. Clin. Psychol.*, 38, 9–14.

ENBURG, R., ROWLEY, V. N. and STONE, B. (1961) Short forms of the WISC for use with emotionally disturbed children. *J. Clin. Psychol.*, 17, 280–284.

ENGIN, A. W. (1975) Prediction of classroom achievement using intelligence and behavioural variables for inner-city children. *Psychol. Rep.*, 36, 67–76.

ERIKSON, R. V. (1967) Abbreviated form of the WISC: A reevaluation. *J. Consult. Psychol.*, 31, 641.

ESCALONA, S. K. and RAPAPORT, D. (1944) The psychological testing of children: Intelligence and emotional adjustment. *Bull. Menninger Clin.*, 8, 205–210.

ESTES, B. W. (1953) Influence of socioeconomic status on Wechsler Intelligence Scale for Children: An exploratory study. *J. Consult. Psychol.*, 17, 58–62.

ESTES, B. W. (1955) Influence of socioeconomic status on Wechsler Intelligence Scale for Children: Addendum. *J. Consult. Psychol.*, 19, 225–226.

ESTES, B. W. (1963) A note on the Satz–Mogel abbreviation of the WAIS. *J. Clin. Psychol.*, 19, 103.

ESTES, S. G. (1946) Deviations of Wechsler–Bellevue subtest scores from Vocabulary level in superior adults. *J. Abnorm. Soc. Psychol.*, 41, 226–228.

EXNER, J. E. (1966) Variations in WISC performances as influenced by differences in pretest rapport. *J. Gen. Psychol.*, 74, 299–306.

EYSENCK, H. J. (1967) Intelligence assessment: A theoretical and experimental approach. *Br. J. Educ. Psychol.*, 37, 81–98.

EYSENCK, H. J. and WHITE, P. O. (1964) Personality and the measurement of intelligence. *Br. J. Educ. Psychol.*, 34, 197–202.

FAGAN-DUBLIN, L. (1974) Lateral dominance and development of cerebral specialization. *Cortex*, 10, 69–74.

FEIFEL, H. (1949) Qualitative differences in the vocabulary responses of normals and abnormals. *Genet. Psychol. Monogr.*, 39, 151–204.

FELDHAUSEN, J. F. and KLAUSMEIER, H. J. (1962) Anxiety, intelligence, and achievement in children of low, average, and high intelligence. *Child Dev.*, 33, 403–409.

FELDMAN, S. E. (1968) Utility of some rapid estimations of intelligence in a college population. *Psychol. Rep.*, 22, 23–26.

FERNALD, P. S. and WISSER, R. E. (1967) Using WISC Verbal-Performance discrepancy to predict degree of acting out. *J. Clin. Psychol.*, 23, 92–93.

FIELD, J. G. (1960a) Two types of tables for use with Wechsler's Intelligence Scales. *J. Clin. Psychol.*, 16, 3–7.

FIELD, J. G. (1960b) The Performance–Verbal IQ discrepancy in a group of sociopaths. *J. Clin. Psychol.*, 16, 321–322.

FINCH, A. J., CHILDRESS, W. B. and OLLENDICK, T. H. (1937a) Comparison of separately administered and abstracted WISC short forms with the Full Scale WISC. *Am. J. Ment. Defic.*, 77, 755–756.

FINCH, A. J., OLLENDICK, T. H. and GINO, F. W. (1973b) WISC short forms with mentally retarded children. *Am. J. Ment. Defic.*, 78, 144–149.

FINCH, A. J., CHILDRESS, W. B. and OLLENDICK, T. H. (1974a) Efficiency of WAIS short forms. *Ment. Retard.*, 12(5), 48–49.

FINCH, A. J., THORNTON, L. J. and MONTGOMERY, L. E. (1974b) WAIS short forms with hospitalized psychiatric patients. *J. Consult. Clin. Psychol.*, 42, 469.

140   THE WECHSLER ENTERPRISE

FINKELSTEIN, M., GERBOTH, R. and WESTERHOLD, R. (1952) Standardization of a short form of the Wechsler subtest. *J. Clin. Psychol.*, 8, 133–135.

FINLEY, C. J. and THOMPSON, J. (1958) An abbreviated Wechsler Intelligence Scale for Children for use with educable mentally retarded. *Am. J. Ment. Defic.*, 63, 473–480.

FINLEY, C. and THOMPSON, J. (1959) Sex differences in intelligence of educable mentally retarded children. *Calif. J. Educ. Res.*, 10, 167–170.

FIRETTO, A. C. and DAVEY, H. (1971) Subjectively reported anxiety as a discriminator of digit span performance. *Psychol. Rep.*, 28, 98.

FISHER, G. C. (1958) Selective and differentially accelerated intellectual dysfunction in specific brain damage. *J. Clin. Psychol.*, 14, 395–398.

FISHER, G. M. (1960) Differences in WAIS V and P IQs in various diagnostic groups of mental retardates. *Am. J. Ment. Defic.*, 65, 256–260.

FISHER, G. M. (1961) Discrepancy in Verbal and Performance IQ in adolescent sociopaths. *J. Clin. Psychol.*, 17, 60.

FISHER, G. M. and SHOTWELL, A. M. (1959) An evaluation of Doppelt's abbreviated form of the WAIS for the mentally retarded. *Am. J. Ment. Defic.*, 64, 476–481.

FISHER, G. M., DOOLEY, M. D. and SILVERSTEIN, A. B. (1960) Wechsler Adult Intelligence Scale performance of familial and undifferentiated mental subnormals. *Psychol. Rep.*, 7, 268.

FITZHUGH, K. B. and FITZHUGH, L. C. (1964) WAIS results for Ss with longstanding, chronic, lateralized and diffuse cerebral dysfunction. *Percept. Motor Skills*, 19, 735–739.

FITZHUGH, K. B. and FITZHUGH, L. C. (1965) Effects of early and later onset of cerebral dysfunction upon psychological test performance. *Percept. Motor Skills*, 20, 1099–1100.

FITZHUGH, K. B., FITZHUGH, L. C. and REITAN, R. M. (1962) Wechsler–Bellevue comparisons in groups with "chronic" and "current" lateralized and diffuse brain lesions. *J. Consult. Psychol.*, 26, 306–310.

FITZHUGH, L. C. and FITZHUGH, K. B. (1964) Relationship between Wechsler–Bellevue Form I and WAIS performance of subjects with longstanding cerebral dysfunction. *Percept. Motor Skills*, 19, 539–543.

FOGEL, M. L. (1965) The proverbs test in the appraisal of cerebral disease. *J. Gen. Psychol.*, 72, 269–275.

FOSTER, A. (1947) Age and the Wechsler–Bellevue scattergraph. *J. Clin. Psychol.*, 3, 396–397.

FOSTER, A. L. (1959) A note concerning the intelligence of delinquents. *J. Clin. Psychol.*, 15, 78–79.

FOX, C. (1947) Vocabulary ability in later maturity. *J. Educ. Psychol.*, 38, 482–492.

FOX, C. and BIRREN, J. E. (1950) The differential decline of subtest scores of the Wechsler–Bellevue Intelligence Scale in 60–69-year-old individuals. *J. Gen. Psychol.*, 77, 313–317.

FRANDSEN, A. N. (1950) The Wechsler–Bellevue Intelligence Scale and high school achievement. *J. Appl. Psychol.*, 34, 406–411.

FRANK, G. H. (1953) Patterning of the schizophrenic on the Wechsler–Bellevue intelligence test. *Psychol. Newslett.*, 46, 7–12.

FRANK, G. H. (1956) The Wechsler–Bellevue and psychiatric diagnosis: A factor analytic approach. *J. Consult. Psychol.*, 20, 67–69.

FRANK, G. H. (1970a) On the nature of borderline psychopathology: A review. *J. Gen. Psychol.*, 83, 61–77.

FRANK, G. H. (1970b) The measurement of personality from the Wechsler Tests. In MAHER, B. (Ed.), *Progress in Experimental Personality Research*. pp. 169–184. New York: Academic Press.

FRANK, G. (1975) *Psychiatric Diagnosis: A Review of Research*. Oxford: Pergamon Press.

FRANK, G. (1976) On the assessment of intelligence and cognition. In WEINER, I. B. (Ed.), *Clinical Methods in Psychology*. pp. 123–186. New York: Wiley.

FRANK, G. H., CORRIE, C. C. and FOGEL, J. (1955) An empirical critique of research with the Wechsler–Bellevue in differential psychodiagnosis. *J. Clin. Psychol.*, 11, 291–293.

FRANKLIN, J. C. (1945) Discriminative value and patterns of the Wechsler–Bellevue Scales in the examination of delinquent negro boys. *Educ. Psychol. Measure.*, 5, 71–85.

FRENCH, E. G. and HUNT, W. A. (1951) The relationship of scatter in test performance to intelligence level. *J. Clin. Psychol.*, 7, 95–98.

FRENCH, J. W., EKSTROM, R. B. and PRICE, L. A. (1963) *Manual for Kit of Reference Tests for Cognitive Factors*. Princeton: Educational Testing Service.

FROST, B. P. (1960) An application of the method of extreme deviations to the Wechsler Intelligence Scale for Children. *J. Clin. Psychol.*, 16, 420.

FROST, B. P. and FROST, R. (1962) The pattern of WISC scores in a group of juvenile sociopaths. *J. Clin. Psychol.*, 18, 354–355.

FULLER, G. B. (1966) A comparison of intelligence and perception in emotionally disturbed children. *J. Clin. Psychol.*, 22, 193–195.

FURTH, H. G. and MILGRAM, N. A. (1965) Verbal factors in performance on WISC similarities. *J. Clin. Psychol.*, 21, 424–427.

GAIER, E. L. and LEE, M. C. (1953) Pattern analysis. The configural approach to predictive measurement. *Psychol. Bull.*, 50, 141–149.

GAINES, T. and MORRIS, R. (1978) Relationships between MMPI measures of psychopathology and WAIS subtest scores and intelligence quotients. *Percept. Motor Skills*, 47, 399–402.

GARFIELD, S. L. (1948) A preliminary appraisal of Wechsler–Bellevue scatter pattern in schizophrenia. *J. Consult. Psychol.*, 12, 32–36.

GARFIELD, S. L. (1949) An evaluation of Wechsler–Bellevue patterns in schizophrenia. *J. Consult. Psychol.*, 13, 279–287.

GARFIELD, S. L. and FEY, W. F. (1948) A comparison of the Wechsler–Bellevue and Shipley–Hartford as measures of mental impairment. *J. Consult. Psychol.*, 12, 259–264.

GARMS, J. D. (1970a) A validational study of the Illinois Test of Psycholinguistic Abilities. *Psychology*, 7, 9–12.

GARMS, J. D. (1970b) Factor analysis of the WISC and ITPA. *Psychology*, 7, 30–31.

GARRETT, H. E. (1943) The discriminant function and its use in psychology. *Psychometrika*, 8, 65–79.

GARRETT, H. E., BRYAN, A. I. and PERL, R. E. (1935) The age factor in mental organization. *Arch. Psychol.*, No. 176.

GAULT, U. (1954) Factoral patterns of the Wechsler Intelligence Scales. *Aust. J. Psychol.*, 6, 85–89.

GAYTON, W. F., WILSON, W. T. and BERNSTEIN, S. (1970) An evaluation of an abbreviated form of the WISC. *J. Clin. Psychol.*, 26, 466–468.

GAZZANIGA, M. S. (1976) The split brain in man. In *Progress in Psychobiology*. pp. 369–374. San Francisco: Freeman.

GEIL, G. A. (1945) A clinically useful abbreviated Wechsler–Bellevue Scale. *J. Psychol.*, 20, 101–108.

GERBOTH, R. (1950) A study of two forms of the Wechsler–Bellevue Intelligence Scale. *J. Consult. Psychol.*, 14, 365–370.

GERSTEIN, R. A. (1949) A suggested method for analyzing and extending the use of Bellevue–Wechsler Vocabulary responses. *J. Consult. Psychol.*, 13, 366–370.

GIANNITIRAPINI, D. (1969) EEG average frequency and intelligence. *Electroenceph. Clin. Neurophysiol.*, 27, 480–486.

GIBBY, R. G. (1949) A preliminary survey of certain aspects of Form II of the Wechsler–Bellevue Scale as compared to Form I. *J. Clin. Psychol.*, 5, 165–169.

GILLILAND, A. R., WITTMAN, P. and GOLDMAN, M. (1943) Patterns and scatter of mental abilities in various psychoses. *J. Gen. Psychol.*, 29, 251–260.

GLICK, I. D. and STERNBERG, D. (1969) Performance IQ as predictor of hospital treatment outcome. *Comp. Psychiat.*, 10, 365–368.

GODDARD, H. H. (1911) Two thousand normal children measured by the Binet measuring scale of intelligence. *Pedagog. Sem.*, 18, 232–259.

GOEBEL, R. A. and SATZ, P. (1975) Profile analysis and the abbreviated Wechsler Adult Intelligence Scale: A multivariate approach. *J. Consult. Clin. Psychol.*, 43, 780–785.

GOLDMAN, R., GREENBLATT, M. and COON, G. P. (1946) Use of the Bellevue–Wechsler Scale in clinical psychiatry with particular reference to cases with brain damage. *J. Nerv. Ment. Dis.*, 104, 144–179.

GOLDMAN, R. D. and HASTING, L. K. (1976) The WISC may not be a valid prediction of school performance for primary-grade minority children. *Am. J. Ment. Defic.*, 80, 583–587.

GOLDSTEIN, K. (1939) The significance of special mental tests for diagnosis and prognosis in schizophrenia. *Am. J. Psychiat.*, 96, 575–588.

GOLLAND, J. H., HERRELL, J. M. and HAHN, M. (1970) Should WAIS subjects explain picture arrangement stories? *J. Consult. Clin. Psychol.*, 35, 157–158.

GOODENOUGH, D. R. and KARP, S. A. (1961) Field dependence and intellectual functioning. *J. Abnorm. Soc. Psychol.*, 63, 241–246.

GOODSTEIN, L. D. and FARBER, I. E. (1957) On the relation between A-scale scores and Digit Symbol performance. *J. Consult. Psychol.*, 21, 152–154.

GOOLISHIAN, H. A. and FOSTER, A. (1954) A note on sex differences on the Wechsler–Bellevue test. *J. Clin. Psychol.*, 10, 298–299.

GOOLISHIAN, H. A. and RAMSAY, R. (1956) The Wechsler–Bellevue Form I and the WAIS: A comparison. *J. Clin. Psychol.*, 12, 147–151.

GORHAM, D. R. (1956) A proverbs tests for clinical and experimental use. *Psychol. Rep.*, Monogr. Suppl., No. 1.

GRAHAM, E. E. (1952) Wechsler–Bellevue and WISC scattergrams of unsuccessful readers. *J. Consult. Psychol.*, 16, 268–271.

GRAHAM, E. E. and KAMANO, D. (1958) Reading failure as a factor in the WAIS subtest patterns of youthful offenders. *J. Clin. Psychol.*, 14, 302–305.

GREEN, R. F. and BERKOWITZ, B. (1964) Changes in intellect with age: II. Factorial analysis of Wechsler–Bellevue scores. *J. Genet. Psychol.*, 104, 3–18.

GREEN, R. F. and BERKOWITZ, B. (1965) Changes in intellect with age: III. The relationship of heterogeneous brain damage to achievement in older people. *J. Genet. Psychol.*, 106, 349–359.

GREEN, R. F., GUILFORD, J. P., CHRISTENSEN, P. R. and COMREY, A. L. (1953) A factor-analytic study of reasoning abilities. *Psychometrika*, 18, 135–160.
GRISSO, J. T. and MEADOW, A. (1967) Test interference in a Rohrschach–WAIS administration sequence. *J. Consult. Psychol.*, 31, 382–386.
GUERTIN, W. H. (1959) Auditory interference with Digit Span performance. *J. Clin. Psychol.*, 15, 349.
GUERTIN, W. H., FRANK, G. H. and RABIN, A. I. (1956) Research with the Wechsler–Bellevue Intelligence Scale: 1950–1955. *Psychol. Bull.*, 53, 235–257.
GUERTIN, W. H., RABIN, A. I., FRANK, G. H. and LADD, C. E. (1962) Research with the Wechsler Intelligence Scales for Adults: 1955–60. *Psychol. Bull.*, 59, 1–26.
GUERTIN, W. H., LADD, C. E., FRANK, G. H., RABIN, A. I. and HIESTER, D. S. (1966) Research with the Wechsler Intelligence Scale for Adults: 1960–1965. *Psychol. Bull.*, 66, 385–409.
GUERTIN, W. H., LADD, C. E., FRANK, G. H., RABIN, A. I. and HIESTER, D. S. (1971) Research with the Wechsler Intelligence Scale for Adults: 1965–1970. *Psychol. Rec.*, 21, 289–339.
GUILFORD, J. P. (1971) Varieties of memory and their implications. *J. Gen. Psychol.*, 85, 207–228.
GURVITZ, M. S. (1945) An alternate short form of the Wechsler–Bellevue test. *Am. J. Orthopsychiat.*, 15, 727–732.
GURVITZ, M. S. (1950) The Wechsler–Bellevue Test and the diagnosis of psychopathic personality. *J. Clin. Psychol.*, 6, 397–401.
GURVITZ, M. S. (1951) The Hillside short form of the Wechsler–Bellevue. *J. Clin. Psychol.*, 7, 131–134.
GURVITZ, M. S. (1952) Some defects of the Wechsler–Bellevue. *J. Consult. Psychol.*, 16, 124–126.
GUTMAN, B. (1950) The application of the Wechsler–Bellevue Scale in the diagnosis of organic brain disorders. *J. Clin. Psychol.*, 6, 195–198.
HAFNER, A. J., POLLIE, D. M. and WAPNER, I. (1960) The relationship between the CMAS and WISC functioning. *J. Clin. Psychol.*, 16, 322–323.
HAFNER, J. L., CORROTTO, L. V. and CURNUTT, R. H. (1978) The development of a WAIS short form for clinical populations. *J. Clin. Psychol.*, 34, 935–937.
HALE, R. L. and LANDINO, S. A. (1981) Utility of WISC-R subtest analysis in discriminating among groups of conduct problem, withdrawn, mixed, and non-problem boys. *J. Consult. Clin. Psychol.*, 49, 91–95.
HALL, L. P. and LADRIERE, L. (1969) Patterns of performance on WISC Similarities in emotionally disturbed and brain-damaged children. *J. Consult. Clin. Psychol.*, 33, 357–364.
HALPERN, F. (1946) Studies of compulsive drinkers: psychological test results. *Q. J. Stud. Alcohol*, 6, 468–479.
HAMM, H., WHEELER, J., McCALLUM, S., HERRIN, M., HUNTER, D. and CATOE, C. (1976) A comparison between WISC and WISC-R among educable mentally retarded students. *Psychol. Sch.*, 13, 4–8.
HAMMER, A. C. (1949) A factor analysis of the Bellevue Intelligence test. *Aust. J. Psychol.*, 1, 108–114.
HANFMANN, E. (1944) Approaches to the intellectual aspects of personality. *Trans. N.Y. Acad. Sci.*, 6, 229–235.
HANNA, J. V. (1950) Estimating intelligence by interview. *Educ. Psychol. Measure.*, 10, 420–429.

HANNON, J. E. and KICKLIGHTER, R. (1970) WAIS versus WISC in adolescents. *J. Consult. Clin. Psychol.*, 35, 179–182.

HARDYCK, C. and PATRINOVICH, L. F. (1963) The patterns of intellectual functioning in Parkinsonian patients. *J. Consult. Psychol.*, 27, 548.

HARPER, A. E. (1950a) Discrimination of the types of schizophrenia by the Wechsler–Bellevue Scale. *J. Consult. Psychol.*, 14, 290–296.

HARPER, A. E. (1950b) Discrimination between matched schizophrenics and normals by the Wechsler–Bellevue Scale. *J. Consult. Psychol.*, 14, 351–357,

HARRIS, A. J. and SHAKOW, D. (1937) The clinical significance of numerical measures of scatter on the Stanford–Binet. *Psychol. Bull.*, 34, 134–150.

HARRIS, D. (1940) Factors affecting college grades: A review of the literature, 1930–1937. *Psychol. Bull.*, 37, 125–166.

HART, B. and SPEARMAN, C. (1914) Mental tests of dementia. *J. Abnorm. Psychol.*, 9, 217–264.

HARTLAGE, L. C. (1970) Differential diagnosis of dyslexia, minimal brain damage and emotional disturbance in school. *Psychol. in the Schl.*, 7, 403–406.

HARTLAGE, L. C. and BOONE, K. E. (1977) Achievement test correlates of Wechsler Intelligence Scale for Children and Wechsler Intelligence Scale for Children – Revised. *Percept. Motor Skills*, 45, 1283–1286.

HARTLAGE, L. C. and GREEN, J. B. (1972) EEG abnormalities and WISC subtest differences. *J. Clin. Psychol.*, 28, 170–171.

HARWOOD, B. T. (1967) Some intellectual correlates of schizoid indicators. *J. Consult. Psychol.*, 31, 218.

HARWOOD, E. and NAYLOR, G. F. (1971) Changes in the constitution of the WAIS intelligence pattern with advancing age. *Aust. J. Psychol.*, 23, 297–303.

HAYNES, J. P. and BENSCH, M. (1981) The P>V sign on the WISC-R and recidivism in delinquents. *J. Consult. Clin. Psychol.*, 49, 480–481.

HAYS, J. R. and SOLWAY, K. S. (1977) Violent behavior and differential Wechsler Intelligence Scale for Children characteristics. *J. Consult. Clin. Psychol.*, 45, 1187.

HAYS, W. and SCHNEIDER, B. (1951) A test–retest evaluation of the Wechsler Forms I and II with mental defectives. *J. Clin. Psychol.*, 7, 140–143.

HEALY, W. (1914) A pictorial completion test. *Psychol. Rev.*, 21, 198–203.

HEALY, W. and FERNALD, G. M. (1911) Tests for practical mental classification. *Psychol. Monog.*, 13, No. 54.

HEIDBREDER, E. (1945) Toward a dynamic psychology of cognition. *Psychol. Rev.*, 52, 1–22.

HEILBRUN, A. B. (1956) Psychological test performance as a function of lateral localization of cerebral lesion. *J. Comp. Physiol. Psychol.*, 49, 10–14.

HEILBRUN, A. B. (1959) Lateralization of cerebral lesion and performance on spatial-temporal tasks. *Arch. Neurol.*, 1, 282–287.

HENDERSON, N. B., BUTLER, B. V. and GOFFENEY, B. (1969) Effectiveness of the WISC and Bender–Gestalt Test in predicting Arithmetic and reading achievement for white and nonwhite children. *J. Clin. Psychol.*, 25, 268–271.

HENDERSON, R. W. and RANKIN, R. J. (1973) WPPSI reliability and predictive validity with disadvantaged Mexican-American children. *J. Sch. Psychol.*, 11, 16–20.

HENNING, J. J. and LEVY, R. H. (1967) Verbal-Performance IQ differences of White and Negro delinquents on the WISC and WAIS. *J. Clin. Psychol.*, 23, 164–168.

HERRELL, J. M. and GOLLAND, J. H. (1969) Should WISC subjects explain picture arrangement stories? *J. Consult. Clin. Psychol.*, 33, 761–762.

HERRING, F. H. (1952) An evaluation of published short forms of the Wechsler–Bellevue Scale. *J. Consult. Psychol.*, 16, 119–123.

HERRING, J. P. (1924) Herring revision of the Binet–Simon tests. *J. Educ. Psychol.*, 15, 172–179.

HERTZKA, A. F., GUILFORD, J. P., CHRISTENSEN, P. R. and BERGER, R. M. (1954) A factor-analytic study of evaluative abilities. *Educ. Psychol. Measure.*, 14, 581–597.

HEWSON, L. R. (1949) The Wechsler–Bellevue Scale and the Substitution test as aids in neuropsychiatric diagnosis. *J. Nerv. Ment. Dis.*, 109, 158–183, 246–266.

HEYER, A. W. (1949) "Scatter analysis" techniques applied to anxiety neurotics from a restricted culturo-educational environment. *J. Gen. Psychol.*, 40, 155–166.

HILDEN, A. H., TAYLOR, J. W. and DuBOIS, P. H. (1952) Empirical evaluation of short W–B scales. *J. Clin. Psychol.*, 8, 232–331.

HILER, E. W. (1958) Wechsler–Bellevue Intelligence as a predictor of continuation in psychotherapy. *J. Clin. Psychol.*, 14, 192–194.

HIMELSTEIN, P. (1957a) Evaluation of an abbreviated WAIS in a psychiatric population. *J. Clin. Psychol.*, 13, 68–69.

HIMELSTEIN, P. (1957b) A comparison of two methods of estimating Full Scale IQ from an abbreviated WAIS. *J. Consult. Psychol.*, 21, 246.

HIMELSTEIN, P. (1957c) A comment on the use of the abbreviated WAIS with homeless men. *Psychol. Rep.*, 3, 440.

HIRSCHENFANG, S. and BENTON, J. C. (1966) Note on intellectual changes in multiple sclerosis. *Percept. Motor Skills*, 22, 786.

HIRT, M. L. and COOK, R. A. (1962) Use of a multiple regression equation to estimate organic impairment from Wechsler scale scores. *J. Clin. Psychol.*, 18, 80–81.

HODGES, W. F. and SPIELBERGER, C. D. (1969) Digit span: an indicant of trait or state anxiety? *J. Consult. Clin. Psychol.*, 33, 430–434.

HOLLENBACK, G. P. and KAUFMAN, A. S. (1973) Factor analysis of the Wechsler Preschool and Primary Scale of Intelligence. *J. Clin. Psychol.*, 29, 41–45.

HOLMES, D. S., ARMSTRONG, H. E., JOHNSON, M. H. and RIES, H. A. (1965) Further evaluation of an abbreviated form of the WAIS. *Psychol. Rep.*, 16, 1163–1164.

HOLMES, D. S., ARMSTRONG, H. E., JOHNSON, M. H. and RIES, H. A. (1966) Validity and clinical utility of the Satz and Mogel abbreviated form of the WAIS. *Psychol. Rep.*, 18, 992–994.

HOLMES, J. S. (1968) Acute psychiatric patient performance on the WAIS. *J. Clin. Psychol.*, 24, 87–91.

HOLROYD, J. (1968) When WISC Verbal IQ is low. *J. Clin. Psychol.*, 24, 457.

HOLROYD, J. and WRIGHT, F. (1965) Neurological implications of WISC Verbal-Performance discrepancies in a psychiatric setting. *J. Consult. Psychol.*, 29, 206–212.

HOLZBERG, J. D. and BELMONT, L. (1952) The relationship between factors on the Wechsler–Bellevue and Rorschach having common psychological rationale. *J. Consult. Psychol.*, 16, 23–29.

HOLZBERG, J. D. and DEANE, M. A. (1950) The diagnostic significance of an objective measure of intratest scatter on the Wechsler–Bellevue Intelligence Scale. *J. Consult. Psychol.*, 14, 180–188.

HOLZINGER, K. J. and HARMAN, H. H. (1938) Comparison of two factorial analyses. *Psychometrika*, 3, 45–60.

HOPKINS, K. D. (1964) An empirical analysis of the efficacy of the WISC in the diagnosis of organicity in children of normal intelligence. *J. Genet. Psychol.*, 105, 163–172.

HORST, P. (1954) Pattern analysis and configural scoring. *J. Clin. Psychol.*, 10, 3–11.

HOWARD, W. (1959) Validities of WAIS short forms in a psychiatric population. *J. Consult. Psychol.*, 22, 282.

HOWELL, R. J. (1955a) Changes in Wechsler subtest scores with age. *J. Consult. Psychol.*, 19, 47–50.

HOWELL, R. J. (1955b) Sex differences and educational influences on a mental deterioration scale. *J. Gerontol.*, 10, 190–193.

HOWELL, R. J., EVANS, L. and DOWNING, L. N. (1958) A comparison of test scores for the 16–17 year age agroup of Navaho Indians with standardized norms for the Wechsler Adult Intelligence Scale (Arizona and New Mexico). *J. Soc. Psychol.*, 47, 355–359.

HUELSMAN, C. B. (1970) The WISC subtest syndrome for disabled readers. *Percept. Motor Skills*, 30, 535–550.

HUGHES, R. B. and LESSLER, K. (1965) A comparison of WISC and Peabody scores of Negro and white rural school children. *Am. J. Ment. Defic.*, 69, 877–880.

HUIZINGA, R. J. (1973) The relationship of the ITPA to the Stanford–Binet Form L-M and the WISC. *J. Learn. Disabil.*, 6, 451–456.

HULICKA, J. M. (1962) Verbal WAIS scores of elderly patients. *Psychol. Rep.*, 10, 250.

HUMPHREYS, L. G. (1968) The fleeting nature of the prediction of academic success. *J. Educ. Psychol.*, 59, 375–380.

HUNT, W. A. and ARNHOFF, F. N. (1955) Some standardized scales for disorganization in schizophrenic thinking. *J. Consult. Psychol.*, 19, 171–174.

HUNT, W. A. and FRENCH, E. G. (1949) Some abbreviated individual intelligence scales containing nonverbal items. *J. Consult. Psychol.*, 13, 119–123.

HUNT, W. A. and FRENCH, E. G. (1952) The CVS abbreviated individual intelligence scale. *J. Consult. Psychol.*, 16, 181–186.

HUNT, W. A. and JONES, N. F. (1958a) The reliability of clinical judgments of asocial tendency. *J. Clin. Psychol.*, 14, 233–235.

HUNT, W. A. and JONES, N. F. (1958b) Clinical judgment of some aspects of schizophrenic thinking. *J. Clin. Psychol.*, 14, 235–239.

HUNT, W. A. and OLDER, H. J. (1944) Psychometric scatter pattern as a diagnostic aid. *J. Abnorm. Soc. Psychol.*, 39, 118–123.

HUNT, W. A. and WALKER, R. E. (1962) A comparison of global and specific clinical judgments across several diagnostic categories. *J. Clin. Psychol.*, 18, 188–194.

HUNT, W. A. and WALKER, R. E. (1971) Cue utilization in diagnostic judgment. *J. Clin. Psychol.*, 27, 62–64.

HUNT, W. A., FRENCH, E. G., KLEBANOFF, S. G., MENSH, I. N. and WILLIAMS, M. (1948a) The clinical possibilities of an abbreviated individual intelligence test. *J. Consult. Psychol.*, 12, 171–173.

HUNT, W. A., KLEBANOFF, S. G., MENSH, I. N. and WILLIAMS, M. (1948b) The validity of some abbreviated individual intelligence scales. *J. Consult. Psychol.*, 12, 48–52.

HUNT, W. A., WALKER, R. E. and JONES, N. F. (1960) The validity of clinical ratings for estimating severity of schizophrenia. *J. Clin. Psychol.*, **16**, 391–393.

HUNT, W., QUAY, H. and WALKER, R. (1966) The validity of clinical judgments of asocial tendency. *J. Clin. Psychol.*, **22**, 116–118.

HUNT, W. L. (1943) The relative rates of decline of Wechsler–Bellevue "Hold" and "Don't Hold" tests. *J. Consult. Psychol.*, **13**, 440–443.

IVNIK, R. J. (1978) Neuropsychological stability in multiple sclerosis. *J. Consult. Clin. Psychol.*, **46**, 913–823.

JACKSON, C. V. (1955) Estimating impairment on Wechsler–Bellevue subtests. *J. Clin. Psychol.*, **11**, 137–143.

JANSEN, D. (1973) WISC and reading achievement of children referred back to the regular classroom or to a special education class after psychological examination. *Percept. Motor Skills*, **37**, 302–304.

JASTAK, J. (1937) Psychometric patterns of State hospital patients. *Del. State Med. J.*, **9**, 87–91.

JASTAK, J. (1946) *Wide Range Achievement Test*. Wilmington: Charles Z. Story.

JASTAK, J. (1948) A plan for the objective measurement of character. *J. Clin. Psychol.*, **4**, 170–178.

JASTAK, J. (1949) Problems of psychometric scatter analysis. *Psychol. Bull.*, **46**, 177–197.

JASTAK, J. (1950) An item analysis of the Wechsler–Bellevue tests. *J. Consult. Psychol.*, **14**, 88–94.

JASTAK, J. (1953) Ranking Bellevue subtests for diagnostic purposes. *J. Consult. Psychol.*, **17**, 403–410.

JASTAK, J. F. and JASTAK, J. R. (1964) Short forms of the WAIS and WISC Vocabulary subtests. *J. Clin. Psychol.*, **20**, 167–199.

JENKIN, N., SPIVACK, G., LEVINE, M. and SAVAGE, W. (1964) Wechsler profiles and academic achievement in emotionally disturbed boys. *J. Consult. Psychol.*, **28**, 290.

JOHNSON, D. T. (1969) Introversion, extraversion and social intelligence: A replication. *J. Clin. Psychol.*, **25**, 181–183.

JOHNSON, E. G. and LYLE, J. G. (1972a) Analysis of WISC Coding: 1. Figure reversibility. *Percept. Motor Skills*, **34**, 195–198.

JOHNSON, E. G. and LYLE, J. G. (1972b) Analysis of WISC Coding: 2. Memory and verbal mediation. *Percept. Motor Skills*, **34**, 659–662.

JOHNSON, E. G. and LYLE, J. G. (1973) Analysis of WISC Coding: 4. Paired-associate learning and performance strategies. *Percept. Motor Skills*, **37**, 695–698.

JOHNSON, L. C. (1949) Wechsler–Bellevue pattern analysis in schizophrenia. *J. Consult. Psychol.*, **13**, 32–33.

JOHNSON, T. F. (1949) Some needs in research with the Wechsler–Bellevue Scale. *J. Gen. Psychol.*, **41**, 33–36.

JOHNSTON, R. A. and CROSS, H. J. (1962) A further investigation of the relation between anxiety and Digit Symbol performance. *J. Consult. Psychol.*, **26**, 390.

JONES, H. E. and CONRAD, H. S. (1933) The growth and decline of intelligence. *Genet. Psychol. Monogr.*, **13**, No. 13.

JONES, H. G. (1956) The evaluation of the significance of differences between scaled scores on the WAIS: Perpetuation of a fallacy. *J. Consult. Psychol.*, **20**, 319–320.

JONES, L. V. (1954) Primary abilities in the Stanford–Binet, age 13. *J. Gen. Psychol.*, **84**, 125–147.

148   THE WECHSLER ENTERPRISE

JONES, N. F. (1959) The validity of clinical judgments of schizophrenic pathology based on verbal responses to intelligence test items. *J. Clin. Psychol.*, **15**, 396–400.

JONES, R. L. (1962) Analytically developed short forms of the WAIS. *J. Consult. Psychol.*, **26**, 289.

JONES, R. L. (1967) Validities of short WAIS batteries. *J. Consult. Psychol.*, **31**, 103.

JORTNER, S. (1970) Overinclusive responses to WAIS Similarities as suggestive of schizophrenia. *J. Clin. Psychol.*, **26**, 346–348.

JURJEVICH, R. M. (1963) Interrelationships of anxiety indices of Wechsler Intelligence Scales and MMPI Scales. *J. Gen. Psychol.*, **69**, 135–142.

JURJEVICH, R. M. (1967) Intellectual assessment with Gorham's Proverbs Test, Raven's Progressive Matrices, and WAIS. *Psychol. Rep.*, **20**, 1285–1286.

KAGAN, J., ROSMAN, B. L., DAY, D., ALBERT, J. and PHILLIPS, W. (1964) Information processing in the child: Significance of analytic and reflective attitudes. *Psychol. Monogr.*, **78**, Whole No. 578.

KAHN, M. W. (1959) A comparison of personality, intelligence, and social history of two criminal groups. *J. Soc. Psychol.*, **49**, 33–40.

KAHN, M. W. (1968) Superior performance IQ of murderers as a function of overt act or diagnosis. *J. Soc. Psychol.*, **76**, 113–116.

KAISER, H. F. (1960) Varimax solution for primary mental abilities. *Psychometrika*, **25**, 153–158.

KALDEGG, A. (1950) The Wechsler test in clinical practice: Comparison of psychiatric and psychosomatic disorders with a control population. *J. Ment. Sci.*, **96**, 908–922.

KALDEGG, A. (1956) Psychological observations in a group of alcoholic patients, with analysis of Rorschach, Wechsler–Bellevue and Bender Gestalt test results. *Q. J. Stud. Alcohol*, **17**, 609–628.

KALDEGG, A. (1960) A note on the application of Doppelt's short form of the Wechsler Adult Intelligence Scale to a clinical population. *Br. J. Med. Psychol.*, **33**, 221–223.

KALLOS, G. L., GRABOW, J. M. and GUARINO, E. A. (1901) The WISC profile of disabled readers. *Person. and Guid. J.*, **39**, 476–478.

KARP, S. A., SILBERMAN, L. and WINTERS, S. (1969) Psychological differentiation and socioeconomic status. *Percept. Motor Skills*, **28**, 55–60.

KARRAS, A. (1963) Predicting full scale WAIS IQs from WAIS subtests for a psychiatric population. *J. Clin. Psychol.*, **19**, 100.

KARSON, S., POOL, K. B. and FREUD, S. L. (1957) The effects of scale and practice on WAIS and W–B I test scores. *J. Consult. Psychol.*, **21**, 241–245.

KASPAR, J. C., THRONE, F. M. and SCHULMAN, J. L. (1968) A study of the inter-judge reliability in scoring the responses of a group of mentally retarded boys to three WISC subscales. *Educ. Psychol. Measure.*, **28**, 469–477.

KAUFMAN, A. S. (1972) A short form of the Wechsler Preschool and Primary Scale of Intelligence. *J. Consult. Clin. Psychol.*, **39**, 361–369.

KAUFMAN, A. S. (1973) The relationship of WPPSI IQs to sex and other background variables. *J. Clin. Psychol.*, **29**, 354–357.

KAUFMAN, A. S. (1975) Factor analysis of the WISC-R at 11 age levels between 6½ and 16½ years. *J. Consult. Clin. Psychol.*, **43**, 135–147.

KAUFMAN, A. S. (1976) A new approach to the interpretation of test scatter on the WISC-R. *J. Learn. Disabil.*, **9**, 160–168.

KAUFMAN, A. S. and HOLLENBECK, G. P. (1974) Comparative structure of the WPPSI for blacks and whites. *J. Clin. Psychol.*, **30**, 316–319.

KAUFMAN, H. L. (1970) Diagnostic indices of employment with the mentally retarded. *Am. J. Ment. Defic.*, **74**, 777–779.

KAY, S. R. (1979) Schizophrenic WAIS pattern by diagnostic subtype. *Percept. Motor Skills*, **48**, 1241–1242.

KENDALL, P. C. and LITTLE, V. L. (1977) Correspondence of brief intelligence measures to the Wechsler Scales with delinquents. *J. Consult. Clin. Psychol.*, **45**, 660–666.

KENDER, J. P. (1972) Is there really a WISC profile for poor readers? *J. Learn. Disabil.*, **57**, 397–400.

KETTNER, N. W., GUILFORD, J. P. and CHRISTENSEN, P. R. (1956) A factor-analytic investigation of the factor called general reasoning. *Educ. Psychol. Measure.*, **16**, 438–453.

KETTNER, N. W., GUILFORD, J. P. and CHRISTENSEN, P. R. (1959) A factor-analytic study across domains of reasoning, creativity and evaluation. *Psychol. Monogr.*, **73**, Whole No. 479.

KIMBRELL, D. L. (1960) Comparison of Peabody, WISC, and academic achievement scores among educable defectives. *Psychol. Rep.*, **7**, 502.

KIMURA, D. (1976) The asymmetry of the human brain. In, *Progress in Psychobiology*. Pp. 360–368. San Francisco: Freeman.

KING, J. D. and SMITH, R. A. (1972) Abbreviated forms of the Wechsler Preschool and Primary Scale of Intelligence for a kindergarten population. *Psychol. Rep.*, **30**, 539–542.

KINGSLEY, L. (1960) Wechsler–Bellevue patterns of psychopaths. *J. Consult. Psychol.*, **24**, 373.

KISSEL, S. (1966a) Schizophrenic patterns on the WISC: a missing control. *J. Clin. Psychol.*, **22**, 201.

KISSEL, S. (1966b) Juvenile delinquency and psychological differentiation: Differences between social and solitary delinquents. *J. Clin. Psychol.*. **22**. 442.

KLATSKIN, E. H., McNAMARA, N. E., SHAFFER, D. and PINCUS, J. H. Minimal organicity in children of normal intelligence: Correspondence between psychological test results and neurologic findings. *J. Learn. Disabil.*, **5**, 213–218.

KLEIN, G. S. (1946) The differentiation of schizophrenics and normals on the Bellevue–Wechsler Test by means of a multiple correlation technique. *Am. Psychol.*, **1**, 263–264.

KLEIN, G. S. (1948) An application of the multiple regression principle to clinical prediction. *J. Gen. Psychol.*, **38**, 159–179.

KLINEBERG, O. (1963) Negro–White difference in intelligence test performance: A new look at an old problem. *Am. Psychol.*, **18**, 198–203.

KLØVE, H. (1959) Relationship of differential electroencephalographic patterns to distribution of Wechsler–Bellevue scores. *Neurology*, **9**, 871–876.

KLØVE, H. and FITZHUGH, K. B. (1962) The relationship of differential EEG patterns to the distribution of Wechsler–Bellevue scores in a chronic epileptic population. *J. Clin. Psychol.*, **18**, 334–337.

KLØVE, H. and REITAN, R. M. (1958) Effect of dysphasia and spatial distortion on Wechsler–Bellevue results. *Arch. Neurol. Psychiat.*, **80**, 708–713.

KLØVE, H. and WHITE, P. T. (1963) The relationship of degree of electroencephalographic abnormality to the distribution of Wechsler–Bellevue scores. *Neurology*, **13**, 423–430.

KNOPF, I. J., MURFETT, B. J. and MILSTEIN, V. (1954) Relationships between the Wechsler—Bellevue Form I and the WISC. *J. Clin. Psychol.*, 10, 261–263.

KNOX, H. A. (1914) A scale based on the work at Ellis Island for estimating mental defect. *J. Am. Med. Assoc.*, 62, 741–747.

KNOX, W. J. and GRIPPALDI, R. (1970) High levels of state or trait anxiety and performance on selected verbal WAIS subtests. *Psychol. Rep.*, 27, 375–379.

KOGAN, W. S. (1950) An investigation into the relationship between psychometric patterns and psychiatric diagnosis. *J. Gen. Psychol.*, 43, 17–46.

KOHS, S. C. (1920) The block-design tests. *J. Exp. Psychol.*, 3, 357–.

KRAEPELIN, E. (1902) *Clinical Psychiatry*. New York: Macmillan.

KRAMER, E. and FRANCIS, P. (1965) Errors in intelligence estimation with short forms of the WAIS. *J. Consult. Psychol.*, 29, 490.

KRAUS, J. (1965a) Psychiatric classification and differential value of WAIS subtest scores. *Aust. J. Psychol.*, 17, 137–139.

KRAUS, J. (1965b) Cattell Anxiety Scale scores and WAIS attainment in three groups of psychiatric patients. *Aust. J. Psychol.*, 17, 229–232.

KRAUS, J. (1966) On the method of indirect assessment of intellectual impairment: a modified WAIS index. *J. Clin. Psychol.*, 22, 66–69.

KRAUS, J. and SELECKI, B. R. (1965) Brain atrophy and assessment of intellectual deterioration on the Wechsler Adult Intelligence Scale. *J. Nerv. Ment. Dis.*, 141, 119–122.

KRAUS, J. and SELECKI, B. R. (1967) Assessment of laterality in diffuse cerebral atrophy using the WAIS. *J. Clin. Psychol.*, 23, 91–92.

KRAUS, J. and WALKER, W. (1969) A pilot study of factors in WAIS "patterns" in diffuse brain atrophy. *Am. J. Ment. Defic.*, 72, 900–904.

KRIEGMAN, G. and HANSEN, F. W. (1947) VIBS: A short form of the Wechsler—Bellevue Intelligence Scale. *J. Clin. Psychol.*, 3, 209–216.

KRIPPNER, S. (1964) WISC Comprehension and Picture Arrangement Subtests as measures of social competence. *J. Clin. Psychol.*, 20, 366–367.

KRUGMAN, M. (1939) Some impressions of the revised Stanford—Binet Scale. *J. Educ. Psychol.*, 30, 594–603.

KUHLMANN, F. (1911a) The present status of the Binet and Simon tests of the intelligence of children. *J. Psycho-Asthenics*, 16, 113–139.

KUHLMANN, F. (1911b) The Binet and Simon tests of intelligence in grading feeble-minded children. *J. Psycho-Asthenics*, 16, 173–193.

KUHLMANN, F. (1941) Retrogressive trends in clinical psychology. *J. Consult. Psychol.*, 5, 97–104.

L'ABATE, L. (1962) The relationship between WAIS-derived indices of maladjustment and MMPI in deviant groups. *J. Consult. Psychol.*, 26, 441–445.

LADD, C. E. (1964) WAIS performance of brain damaged and neurotic patients. *J. Clin. Psychol.*, 20, 114–117.

LAIRD, D. S. (1957) The performance of two groups of eleven-year-old boys on the Wechsler Intelligence Scale for Children. *J. Educ. Res.*, 51, 101–107.

LANSDELL, H. and SMITH, F. J. (1975) Asymmetrical cerebral function for two WAIS factors and their recovery after brain injury. *J. Consult. Clin. Psychol.*, 43, 923.

LARRABEE, G. J. and HOLROYD, R. G. (1976) Comparison of WISC and WISC-R using a sample of highly intelligent children. *Psychol. Rep.*, 38, 1071–1074.

LELI, D. A. and FILSKOV, S. B. (1981) Actuarial detection and description of brain impairment with the W—B Form I. *J. Clin. Psychol.*, 37, 615–622.

LETON, D. A. (1972) A factor analysis of ITPA and WISC scores of learning-disabled pupils. *Psychol. Sch.*, 9, 31–36.

LEVI, J. (1943) A psychometric pattern of the adolescent psychopathic personality. Unpublished doctoral dissertation, New York University.

LEVI, J., OPPENHEIM, S. and WECHSLER, D. (1945) Clinical use of the Mental Deterioration Index of the Bellevue–Wechsler Scale. *J. Abnorm. Soc. Psychol.*, 40, 405–407.

LEVINE, B. and ISCOE, I. (1954) A comparison of Raven's Progressive Matrices (1938) with a short form of the Wechsler–Bellevue. *J. Consult. Psychol.*, 18, 10.

LEVINE, L. S. (1949) The utility of Wechsler's patterns in the diagnosis of schizophrenia. *J. Consult. Psychol.*, 13, 28–31.

LEVINE, M., SPIVACK, G., FUSCHILLO, J. and TAVERNIER, A. (1959) Intelligence, and measures of inhibition and time sense. *J. Clin. Psychol.*, 15, 224–226.

LEVINSON, B. M. (1957) Use of the abbreviated WAIS with homeless men. *Psychol. Rep.*, 3, 287.

LEVINSON, B. M. (1958) Cultural pressure and WAIS scatter in a traditional Jewish setting. *J. Gen. Psychol.*, 93, 277–286.

LEVINSON, B. M. (1959) Traditional Jewish cultural values and performance on the Wechsler tests. *J. Educ. Psychol.*, 50, 177–181.

LEVINSON, B. M. (1960) Subcultural variations in verbal and performance ability at the elementary school level. *J. Genet. Psychol.*, 97, 149–160.

LEVINSON, B. M. (1962) Jewish subculture and WAIS performance among Jewish aged. *J. Genet. Psychol.*, 100, 55–68.

LEVINSON, B. M. (1963a) The WAIS quotient of subcultural deviation. *J. Genet. Psychol.*, 103, 123–131.

LEVINSON, B. M. (1963b) Wechsler M–F index. *J. Gen. Psychol.*, 69, 217–220.

LEVINSON, B. M. (1964) A comparative study of the WAIS performance of native-born Negro and white homeless. *J. Genet. Psychol.*, 105, 211–218.

LEVY, P. (1968) Short-form tests: A methodological review. *Psychol. Bull.*, 69, 410–416.

LEWANDOWSKI, D. G. and SACCUZZO, D. P. (1975) Possible differential WISC patterns for retarded delinquents. *Psychol. Rep.*, 37, 887–894.

LEWANDOWSKI, N., SACCUZZO, D. P. and LEWANDOWSKI, D. G. (1977) The WISC as a measure of personality types. *J. Clin. Psychol.*, 33, 285–291.

LEWIN, K. (1935) *A Dynamic Theory of Personality*, New York: McGraw-Hill.

LEWINSKI, R. J. (1943) Intertest variability of subnormal Naval recruits on the Bellevue Verbal Scale. *J. Abnorm. Soc. Psychol.*, 38, 540–544.

LEWINSKI, R. J. (1944) Discriminative value of the sub-tests of the Bellevue Verbal Scale in the examination of naval recruits. *J. Gen. Psychol.*, 31, 95–99.

LEWINSKI, R. J. (1945) The psychometric pattern: I. Anxiety neurosis. *J. Clin. Psychol.*, 1, 214–221.

LEWINSKI, R. J. (1947) The psychometric pattern. III. Epilepsy. *Am. J. Orthopsychiat.*, 17, 714–722.

LIGHT, M. L. and CHAMBERS, W. R. (1958) A comparison of the Wechsler Intelligence Scale and Wechsler–Bellevue II with mental defectives. *Am. J. Ment. Defic.*, 62, 878–881.

LIN, Y. and RENNICK, P. M. (1973) WAIS correlates of the Minnesota Percepto-Diagnostic Test in a sample of epileptic patients: differential patterns for men and women. *Percept. Motor Skills*, 37, 643–646.

LIN, Y. and RENNICK, P. M. (1974) Correlations between performance on the Category Test and the Wechsler Adult Intelligence Scale in an epileptic sample. *J. Clin. Psychol.*, 30, 62–65.

LITTELL, W. M. (1960) The Wechsler Intelligence Scale for Children: a review of a decade of research. *Psychol. Bull.*, 57, 132–156.

LORO, B. and WOODWARD, J. A. (1976) Verbal and performance IQ for discrimination among psychiatric diagnostic groups. *J. Clin. Psychol.*, 32, 107–114.

LOTSOF, E. J., COMREY, A., BOGARTZ, W. and ARNSFIELD, P. (1958) A factor analysis of the WISC and Rorschach. *J. Project. Techniq.*, 22, 297–301.

LOVE, H. G. (1969) Validity of the Doppelt short form WAIS in a psychiatric population. *Br. J. Soc. Clin. Psychol.*, 8, 185–186.

LOWE, C. M. (1967) Prediction of posthospital work adjustment by use of psychological tests. *J. Counsel. Psychol.*, 14, 248–252.

LURIA, A. R. (1976) The functional organization of the brain. In *Progress in Psychobiology*. Pp. 375–382. San Francisco: Freeman.

LUZKI, M. B., LAYWELL, H. R., SCHULTZ, W. and DAWES, R. M. (1970) Long search for a short WAIS: stop looking. *J. Consult. Psychol.*, 34, 425–431.

LYLE, J. G. and JOHNSON, E. G. (1973) Analysis of WISC Coding: 3. Writing and copying speed, and motivation. *Percept. Motor Skills*, 36, 211–214.

MACHOVER, S. (1943) Cultural and racial variations in patterns of intellect: Performance of Negro and White criminals on the Bellevue Adult Intelligence Scale. Unpublished doctoral dissertation, Teachers College, Columbia University.

MACPHEE, H. M., WRIGHT, H. F. and CUMMINGS, S. B. (1947) The performance of mentally subnormal rural Southern Negroes on the verbal scale of the Bellevue Intelligence Examination. *J. Soc. Psychol.*, 25, 217–229.

MADONICK, M. J. and SOLOMON, M. (1947) The Wechsler–Bellevue Scale in individuals past sixty. *Geriatrics*, 2, 34–40.

MAGARET, A. (1942) Parallels in the behavior of schizophrenics, paretics, and pre-senile non-psychotics. *J. Abnorm. Soc. Psychol.*, 37, 511–528.

MAGARET, A. and WRIGHT, C. (1943) Limitations in the use of intelligence test performance to detect mental disturbance. *J. Appl. Psychol.*, 27, 387–398.

MALEY, R. F. (1970) The relationship of premorbid social activity level of psychiatric patients to test performance on the WAIS and the MMPI. *J. Clin. Psychol.*, 26, 75–76.

MALONEY, M. P., DEYOUNG, R. and MAJOVSKY, L. (1975) Performance of hospitalized schizophrenics on picture vocabulary (QT) and verbal vocabulary (WAIS) measures. *Psychol. Rep.*, 37, 217–218.

MANDLER, G. and SARASON, S. B. (1952) A study of anxiety and learning. *J. Abn. Soc. Psychol.*, 47, 166–173.

MANNE, S. H., KANDEL, A. and ROSENTHAL, D. (1962) Differences between Performance IQ and Verbal IQ in a severely sociopathic population. *J. Clin. Psychol.*, 18, 73–77.

MANNE, S. H., KANDEL, A. and ROSENTHAL, D. (1963) The relationship between performance minus verbal scores and extraversion in a severely sociopathic population. *J. Clin. Psychol.*, 19, 96–97.

MANSON, G. E. (1925) Personality difference in intelligence test performance. *J. Appl. Psychol.*, 9, 230–255.

MARKS, J. B. and KLAHN, J. E. (1961) Verbal and perceptual components in WISC performance and their relation to social class. *J. Consult. Psychol.*, 25, 273.

MARKS, M. R. (1953) A criticism of the use of the Wechsler–Bellevue Scale as a diagnostic instrument. *J. Gen. Psychol.*, 49, 143–152.

MARKWELL, E. D., WHEELER, W. M. and KITZINGER, H. (1953) Changes in Wechsler–Bellevue test performance following prefrontal lobotomy. *J. Consult. Psychol.*, 17, 229–231.

MARSDEN, G. and KALTER, N. (1969) Bodily concerns and the WISC Object Assembly subtest. *J. Consult. Clin. Psychol.*, 33, 391–395.

MARSH, G. G. (1973) Satz–Mogel abbreviated WAIS and CNS-damaged patients. *J. Clin. Psychol.*, 29, 451–455.

MARSHALL, W., HESS, A. K. and LAIR, C. V. (1978) The WISC-R and WRAT as indicators of arithmetic achievement in juvenile delinquents. *Percept. Motor Skills*, 47, 408–410.

MARTIN, A. W. and WIECHERS, J. E. (1954) Raven's Colored Progressive Matrices and the Wechsler Intelligence Scale for Children. *J. Consult. Psychol.*, 18, 143–144.

MARTIN, J. D., BLAIR, G. E., STOKES, E. H. and ARMSTRONG, G. (1977) Correlation of the Object Assembly and Block Design tests of the Wechsler Adult Intelligence Scale and the Torrance Test of Creative Thinking. *Educ. Psychol. Measure.*, 37, 1095–1097.

MASLING, J. (1959) The effects of warm and cold interaction on the administration and scoring of an intelligence test. *J. Consult. Psychol.*, 23, 336–341.

MASLING, J. (1960) The influence of situational and interpersonal variables in projective testing. *Psychol. Bull.*, 57, 65–85.

MATARAZZO, J. D. (1976) *Wechsler's Measurement and Appraisal of Adult Intelligence*. Baltimore: Williams & Wilkins.

MATARAZZO, J. D. and PHILLIPS, J. S. (1955) Digit Symbol performance as a function of increasing levels of anxiety. *J. Consult. Psychol.*, 19, 131–134.

MATARAZZO, J. D., ULETT, G. A., GUZE, S. B. and SASLOW, G. (1954) The relationship between anxiety level and several measures of intelligence. *J. Consult. Psychol.*, 18, 201–205.

MATARAZZO, R. G. (1955) The relationship of manifest anxiety to Wechsler–Bellevue performance. *J. Consult. Psychol.*, 19, 218.

MATEER, F. (1918) The diagnostic fallibility of intelligence ratios. *Pedagog. Sem.*, 25, 369–392.

MATTHEWS, C. G. and REITAN, R. M. (1964) Correlations of Wechsler–Bellevue rank orders of subtest means in laterialized and non-lateralized brain-damaged groups. *Percept. Motor Skills*, 19, 391–399.

MATTHEWS, C. G., GUERTIN, W. H. and REITAN, R. M. (1962) Wechsler–Bellevue subtest mean rank orders in diverse diagnostic groups. *Psychol. Rep.*, 11, 3–9.

MAUPIN, E. W. and HUNTER, D. (1966) Digit span as a measure of attention: Attempted validation studies. *Psychol. Rep.*, 18, 457–458.

MAXWELL, A. E. (1959) Tables to facilitate the comparison of subtest scores on the WISC. *J. Clin. Psychol.*, 15, 293–295.

MAXWELL, A. E. (1972) The WPPSI: A marked discrepancy in the correlations of the subtests for good and poor readers. *Br. J. Math. Stat. Psychol.*, 25, 283–291.

MAXWELL, E. (1957) Validities of abbreviated WAIS Scales. *J. Consult. Psychol.*, 21, 121–126.

MAYZNER, M. S., SERSEN, E. and TRESSELT, M. E. (1955) The Taylor Manifest Anxiety Scale and intelligence. *J. Consult. Psychol.*, 19, 401–403.

McCULLOUGH, M. W. (1950) Wechsler–Bellevue changes following prefrontal lobotomy. *J. Clin. Psychol.*, 6, 270–277.

McFIE, J. (1960) Psychological testing in clinical neurology. *J. Nerv. Ment. Dis.*, 131, 383-393.

McFIE, J. and PIERCY, M. F. (1952) Intellectual impairment with localized cerebral impairment. *Brain*, 75, 292-311.

McHUGH, A. F. (1963) WISC performance in neurotic and conduct disorders. *J. Clin. Psychol.*, 19, 423-424.

McINTOSH, W. J. (1974) The use of a Wechsler subtest ratio as an index of brain damage in children. *J. Learn. Disabil.*, 7, 161-163.

McKEEVER, W. F. and GERSTEIN, A. I. (1954) Validity of the Hewson ratios: Investigation of a fundamental methodological consideration. *J. Consult. Psychol.*, 22, 150.

McKENZIE, R. E. (1951) A study of the Wechsler–Bellevue Intelligence Scale and the VIBS Short Form in an institute for the mentally defective. *Am. J. Ment. Defic.*, 56, 174-176.

McKERRACHER, D. W. and ORRITT, C. P. (1972) Prediction of vocational and social skill acquisition in a developmentally handicapped population: A pilot study. *Am. J. Ment. Defic.*, 76, 574-580.

McKERRACHER, D. W. and WATSON, R. A. (1968) Validation of a short form WISC with clinic children. *Br. J. Educ. Psychol.*, 38, 205-208.

McKERRACHER, D. W., WATSON, R. A., LITTLE, A. J. and WINTER, K. S. (1968) Validation of a short form estimation of WAIS in subnormal and psychopathic patients. *J. Ment. Subnormal.*, 14, 96-97.

McLEAN, O. S. (1954) Divergent scores on the Wechsler–Bellevue Scale as indicators of learning ability. *J. Clin. Psychol.*, 10, 264-266.

McMAHON, R. C. and KUNCE, J. T. (1981) A comparison of the factor structure of the WISC and WISC-R in normal and exceptional groups. *J. Clin. Psychol.*, 37, 408-410.

McNEMAR, Q. (1942) *The Revision of the Stanford–Binet Scale*. Boston: Houghton-Mifflin.

McNEMAR, Q. (1950) On abbreviated Wechsler–Bellevue Scales. *J. Consult. Psychol.*, 14, 79-81.

McNEMAR, Q. (1957) On WAIS difference scores. *J. Consult. Psychol.*, 21, 239-240.

McNEMAR, Q. (1964) Lost: Our intelligence: Why? *Am. Psychol.*, 19, 871-882.

McQUITTY, L. L. (1956) Agreement analysis: Classifying persons by predominant patterns of responses. *Br. J. Stat. Psychol.*, 9, 5-16.

MECH, E. (1953) Item analysis and discriminative value of selected Wechsler–Bellevue subtests. *J. Educ. Res.*, 47, 241-260.

MEEHL, P. (1954) *Clinical versus Statistical Prediction*. Minneapolis: University of Minnesota Press.

MEEHL, P. (1973) Why I do not attend case conferences. In, *Psychodiagnosis: Selected Papers*. Pp. 225-302. Minneapolis: University of Minnesota Press.

MEIER, M. J. and FRENCH, L. A. (1966) Longitudinal assessment of intellectual functioning following unilateral temporal lobectomy. *J. Clin. Psychol.*, 22, 22-27.

MEIKLE, S. (1968) The effect on subtest differences of abbreviating the WAIS. *J. Clin. Psychol.*, 24, 196-197.

MERRILL, R. M. and HEATHERS, L. B. (1952) Deviations of Wechsler–Bellevue subtest scores from Vocabulary level in university counseling-center clients. *J. Consult. Psychol.*, 16, 469-472.

MERRILL, R. M. and HEATHERS, L. B. (1953) A comparison of the Wechsler–

Bellevue and ACE tests on a university counseling center group. *J. Consult. Psychol.*, 17, 63–66.

MEYER, A. (1906) The relation of emotional and intellectual functions in paranoia and obsessions. *Psychol. Bull.*, 3, 255–274.

MEYER, V. (1959) Cognitive changes following temporal lobectomy for the relief of temporal lobe epilepsy. *Arch. Neurol. Psychiat.*, 81, 299–309.

MEYER, V. and JONES, H. G. (1957) Patterns of cognitive test performance as functions of the lateral localization of cerebral abnormalities in the temporal lobe. *J. Ment. Sci.*, 103, 758–772.

MILBERG, W., GREIFTENSTEIN, M., LEWIS, R. and ROURKE, D. (1980) Differentiation of temporal lobe and generalized seizure patients with the WAIS. *J. Consult. Clin. Psychol.*, 48, 39–42.

MILLHAM, J., JACOBSON, L. I. and BERGER, S. E. (1971) Effects of intelligence, information processing, and mediation conditions on conceptual learning. *J. Educ. Psychol.*, 62, 293–299.

MILLIREN, A. P. and NEWLAND, T. E. (1968) Statistically significant differences between subtest scaled scores for the WPPSI. *J. Sch. Psychol.*, 7 (3), 16–19.

MISHRA, S. P. (1971) Wechsler Adult Intelligence Scale: Examiner vs. machine administration. *Psychol. Rep.*, 29, 759–762.

MOGEL, S. and SATZ, P. (1963) Abbreviation of the WAIS for clinical use: An attempt at validation. *J. Clin. Psychol.*, 19, 298–300.

MOLDAWSKY, S. and MOLDAWSKY, P. C. (1952) Digit span as an anxiety indicator. *J. Consult. Psychol.*, 16, 115–118.

MONROE, J. J. (1952) The effects of emotional adjustment and intelligence upon Bellevue scatter. *J. Consult. Psychol.*, 16, 110–114.

MONROE, K. L. (1966) Note on the estimation of the WAIS Full Scale IQ. *J. Clin. Psychol.*, 22, 79–81.

MOON, W. H. and LAIR, C. V. (1970) Manifest anxiety, induced anxiety and digit symbol performance. *Psychol. Rep.*, 26, 947–950.

MORAN, L. J. (1953) Vocabulary knowledge and usage among normal and schizophrenic subjects. *Psychol. Monogr.*, 67, No. 370.

MORAN, L. J., MORAN, F. A. and BLAKE, R. R. (1954) An investigation of the vocabulary performance of shizophrenics: II. Conceptual level of definitions. *J. Abnorm. Soc. Psychol.*, 49, 183–195.

MORRIS, L. W. and LIEBERT, R. M. (1969) Effects of anxiety on timed and untimed intelligence tests: Another look. *J. Consult. Clin. Psychol.*, 33, 240–244.

MORROW, R. S. and MARK, J. C. (1955) The correlation of intelligence and neurological findings on twenty-two patients autopsied for brain damage. *J. Consult. Psychol.*, 19, 283–289.

MUMPOWER, D. L. (1964) The fallacy of the short form. *J. Clin. Psychol.*, 20, 111–113.

MUNFORD, P. R. (1978) A comparison of the WISC and WISC-R on Black child psychiatric outpatients. *J. Clin. Psychol.*, 34, 938–943.

MUNFORD, P. R. and MEYEROWITZ, B. E. (1980) A comparison of Black and White children's WISC/WISC-R differences. *J. Consult. Clin. Psychol.*, 36, 471–475.

MUNFORD, P. R. and MUNOZ, A. (1980) A comparison of the WISC and WISC-R on Hispanic children. *J. Consult. Clin. Psychol.*, 36, 452–458.

MURPHY, D. B. and LANGSTON, R. D. (1956) A short form of the Wechsler–Bellevue and the Army Classification Battery as measures of intelligence. *J. Consult. Psychol.*, 20, 405.

MURRAY, H. A. (1933) The effect of fear upon estimates of the maliciousness of other personalities. *J. Soc. Psychol.*, 4, 310–329.
MURSTEIN, B. I. and LEIPOLD, W. D. (1961) The role of learning and motor abilities in the Wechsler–Bellevue Digit Symbol subtest. *Educ. Psychol. Measure.*, 21, 103–112.
MUZYCZKA, M. J. and ERICKSON, M. T. (1976) WISC characteristics of reading disabled children by three objective methods. *Percept. Motor Skills*, 43, 595–602.
NALVEN, F. B. (1967) Relationship between Digit Span and distractibility ratings in emotionally disturbed children. *J. Clin. Psychol.*, 23, 466–467.
NALVEN, F. B. (1969) Classroom-administered Digit Span and distractibility ratings for elementary school pupils. *Psychol. Rep.*, 24, 734.
NALVEN, F. B. and BIERBRYER, B. (1969) Predicting elementary school children's classroom comprehension from their WISC results. *J. Clin. Psychol.*, 25, 75–76.
NALVEN, F. B. and PULEO, V. T. (1968) Relationship between Digit Span and classroom distractibility in elementary school children. *J. Clin. Psychol.*, 24, 85–87.
NEFF, W. S. (1937) Perceiving and symbolizing: An experimental study. *Am. J. Psychol.*, 49, 376–418.
NEFF, W. S. (1938) Socioeconomic status and intelligence: A critical survey. *Psychol. Bull.*, 35, 727–757.
NEURINGER, C. (1963a) The form equivalence between the Wechsler–Bellevue Intelligence Scale, Form I and the Wechsler Adult Intelligence Scale. *Educ. Psychol. Measure.*, 23, 755–763.
NEURINGER, C. (1963b) Effect of intellectual level and neuropsychiatric status on the diversity of intensity of semantic differential ratings. *J. Consult. Psychol.*, 27, 280.
NEURINGER, C., WHEELER, G. R. and BEARDSLEY, J. V. (1969) Rating diversity and measures of convergent and divergent intelligence. *J. Gen. Psychol.*, 80, 73–79.
NEWLAND, T. E. and SMITH, P. A. (1967) Statistically significant differences between subtest scaled scores on the WISC and WAIS. *J. Sch. Psychol.*, 2, 122–127.
NEWMAN, J. R. and LOOS, F. M. (1955) Differences between verbal and performance IQs with mentally defective children on the Wechsler Intelligence Scale for Children. *J. Consult. Psychol.*, 19, 16.
NICHOLS, R. C. (1959) The effect of ego involvement and success experience on intelligence test results. *J. Consult. Psychol.*, 23, 92.
NICKOLS, J. E. (1962) Brief forms of the Wechsler Intelligence Scales for research. *J. Clin. Psychol.*, 18, 167.
NICKOLS, J. (1963) Structural efficiency of WAIS subtests. *J. Clin. Psychol.*, 19, 420–423.
NICKOLS, J. and NICKOLS, M. (1963) Brief forms of the WISC for research. *J. Clin. Psychol.*, 19, 425.
NORMAN, R. D. (1953) Sex differences and other aspects of young superior adult performance on the Wechsler–Bellevue. *J. Consult. Psychol.*, 17, 411–418.
NORMAN, R. D. (1966) A revised deterioration formula for the Wechsler Adult Intelligence Scale. *J. Clin. Psychol.*, 22, 287–294.
NORMAN, R. D. and DALEY, M. F. (1959) Senescent changes in intellectual ability among superior older women. *J. Gerontol.*, 14, 457–464.
NORMAN, R. P. and WILENSKY, H. (1961) Item difficulty of the WAIS Information subtest for a chronic schizophrenic sample. *J. Clin. Psychol.*, 17, 56–57.

OAKLAND, J. A. (1969) WISC Coding as a measure of motivation. *J. Clin. Psychol.*, 25, 411–412.

OATES, D. W. (1928) A statistical and psychological investigation of intelligence tests. *Forum Educ.*, 6, 38–62.

OLCH, D. R. (1948) Psychometric pattern of schizophrenics on the Wechsler–Bellevue Intelligence Test. *J. Consult. Psychol.*, 12, 127–136.

OLIN, T. D. and REZNIKOFF, M. (1957) The use of Doppelt's short form of the Wechsler Adult Intelligence Scale with psychiatric patients. *J. Consult. Psychol.*, 21, 27–28.

ORME, J. E. (1957) Non-verbal and verbal performance in normal old age, senile dementia, and elderly depressives. *J. Gerontol.*, 12, 408–413.

OROS, J. A., JOHNSON, J. J. and LEWIS, M. L. (1972) The effect of induced anxiety on the Wechsler Intelligence Scale for Children. *Psychol. Sch.*, 9, 388–392.

OSBORNE, R. T. (1963) Factorial composition of the Wechsler Intelligence Scale for children at the pre-school level. *Psychol. Rep.*, 13, 443–448.

OSBORNE, R. T. and ALLEN, J. (1962) Validity of short forms of the WISC for mental retardates. *Psychol. Rep.*, 11, 167–170.

OVERALL, J. E. and LEVIN, H. S. (1978) Correcting for cultural factors in evaluating intellectual deficit on the WAIS. *J. Clin. Psychol.*, 34, 910–915.

OVERALL, J. E., HOFFMAN, N. G. and LEVIN, H. (1978) Effects of aging, organicity, alcoholism, and functional psychopathology on WAIS subtest profiles. *J. Consult. Clin. Psychol.*, 46, 1315–1322.

PANTON, J. H. (1960) Beta-WAIS comparisons and WAIS subtest configurations within a state prison population. *J. Clin. Psychol.*, 16, 312–317.

PARSONS, O. A. and KEMP, D. E. (1960) Intellectual functioning in temporal lobe epilepsy. *J. Consult. Psychol.*, 24, 408–414.

PARSONS, O. A., VEGA, A. and BURN, J. (1969) Different psychological effects of lateralized brain damage. *J. Consult. Clin. Psychol.*, 33, 551–557.

PATALANO, F. (1976) Comments on criminal offenders and the WAIS Picture Arrangement "hold-up" item. *Psychol. Rep.*, 39, 1148–1150.

PATTERSON, C. H. (1946a) The Wechsler–Bellevue Scale as an aid in psychiatric diagnosis. *J. Clin. Psychol.*, 2, 348–353.

PATTERSON, C. H. (1946b) A comparison of various "short forms" of the Wechsler–Bellevue Scale. *J. Consult. Psychol.*, 10, 260–267.

PATTERSON, C. H. (1948) A further study of two short forms of the Wechsler–Bellevue Scale. *J. Consult. Psychol.*, 12, 147–152.

PAUKER, J. D. (1963) A split-half abbreviation of the WAIS. *J. Clin. Psychol.*, 19, 98–100.

PAULSON, M. J. and LIN, T. (1970) Age: the neglected variable in constructing an abbreviated WAIS. *J. Clin. Psychol.*, 26, 336–343.

PAYNE, D. A. and LEHMANN, I. J. (1966) A brief WAIS item analysis. *J. Clin. Psychol.*, 22, 296–297.

PEARSON, K. (1906) On the relationship of intelligence to size and shape of head, and to other physical and mental characters. *Biometrika*, 5, 105–146.

PENNINGTON, H., GALLIANI, C. A. and VOEGELE, G. E. (1965) Unilateral electroencephalographic dysrhythmia and children's intelligence. *Child Devel.*, 36, 539–546.

PEREZ, F. I., GAY, J. R. A. and TAYLOR, R. L. (1975) WAIS performance of neurologically impaired aged. *Psychol. Rep.*, 37, 1043–1047.

PHILLIPS, W. M. (1979) Structure of WAIS scores for private psychiatric inpatients. *Psychol. Rep.*, **44**, 119–126.

PICKERING, J. W., JOHNSON, D. L. and STARY, J. E. (1977) Systematic VIQ/PIQ differences on the WAIS: an artifact of this instrument? *J. Clin. Psychol.*, **33**, 1061–1064.

PIHL, R. O. (1968) The degree of verbal-performance discrepancy on the WISC and the WAIS and severity of EEG abnormality in epileptics. *J. Clin. Psychol.*, **24**, 418–420.

PILLEY, J., HARRIS, C., MILLER, J. and RICE, D. (1975) Correlation of scores on the Wechsler Intelligence Scale for Children and the Peabody Picture Vocabulary Test for adolescents in a special education program. *Psychol. Rep.*, **37**, 139–144.

PINTNER, R. (1919) A non-language group intelligence test. *J. Appl. Psychol.*, **3**, 199–214.

PINTNER, R. (1923) *Intelligence Testing: Methods and Results.* New York: Holt.

PINTNER, R. and PATTERSON, D. G. (1917) *A Scale of Performance Testing.* New York: Appleton.

PIOTROWSKI, R. J. (1978) Abnormality of subtest score differences on the WISC-R. *J. Consult. Clin. Psychol.*, **46**, 569–570.

PIOTROWSKI, R. J. and GRUBB, R. D. (1976) Significant subtest score differences on the WISC-R. *J. Sch. Psychol.*, **14**, 202–206.

PLANT, W. T. and LYND, C. (1959) A validity study and a college freshman norm group for the Wechsler Adult Intelligence Scale. *Person. Guid. J.*, **37**, 578–580.

PLUMB, G. R. and CHARLES, D. C. (1955) Scoring difficulty of Wechsler comprehension responses. *J. Educ. Psychol.*, **46**, 179–183.

POFFENBERGER, A. T. and CARPENTER, F. L. (1924) Character traits in school success. *J. Exp. Psychol.*, **7**, 67–74.

PRADO, W. M. and SCHNADT, F. (1965) Differences in WAIS-WB functioning of three psychiatric groups. *J. Clin. Psychol.*, **21**, 184–186.

PRESSEY, S. L. (1917) Distinctive features in psychological test measurement made upon dementia praecox and chronic alcoholic patients. *J. Abnorm. Psychol.*, **12**, 130–139.

PRESSEY, S. L. and COLE, L. W. (1918) Irregularity in a psychological examination as a measure of mental deterioration. *J. Abnorm. Psychol.*, **13**, 285–294.

PRESTON, J. (1978) Abbreviated forms of the WISC-R. *Psychol. Rep.*, **42**, 883–887.

PRICE, A. C. and GENTRY, W. D. (1968) Schizophrenic thought process: Analysis of the WAIS. *Psychol. Rep.*, **22**, 1099–1100.

PRICE, J. R. and THORNE, G. D. (1955) A statistical comparison of the WISC and Wechsler–Bellevue, Form I. *J. Consult. Psychol.*, **19**, 479–482.

PRISTO, L. J. (1978) Comparing WISC and WISC-R scores. *Psychol. Rep.*, **42**, 515–518.

PURCELL, C. K., DREVDAHL, J. and PURCELL, K. (1952) The relationship between altitude-IQ discrepancy and anxiety. *J. Clin. Psychol.*, **8**, 82–85.

PURCELL, K. (1956) A note on Porteus Maze and Wechsler–Bellevue scores as related to antisocial behavior. *J. Consult. Psychol.*, **20**, 361–364.

PYKE, S. and AGNEW, N. McK. (1963) Digit Span performance as a function of noxious stimulation. *J. Consult. Psychol.*, **27**, 281.

QUAY, H. C. and PETERSON, D. R. (1979) *Manual for the Behavior Problem Checklist.* New Brunswick, NJ: School of Professional Psychology, Busch Campus, Rutgers State University.

QUERESHI, M. Y. (1968a) The comparability of WAIS and WISC subtest scores and IQ estimates. *J. Psychol.*, 68, 73–82.

QUERESHI, M. Y. (1968b) Intelligence test scores as a function of sex of experimenter and sex of subject. *J. Psychol.*, 69, 277–284.

QUERESHI, M. Y. (1973) Patterns of intellectual development during childhood and adolescence. *Genet. Psychol. Monogr.*, 87, 313–344.

QUERESHI, M. Y. and MILLER, J. M. (1970) The comparability of the WAIS, WISC and WB II. *J. Educ. Measure.*, 7, 105–111.

RABIN, A. I. (1941) Test-score patterns in schizophrenia and non-psychotic states. *J. Psychol.*, 12, 91–100.

RABIN, A. I. (1942a) Differentiating psychometric patterns in schizophrenia and manic-depressive psychoses. *J. Abnorm. Soc. Psychol.*, 37, 270–272.

RABIN, A. I. (1942b) Wechsler–Bellevue test results in senile and arteriosclerotic patients. *Psychol. Bull.*, 39, 510.

RABIN, A. I. (1943) A short form of the Wechsler–Bellevue test. *J. Appl. Psychol.*, 27, 320–324.

RABIN, A. I. (1944a) The relationship between Vocabulary levels and level of general intelligence in psychotic and non-psychotic individuals of a wide age-range. *J. Educ. Psychol.*, 35, 411–422.

RABIN, A. I. (1944b) Fluctuations in the mental level of schizophrenics. *Psychiat. Q.*, 18, 78–91.

RABIN, A. I. (1945a) Psychometric trends in senility and psychoses of the senium. *J. Gen. Psychol.*, 32, 149–162.

RABIN, A. I. (1945b) The use of the Wechsler–Bellevue scale with normal and abnormal persons. *Psychol. Bull.*, 42, 410–422.

RABIN, A. I. (1965) Diagnostic use of intelligence tests. In, B. B. WOLMAN, Ed., *Handbook of Clinical Psychology*. Pp. 477–497. New York: McGraw-Hill.

RABIN, A. I. and GUERTIN, W. H. (1951) Research with the Wechsler–Bellevue test: 1945–1950. *Psychol. Bull.*, 48, 211–248.

RABIN, A. I., DAVIS, J. C. and SANDERSON, M. H. (1946) Item difficulty of some Wechsler–Bellevue subtests. *J. Appl. Psychol.*, 30, 443–500.

RADCLIFFE, J. A. (1966) WAIS factorial structure and factor scores for ages 18 to 54. *Aust. J. Psychol.*, 15, 228–238.

RAMANAIAH, N. V., O'DONNELL, J. P. and RIBICH, F. (1976) Multiple-factor analysis of the Wechsler Scale for Children. *J. Clin. Psychol.*, 32, 829–831.

RAMANAUSKAS, S. and BURROW, W. H. (1973) WISC profiles: Above average and MR good and poor readers. *Ment. Retard.*, 11(2), 12–14.

RANDOLPH, M. H., RICHARDSON, H. and JOHNSON, R. C. (1961) A comparison of social and solitary male delinquents. *J. Consul. Psychol.*, 25, 293–295.

RAPAPORT, D. (1942) Principles underlying projective techniques. *Character Personal.*, 10, 213–219.

RAPAPORT, D. (1946) Principles underlying non-projective tests of personality. *Ann. N.Y. Acad. Sci.*, 46, 643–652.

RAPAPORT, D., GILL, M. and SCHAFER, R. (1945) *Diagnostic Psychological Testing*. Vol. 1. Chicago: Yearbook Publishers.

RAPPAPORT, S. R. (1953) Intellectual deficit in organics and schizophrenics. *J. Consult. Psychol.*, 17, 389–395.

RASBURY, W. C., FALGOUT, J. C. and PERRY, N. W. (1978) A Yudin-type short form of the WISC-R: two aspects of validation. *J. Clin. Psychol.*, 34, 120–126.

RAVENETTE, A. T. and KAHN, J. H. (1962) Intellectual ability of disturbed children in a working-class area. *Br. J. Soc. Clin. Psychol.*, 1, 208–212.

RAWLINGS, E. (1921) Intellectual status of patients with paranoid dementia preacox: its relation to organic changes. *Arch. Neurol. Psychia.*, 5, 283–295.

REED, H. B. C. and FITZHUGH, K. B. (1966) Patterns of deficits in relation to severity of cerebral dysfunction in children and adults. *J. Consult. Psychol.*, 30, 98–102.

REED, H. B. C. and REITAN, R. M. (1963) Intelligence test performances of brain-damaged subjects with lateralized motor deficits. *J. Consult. Psychol.*, 27, 102–106.

REED, H. B. C., REITAN, R. M. and KLØVE, H. (1965) Influence of cerebral lesion on psychological test performance of older children. *J. Consult. Psychol.*, 29, 247–256.

REED, J. C. (1967) Reading achievement as related to differences between WISC Verbal and Performance IQs. *Child Devel.*, 38, 835–840.

REED, J. C. and FITZHUGH, K. B. (1967) Factor analysis of WB-I and WAIS scores of patients with chronic cerebral dysfunction. *Percept. Motor Skills*, 25, 517–521.

REED, J. C. and REITAN, R. M. (1969) Verbal and performance differences among brain-injured children with lateralized motor deficits. *Percept. Motor Skills*, 29, 747–752.

REICHARD, S. and SCHAFER, R. (1943) The clinical significance of the scatter on the Bellevue Scale. *Bull. Menninger Clin.*, 7, 93–98.

REID, W. B., MOORE, D. and ALEXANDER, D. (1968) Abbreviated form of the WISC for use with brain-damaged and mentally retarded children. *J. Consult. Clin. Psychol.*, 32, 236.

REID, W. R. and SCHOER, L. A. (1966) Reading achievement, social-class and subtest pattern on the WISC. *J. Educ. Res.*, 59, 469–472.

REITAN, R. M. (1955) Certain differential effects of left and right cerebral lesions in human adults. *J. Comp. Physiol Psychol.*, 48, 474–477.

REITAN, R. M. (1958) Qualitative versus quantitative changes following brain damage. *J. Psychol.*, 46, 339–346.

REITAN, R. M. (1959) The comparative effects of brain damage on the Halstead Impairment Index and the Wechsler–Bellevue Scale. *J. Clin. Psychol.*, 15, 281–285.

REITAN, R. M. and FITZHUGH, K. B. (1971) Behavioral deficits in groups with cerebral vascular lesions. *J. Consult. Clin. Psychol.*, 37, 215–223.

RESCHLY, D. J. (1978) WISC-R factor structures among Anglos, Blacks, Chicanos and native-American Papagos. *J. Consult. Clin. Psychol.*, 46, 417–422.

RESNICK, R. J. and ENTIN, A. D. (1971) Is an abbreviated form of the WISC valid for Afro-American children? *J. Consult. Clin. Psychol.*, 36, 97–99.

REYNELL, W. R. (1944) A psychometric method of determining intellectual loss following head injury. *J. Ment. Sci.*, 90, 710–719.

REYNOLDS, C. R. and GUTKIN, T. B. (1980) Stability of the WISC-R factor structure across sex at two age levels. *J. Consult. Clin. Psychol.*, 36, 775–777.

RICHMAN, J. (1964) Symbolic distortion in the vocabulary definition of schizophrenics. *J. Gen. Psychol.*, 71, 1–8.

RIEGEL, R. M. and RIEGEL, K. F. (1962) A comparison of reinterpretation of factor structures of the W-B., the WAIS, and the HAWIE on aged persons. *J. Consult. Psychol.*, 26, 31–37.

RIMOLDI, H. J. A. (1951) The central intellective factor. *Psychometrika*, 16, 75–101.

ROBECK, M. C. (1960) Subtest patterning of problem readers on WISC. *Calif. J. Educ. Res.*, 11, 110–115.

ROBERTSON, J. P. S. and BATCHELDOR, K. J. (1956) Cultural aspects of the Wechsler Adult Intelligence Scale in relation to British mental patients. *J. Ment. Sci.*, 102, 612–618.

ROCKWELL, G. J. (1967) WISC object assembly and bodily concern. *J. Consult. Psychol.*, 31, 221.

ROE, A. and SHAKOW, D. (1942) Intelligence in mental disorder. *Ann. N.Y. Acad. Sci.*, 42, 361–390.

ROGERS, L. S. (1950a) A comparative evaluation of the Wechsler–Bellevue Mental Deterioration Index for various adult groups. *J. Clin. Psychol.*, 6, 199–202.

ROGERS, L. S. (1950b) A note on Allen's index of deterioration. *J. Clin. Psychol.*, 6, 203.

ROGERS, L. S. (1951) Differences between neurotic and schizophrenics on the Wechsler–Bellevue Scale. *J. Consult. Psychol.*, 15, 151–153.

ROSS, R. T. and MORLEDGE, J. (1967) Comparison of the WISC at chronological age sixteen. *J. Consult. Psychol.*, 31, 331–332.

ROURKE, B. P., YOUNG, G. C. and FLEWELLING, R. W. (1971) The relationship between WISC Verbal-Performance discrepancies and selected verbal, auditory-perceptual, visual-perceptual, and problem-solving abilities in children with learning disabilities. *J. Clin. Psychol.*, 27, 475–479.

ROURKE, B. P., DIETRICH, D. M. and YOUNG, G. C. (1973) Significance of WISC Verbal-Performance discrepancies for younger children with learning disabilities. *Percept. Motor Skills*, 36, 275–282.

ROWLEY, V. N. (1961) Analysis of the WISC performance of brain-damaged and emotionally disturbed children. *J. Consult. Psychol.*, 25, 553.

ROWLEY, V. N. and STONE, F. B. (1963) A further note on the relationship between WISC functioning and the CMAS. *J. Clin. Psychol.*, 19, 426.

ROYER, F. L. and JANOWITCH, L. (1973) Performance of process and reactive schizophrenics on a symbol-digit substitution task. *Percept. Motor Skills*, 37, 63–70.

RUBIN-RABSON, G. (1956) Item order and difficulty in four verbal subtests of the Bellevue–Wechsler Scale. *J. Genet. Psychol.*, 88, 167–174.

RUGEL, R. (1974) The factor structure of the WISC in two populations of disabled readers. *J. Learn. Disabil.*, 7, 581–585.

RUSSELL, E. W. (1972) WAIS factor analysis with brain-damaged subjects using criterion measures. *J. Consult. Clin. Psychol.*, 39, 133–139.

RUSSELL, E. W. (1979) Three patterns of brain damage on the WAIS. *J. Clin. Psychol.*, 35, 611–620.

RUST, J. O., BARNARD, D. and OSTER, G. D. (1979) WAIS Verbal-performance differences among elderly when controlling for fatigue. *Psychol. Rep.*, 44, 489–490.

SACCUZZO, D. P. and LEWANDOWSKI, D. G. (1976) The WISC as a diagnostic tool. *J. Clin. Psychol.*, 32, 115–125.

SAN DIEGO, E. A., FOLEY, J. M. and WALKER, R. E. (1970) WAIS scores for highly educated young adults from the Philippines and the United States. *Psychol. Rep.*, 27, 511–515.

162   THE WECHSLER ENTERPRISE

SANFORD, R. N. (1936) The effect of abstinence from food upon imaginal processes. *J. Psychol.*, **2**, 129–136.

SANFORD, R. N. (1937) The effect of abstinence from food upon imaginal processes: A further experiment. *J. Psychol.*, **3**, 145–159.

SARASON, I. G. and MINARD, J. (1962) Test anxiety, experimental instructions and the Wechsler Adult Intelligence Scale. *J. Educ. Psychol.*, **53**, 299–302.

SARTAIN, A. Q. (1946) A comparison of the new Revised Stanford–Binet, the Bellevue Scale, and certain group tests of intelligence. *J. Soc. Psychol.*, **23**, 237–239.

SATTLER, J. M. and THEYE, F. (1967) Procedures, situational and interpersonal variables in individual intelligence testing. *Psychol. Bull.*, **68**, 347–360.

SATTLER, J. M., WINGET, B. M. and ROTH, R. J. (1969) Scoring difficulty of WAIS and WISC Comprehension, Similarities, and Vocabulary responses. *J. Clin. Psychol.*, **25**, 175–177.

SATZ, P. and MOGEL, S. (1962) An abbreviation of the WAIS for clinical use. *J. Clin. Psychol.*, **18**, 77–79.

SATZ, P., RICHARD, W. and DANIELS, A. (1967a) The alteration of intellectual performance after lateralized brain-injury in man. *Psychonom. Sci.*, **7**, 369–370.

SATZ, P., VAN DE RIET, H. and MOGEL, S. (1967b) An abbreviation of the WISC for clinical use. *J. Consult. Psychol.*, **31**, 108.

SAUNDERS, D. R. (1961) Digit Span and alpha frequency: a cross-validation. *J. Clin. Psychol.*, **17**, 165–167.

SAUNDERS, D. R. (1959) On the dimensionality of the WAIS battery for two groups of normal males. *Psychol. Rep.*, **5**, 529–541.

SAUNDERS, D. R. (1960a) A factor analysis of the Picture Completion items of the WAIS. *J. Clin. Psychol.*, **16**, 146–149.

SAUNDERS, D. R. (1960b) A factor analysis of the Information and Arithmetic items of the WAIS. *Psychol. Rep.*, **16**, 367–383.

SCHAFER, R. (1944) The significance of scatter in research and practice of clinical psychology. *J. Psychol.*, **18**, 119–124.

SCHAFER, R. (1946) The expression of personality and maladjustment in intelligence test results. *Ann. N.Y. Acad. Sci.*, **46**, 609–623.

SCHAFER, R. (1948) *The Clinical Application of Psychological Tests.* New York: International Universities Press.

SCHAFER, R. and RAPAPORT, D. (1944) The scatter: In diagnostic intelligence testing. *Charact. Personal.*, **12**, 275–284.

SCHEERER, M. (1946) Problems of performance analysis in the study of personality. *Ann. N.Y. Acad. Sci.*, **46**, 653–678.

SCHEERER, M. (1953) Personality functioning and cognitive psychology. *J. Personal.*, **22**, 1–16.

SCHILL, T. (1966) The effects of MMPI social introversion on WAIS PA performance. *J. Clin. Psychol.*, **22**, 72–74.

SCHILL, T., KAHN, M. and MEUHLEMAN, T. (1968) WAIS PA performance and participation in extracurricular activities. *J. Clin. Psychol.*, **24**, 95–96.

SCHILLER, B. (1934) Verbal, numerical and spatial abilities of young children. *Arch. Psychol.*, No. 161.

SCHLOSSER, J. R. and KANTOR, R. E. (1948) A comparison of Wechsler's deterioration ratio in psychoneurosis and schizophrenia. *J. Consult. Psychol.*, **13**, 108–110.

SCHNADT, F. (1952) Certain aspects of Wechsler–Bellevue scatter at low IQ levels. *J. Consult. Psychol.*, **16**, 456–461.

SCHNEYER, S. (1957) A short form of the Wechsler–Bellevue Scale, Form II, for alcoholic outpatients. *Q. J. Stud. Alcohol*, 18, 382–387.

SCHOFIELD, W. (1952) Critique of scatter and profile analysis of psychometric data. *J. Clin. Psychol.*, 8, 16–22.

SCHOONOVER, S. M. and HARTEL, R. K. (1970) Diagnostic and implications of WISC scores. *Psychol. Rep.*, 26, 967–973.

SCHROEDER, H. E. and KLEINSASSER, L. D. (1972) Examiner bias: A determinant of children's verbal behavior on the WISC. *J. Consult. Clin. Psychol.*, 39, 451–454.

SCHWARTZ, L. and LEVITT, E. I. (1960) Short-forms of the Wechsler Intelligence Scale for Children in the educable, non-institutionalized, mentally retarded. *J. Educ. Psychol.*, 51, 187–190.

SCHWARTZ, M. L. (1966) The scoring of WAIS Comprehension responses by experienced and inexperienced judges. *J. Clin. Psychol.*, 22, 425–427.

SCHWARTZ, M. L. and DENNERLL, R. D. (1970) Neuropsychological assessment of children with, without, and with questionable epileptogenic dysfunction. *Percept. Motor Skills*, 30, 111–121.

SEARS, R. R. (1936) Experimental studies of projection: I. Attribution of traits. *J. Soc. Psychol.*, 7, 151–163.

SEARS, R. R. (1937) Experimental studies of projection: II. Ideas of reference. *J. Soc. Psychol.*, 8, 389–400.

SEASHORE, H. G. (1951) Differences between Verbal and Performance IQs on the Wechsler Intelligence Scale for Children. *J. Consult. Psychol.*, 15, 62–67.

SEGUIN, E. (1866) *Idiocy and Its Treatment by the Physiological Method*. Albany, N.Y.: Brandow Publishing.

SEMLER, I. J. and ISCOE, I. (1966) Structure of intelligence in Negro and White children. *J. Educ. Psychol.*, 57, 326–336.

SEWELL, T. E. and SEVERSON, R. A. (1975) Intelligence and achievement in first-grade black children. *J. Consult. Clin. Psychol.*, 43, 112.

SHAW, D. J. (1965) Sexual bias in the WAIS. *J. Consult. Psychol.*, 29, 590–591.

SHAW, D. J. (1967) Factor analysis of the collegiate WAIS. *J. Consult. Psychol.*, 31, 217.

SHAWVER, L. and JEW, C. (1978) Predicting violent behavior from WAIS characteristics: A replication failure. *J. Consult. Clin. Psychol.*, 46, 206.

SHERIF, M. (1935) A study of some social factors in perception. *Arch. Psychol.*, No. 187.

SHERMAN, A. R. and BLATT, S. J. (1968) WAIS Digit Span, Digit Symbol, and Vocabulary performance as a function of prior experience of success and failure. *J. Consult. Clin. Psychol.*, 32, 407–412.

SHERMAN, M., CHINSKY, J. M. and MAFFEO, P. (1974) Wechsler Preschool and Primary Scale of Intelligence Animal House as measure of learning and motor disabilities. *J. Consult. Clin. Psychol.*, 42, 470.

SHIEK, D. A. and MILLER, J. E. (1978) Validity generalization of the WISC-R factor structure with 10½-year-old children. *J. Consult. Clin. Psychol.*, 46, 583.

SHIMKUNAS, A. M., GROHMANN, M. and ZWIBELMAN, B. (1971) Sources of intellectual inefficiency. *Psychol. Rep.*, 29, 747–754.

SHOBEN, E. J. (1950) The Wechsler–Bellevue in the detection of anxiety: A test of the Rashkis–Welsh hypothesis. *J. Consult. Psychol.*, 14, 40–45.

SHORE, C., SHORE, H. and PIHL, R. O. (1971) Correlations between performance

164   THE WECHSLER ENTERPRISE

on the Category Test and the Wechsler Adult Intelligence Scale. *Percept. Motor Skills*, 32, 70.

SIEGMAN, A. W. (1956) The effect of manifest anxiety on a concept formation task, a nondirected learning task, and on timed and untimed intelligence tests. *J. Consult. Psychol.*, 20, 176–178.

SIGEL, I. E. (1963) How intelligence tests limit understanding of intelligence. *Merrill-Palmer Q.*, 9, 39–56.

SIGEL, I. E. (1967) Styles of categorization and their intellectual and personality correlations in young children. *Hum. Devel.*, 10, 1–17.

SILVERSTEIN, A. B. (1960) Relations between intelligence and conceptual levels in active and passive concept formation. *Psychol. Rep.*, 7, 202.

SILVERSTEIN, A. B. (1967a) Validity of WAIS short forms. *Psychol. Rep.*, 20, 37–38.

SILVERSTEIN, A. B. (1967b) A short form of the WISC and WAIS for screening purposes. *Psychol. Rep.*, 20, 682.

SILVERSTEIN, A. B. (1967c) Estimating Full Scale IQs in WISC short forms. *Psychol. Rep.*, 20, 1264.

SILVERSTEIN, A. B. (1967d) A short form of Wechsler's Scale for screening purposes. *Psychol. Rep.*, 21, 842.

SILVERSTEIN, A. B. (1967e) Validity of WISC short forms at three age levels. *J. Consult. Psychol.*, 31, 635–636.

SILVERSTEIN, A. B. (1968a) Validity of WPPSI short forms. *J. Consult. Clin. Psychol.*, 32, 229–230.

SILVERSTEIN, A. B. (1968b) Evaluation of a split-half short form of the WAIS. *Am. J. Ment. Defic.*, 72, 839–840.

SILVERSTEIN, A. B. (1968c) Validity of a new approach to the design of WAIS, WISC, and WPPSI short forms. *J. Consult. Clin. Psychol.*, 32, 478–479.

SILVERSTEIN, A. B. (1968d) Variance components in five psychological tests. *Psychol. Rep.*, 23, 141–142.

SILVERSTEIN, A. B. (1969) An alternative factor analytic solution for Wechsler's intelligence scales. *Educ. Psychol. Measure.*, 29, 763–767.

SILVERSTEIN, A. B. (1973) Factor structure of the Wechsler Intelligence Scale for Children for three ethnic groups. *J. Educ. Psychol.*, 65, 408–410.

SILVERSTEIN, A. B. (1970a) Reappraisal of the validity of a short short form of Wechsler's Scales. *Psychol. Rep.*, 26, 559–561.

SILVERSTEIN, A. B. (1970b) Reappraisal of the validity of WAIS, WISC, and WPPSI short forms. *J. Consult. Clin. Psychol.*, 34, 12–14.

SILVERSTEIN, A. B. (1971) A corrected formula for assessing the validity of WAIS, WISC, and WPPSI short forms. *J. Clin. Psychol.*, 27, 212–213.

SILVERSTEIN, A. B. (1975) Validity of WISC-R short forms. *J. Clin. Psychol.*, 31, 696–697.

SILVERSTEIN, A. B. and FISHER, G. M. (1960) Reanalysis of sex differences in the standardization data of the Wechsler Adult Intelligence Scale. *Psychol. Rep.*, 7, 405–406.

SIMENSEN, R. J. (1974) Correlations among Bender–Gestalt, WISC Block Design, memory-for-designs, and the Pupil Rating Scale. *Percept. Motor Skills*, 38, 1249–1250.

SIMKIN, J. A. (1951) An investigation of differences in intellectual factors between normal and schizophrenic adults. *Am. Psychol.*, 6, 335. (Abstract)

SIMPSON, C. D. and VEGA, A. (1971) Unilateral brain damage and patterns of age-corrected WAIS subtest scores. *J. Clin. Psychol.*, 27, 204–208.

SIMPSON, R. L. (1970a) Study of the comparability of the WISC and the WAIS. *J. Consult. Clin. Psychol.*, 34, 156–158.

SIMPSON, R. L. (1970b) Reading tests versus intelligence tests as predictors of high school graduation. *Psychol. Sch.*, 7 (4), 363–365.

SIMPSON, W. H. and BRIDGES, C. C. (1959) A short form of the Wechsler Intelligence Scale for Children. *J. Clin. Psychol.*, 15, 424.

SINES, L. K. and SIMMONS, H. (1959) The Shipley–Hartford Scale and the Doppelt Short Form as estimators of WAIS IQ in a state hospital population. *J. Clin. Psychol.*, 15, 452–453.

SINNETT, K. and MAYMAN, M. (1960) The Wechsler Adult Intelligence Scale as a clinical diagnostic tool: A review. *Bull. Menninger Clin.*, 24, 80–84.

SLOAN, W. (1947) Validity of Wechsler's deterioration quotient in high grade mental defectives. *J. Clin. Psychol.*, 3, 287–288.

SLOAN, W. and CUTTS, R. A. (1945) Test patterns of defective delinquents on the Wechsler–Bellevue test. *Am. J. Ment. Defic.*, 50, 95–97.

SLOAN, W. and NEWMAN, J. R. (1955) The development of a Wechsler–Bellevue II short form. *Personn. Psychol.*, 8, 347–353.

SMITH, A. (1966) Verbal and non-verbal test performance of patients with "acute" lateralization brain lesions (tumors). *J. Nerv. Ment. Dis.*, 141, 517–523.

SMITH, N. C. (1971) A comparison of short-form estimation methods in the WISC in juvenile public offenders. *J. Clin. Psychol.*, 27, 77–79.

SMITH, T. A. and CALDWELL, M. B. (1969) Intellectual differences in Negro and white mental defectives. *Psychol. Rep.*, 25, 559–565.

SOLKOFF, N. (1964) Frustration and WISC Coding performance among brain-injured children. *Percept. Motor Skills*, 18, 54.

SOLKOFF, N. (1972) Race of experimenter as a variable in research with children. *Devel. Psychol.*, 7, 70–75.

SOLKOFF, N. (1974) Race of examiner and performance on the Wechsler Intelligence Scale for Children: A replication. *Percept. Motor Skills*, 39, 1063–1066.

SOLKOFF, N. and CHRISIEN, G. (1963) Frustration and perceptual-motor performance. *Percept. Motor Skills*, 17, 282.

SOLWAY, K. S., HAYS, J. R., ROBERTS, T. K. and CODY, J. A. (1975) Comparison of WISC profiles of alleged juvenile delinquents living at home versus those incarcerated. *Psychol. Rep.*, 37, 403–407.

SOLWAY, K. S., COOK, T. H. and HAYS, J. R. (1976) WISC subtest patterns of delinquent female retardates. *Psychol. Rep.*, 38, 42.

SPANER, F. E. (1950) An analysis of the relationship between some Rorschach Test determinants and subtest scores on the Wechsler–Bellevue Adult Scale. Unpublished doctoral dissertation, Purdue University.

SPEARMAN, C. (1904) "General intelligence," objectively determined and measured. *Am. J. Psychol.*, 15, 201–293.

SPEARMAN, C. (1923) *The Nature of "Intelligence" and the Principles of Cognition.* London: Macmillan.

SPEARMAN, C. (1927) *The Abilities of Man: Their Nature and Measurement.* New York: Macmillan.

SPEARMAN, C. (1939) "Intelligence" tests. *Eugen. Rev.,* 30, 249–254.

SPENCE, J. T. (1963) Patterns of performance on WAIS Similarities in schizophrenic, brain-damaged and normal subjects. *Psychol. Rep.*, 13, 431–436.

SPERBA, Z. and ADLERSTEIN, A. M. (1961) The accuracy of clinical psychologists' estimates of interviewees' intelligence. *J. Consult. Psychol.*, 25, 521–524.

SPRAGUE, R. L. and QUAY, H. C. (1966) A factor analytic study of the responses of mental retardates on the WAIS. *Am. J. Ment. Defic.*, 70, 595–600.

SPRINGER, N. N. (1946) A short form of the Wechsler–Bellevue Intelligence Test as applied to normal personnel. *Am. J. Orthopsychiat.*, 16, 341–344.

STACEY, C. L. and PORTNOY, B. (1950) A study of the differential responses on the vocabulary sub-test of the Wechsler Intelligence Scale for Children. *J. Clin. Psychol.*, 6, 401–403.

STAFF, PERSONNEL RESEARCH SECTION, PERSONNEL RESEARCH and PROCEDURES BRANCH, THE ADJUTANT GENERAL'S OFFICE (1946) Use of ability sub-test scores in differentiating between diagnostic categories among psychiatric patients. *Am. Psychol.*, 1, 263.

STEMPEL, E. F. (1953) The WISC and the SRA Primary Mental Abilities tests. *Child Devel.*, 24, 257–261.

STEPHENSON, W. (1931) Tetrad-differences for non-Verbal subtests. *J. Educ. Psychol.*, 22, 167–185.

STERN, W. (1914) The psychological methods of testing intelligence. *Educ. Psychol. Monogr.*, No. 13.

STERN, W. (1938) *General Psychology from the Personalistic Standpoint*. New York: Macmillan.

STERNE, D. M. (1957) A note on the use of Doppelt's short form of the WAIS with psychiatric patients. *J. Consult. Psychol.*, 21, 502.

STERNLICHT, M., SIEGEL, L. and DEUTSCH, M. R. (1968) WAIS subtest characteristics of institutionalized retardates. *Educ. Psychol. Measure.*, 28, 465–468.

STEWART, D. W. (1976) Effects of sex and ethnic variables on the profiles of the Illinois Test of Psycholinguistics and Wechsler Intelligence Scale for Children. *Psychol. Rep.*, 38, 53–54.

STEWART, D. J., POWERS, J. and GOUAUX, C. (1973) The Wechsler in personality assessment: Object assembly subtest as predictive of bodily concerns. *J. Consult. Clin. Psychol.*, 40, 488.

STEWART, K. J. and DAVIS, W. E. (1974) Deficit in Digit Span performance: state anxiety of aroused emotional state? *J. Consult. Clin. Psychol.*, 42, 147.

STRANGE, F. B. and PALMER, J. O. (1953) A note on sex differences on the Wechsler–Bellevue subtests. *J. Clin. Psychol.*, 9, 85–87.

STRICKER, G., MERBAUM, M. and TANGEMAN, P. (1969) WAIS short forms, information transmission and approximations of Full Scale IQ. *J. Clin. Psychol.*, 25, 170–172.

STROUD, J. B. (1957) The intelligence test in school use: Some persistent issues. *J. Educ. Psychol.*, 48, 77–86.

STROUD, J., BLOMMERS, P. and LAUBT, M. (1957) Correlation analysis of WISC and achievement tests. *J. Educ. Psychol.*, 48, 18–26.

SUTKER, P. B., MOAN, C. E. and ALLAIN, A. N. (1974) WAIS performance in unincarcerated groups of MMPI-defined sociopaths and normal controls. *J. Consult. Clin. Psychol.*, 42, 307–308.

TARKINGTON, L. W. and RICKER, G. A. (1969) A short form of the WISC for use with the mentally retarded. *Psychol. Rep.*, 25, 461–462.

TAYLOR, J. A. (1953) A personality scale of manifest anxiety. *J. Abnorm. Soc. Psychol.*, 48, 285–290.

TAYLOR, J. B. (1964) The structure of ability in the lower intellectual range. *Am. J. Ment. Defic.*, 68, 766–774.

TEAHAN, J. E. and DREWS, E. M. (1962) A comparison of northern and southern Negro children on the WISC. *J. Consult. Psychol.*, 26, 292.

TEICHER, M. I. and SINGER, E. (1946) A report on the use of the Wechsler–Bellevue Scales in an overseas general hospital. *Am. J. Psychiat.*, 103, 91–93.

TELEGDY, G. A. (1973) The relationship between socio-economic status and patterns of WISC scores in children with learning disabilities. *Psychol. Sch.*, 10, 427–430.

TELLEGEN, A. and BRIGGS, P. F. (1967) Old wine in new skins: Grouping Wechsler subtests into new scales. *J. Consult. Psychol.*, 31, 499–506.

TEMPLER, D. I. and HARTLAGE, L. C. (1969) Physicians' IQ estimates and Kent IQ compared with WAIS IQ. *J. Clin. Psychol.*, 25, 74–75.

TENDLER, A. D. (1923) The mental status of psychoneurotics. *Arch. Psychol.*, No. 60.

TERMAN, L. M. (1911) The Binet–Simon Scale for measuring intelligence. *Psychol. Clin.*, 5, 199–206.

TERMAN, L. M. (1913a) Suggestions for revising, extending and supplementing the Binet intelligence tests. *J. Psycho-Asthenics*, 18, 20–33.

TERMAN, L. M. (1913b) Psychological principles underlying the Binet–Simon Scale and some practical considerations for its correct use. *J. Psycho-Asthenics*, 18, 93–104.

TERMAN, L. M. (1916) *The Measurement of Intelligence*. Boston: Houghton.

TERMAN, L. M. (1918) The Vocabulary test as a measurement of intelligence. *J. Educ. Psychol.*, 9, 452–466.

TERMAN, L. M. and CHAMBERLAIN, M. B. (1918) Twenty-three serial tests of intelligence and their intercorrelations. *J. Appl. Psychol.*, 2, 341–354.

TERMAN, L. M. and CHILDS, H. G. (1912) A tentative revision and extension of the Binet–Simon Scale of Intelligence. *J. Educ. Psychol.*, 3, 277–289.

TERMAN, L. M. and MERRILL, M. A. (1937) *Measuring Intelligence*. Boston: Houghton Mifflin.

THOMPSON, J. M. and FINLEY, C. J. (1962) The validation of an abbreviated Wechsler Intelligence Scale for Children for use with the educable mentally retarded. *Educ. Psychol. Measure.*, 22, 539–542.

THOMPSON, R. J. (1980) The dignostic utility of WISC-R measures with children referred to a developmental evaluation center. *J. Consult. Clin. Psychol.*, 48, 440–447.

THORNDIKE, E. L. (1920) Intelligence examinations for college entrance. *J. Educ. Res.*, 1, 329–337.

THORNDIKE, E. L., BREGMAN, M. V. and COBB, E. W. (1920) *The Measurement of Intelligence*. New York: Teachers College Publications.

THORNDIKE, E. L., TERMAN, L. M., FREEMAN, F. N., COLVIN, S. S., PINTNER, R., RUML, B., PRESSEY, S. L., HENMON, V. A. C., PETERSON, J., THURSTONE, L. L., WOODROW, H., DEARBORN, W. F. and HAGGERTY, M. E. (1921) Intelligence and its measurement: A symposium. *J. Educ. Psychol.*, 12, 123–147, 195–216.

THURSTONE, L. L. (1921) A cycle-omnibus intelligence test for college students. *J. Educ. Res.*, 4, 265–278.

THURSTONE, L. L. (1925) A method of scaling psychological and educational tests. *J. Educ. Psychol.*, 16, 433–451.

168   THE WECHSLER ENTERPRISE

THURSTONE, L. L. (1928) The absolute zero in intelligence measurement. *Psychol. Rev.*, 35, 175–197.
THURSTONE, L. L. (1931) A cycle-omnibus intelligence test for college students. *J. Educ. Res.*, 4, 265–278.
THURSTONE, L. L. (1935) *The Vectors of Mind: Multiple-factor Analysis for the Isolation of Primary Traits.* Chicago: University of Chicago Press.
THURSTONE, L. L. (1936) The factorial isolation of primary abilities. *Psychometrika*, 1, 175–182.
THURSTONE, L. L. (1938) Primary mental abilities. *Psychomet. Monogr.*, No. 1.
THURSTONE, L. L. (1940) Experimental study of simple structure. *Psychometrika*, 5, 153–168.
THURSTONE, L. L. and THURSTONE, T. E. (1941) Factorial studies of intelligence. *Psychomet. Monogr.*, No. 2.
TIPTON, R. M. and STROUD, L. (1971) Abbreviated forms of the WAIS. *Am. J. Ment. Defic.*, 78, 150–152.
TODD, J., COOLIDGE, F. and SATZ, P. (1977) The Wechsler Adult Intelligence Scale Discrepancy Index: A neuropsychological evaluation. *J. Consult. Clin. Psychol.*, 45, 450–454.
TORRANCE, E. P. (1966) *Torrance Tests of Creative Thinking, Norms – Technical Manual.* Princeton: Personnel Press.
TRAVERS, R. M. W. (1939) The use of a discriminant function in the treatment of psychological group differences. *Psychometrika*, 4, 25–32.
TREHUB, A. and SCHERER, I. W. (1958) Wechsler–Bellevue scatter as an index of schizophrenia. *J. Consult. Psychol.*, 22, 147–149.
TSENG, M. S. (1972) Predicting vocational rehabilitation dropouts from psychometric attributes and work behaviors. *Rehabil. Counsel. Bull.*, 15, 154–159.
TSUSHIMA, W. T. and BRATTON, J. C. (1977) Effects of geographic region upon Wechsler Adult Intelligence Scale results: A Hawaii-Mainland United States comparison. *J. Consult. Clin. Psychol.*, 45, 501–502.
TURNER, R. G. and WILLERMAN, L. (1977) Sex differences in WAIS item performance. *J. Clin. Psychol.*, 33, 795–797.
TURNER, R. G., WILLERMAN, L. and HORN, J. M. (1976) Personality correlates of WAIS performance. *J. Clin. Psychol.*, 32, 349–354.
VANCE, H. B. and ENGIN, A. (1978) Analysis of cognitive abilities of Black children's performance on WISC-R. *J. Clin. Psychol.*, 34, 452–456.
VANCE, H. B. and WALLBROWN, F. H. (1979) Hierarchical factor structure of the WISC-R for referred children and adolescents. *Psychol. Rep.*, 41, 699–702.
VANCE, H. B., GAYNOR, P. and COLEMAN, M. (1976) Analysis of cognitive abilities for learning disabled children. *Psychol. Sch.*, 13, 477–483.
VANCE, H. B., SINGER, M. G. and ENGIN, A. W. (1980) WISC-R subtest differences for male and female LD children and youth. *J. Clin. Psychol.*, 36, 953–957.
VANDERHOST, L., SLOAN, W. and BENSBERG, G. J. (1953) Performance of mental defectives on the Wechsler–Bellevue and the WISC. *Amer. J. Ment. Defic.*, 57, 481–483.
VEGA, A. and PARSONS, O. A. (1969) Relationship between sensory-motor deficits and WAIS Verbal and Performance scores in unilateral brain damage. *Cortex*, 5, 229–241.
VIDLER, D. C. and RAWAN, H. R. (1974) Construct validation of a scale of academic curiosity. *Psychol. Rep.*, 35, 263–266.

VIGOTSKY, L. (1934) Thought in schizophrenia. *Arch. Neurol. Psychiat.*, 31, 1063–1077.

VOGT, A. T. and HEATON, R. K. (1977) Comparison of Wechsler Adult Intelligence Scale indices of cerebral dysfunction. *Percept. Motor Skills*, 45, 607–615.

WACHTEL, P. L. and BLATT, S. J. (1965) Energy deployment and achievement. *J. Consult. Psychol.*, 29, 302–308.

WALDFOGEL, S. and GUY, W. (1951) Wechsler–Bellevue subtest scatter in the affective disorders. *J. Clin. Psychol.*, 7, 135–139.

WALKER, R. E. and SPENCE, J. T. (1964) Relationship between digit span and anxiety. *J. Consult. Psychol.*, 28, 220–223.

WALKER, R. E., HUNT, W. A. and SCHWARTZ, M. L. (1965a) The difficulty of WAIS Comprehension scoring. *J. Clin. Psychol.*, 21, 427–429.

WALKER, R. E., NEILSON, M. K. and NICOLAY, R. C. (1965b) The effects of failure and anxiety on intelligence test performance. *J. Clin. Psychol.*, 21, 400–402.

WALKER, R. E., SANNITO, T. C. and FIRETTO, A. C. (1970) The effect of subjectively reported anxiety on intelligence test performance. *Psychol. Sch.*, 7, 241–243.

WALL, H. W., MARKS, E., FORD, D. H. and ZEIGLER, M. L. (1962) Estimates of the concurrent validity of the WAIS and normative distributions for college freshmen. *Personn. Guid. J.*, 40, 717–722.

WALLBROWN, F. H., BLAHA, J. and WHERRY, R. J. (1973) The hierarchical factor structure of the Wechsler Preschool and Primary Scale of Intelligence. *J. Consult. Clin. Psychol.*, 41, 356–362.

WALLBROWN, F. H., BLAHA, J. and WHERRY, R. J. (1974a) The hierarchical factor structure of the Wechsler Adult Intelligence Scale. *Br. J. Educ. Psychol.*, 44, 47–56.

WALLBROWN, F. H., BLAHA, J., COUNTS, D. H. and WALLBROWN, J. D. (1974b) The hierarchical factor structure of the WISC and revised ITPA for reading disabled children. *J. Psychol.*, 88, 65–76.

WALLIN, J. E. W. (1917) The phenomenon of scattering in the Binet–Simon Scale. *Psychol. Clin.*, 11, 179–195.

WALLIN, J. E. W. (1918) A further comparison of scattering and of the Mental Rating by the 1908 and 1911 Binet–Simon Scales. *J. Delinq.*, 3, 12–27.

WALLIN, J. E. W. (1922) Intelligence irregularity as measured by scattering in the Binet Scales. *J. Educ. Psychol.*, 13, 140–151.

WALLIN, J. E. W. (1927) A further note on scattering in the Binet Scale. *J. Appl. Psychol.*, 11, 143–154.

WALLIN, J. E. W. (1929) A statistical study of the individual tests in ages VIII and IX in the Stanford–Binet Scale. *Ment. Measure. Monogr.*, No. 6.

WALTERS, R. H. (1953) Wechsler–Bellevue test results of prison inmates. *Aust. J. Psychol.*, 5, 46–54.

WANG, H. S., OBRIST, W. D. and BUSSE, E. W. (1970) Neurophysiological correlates of the intellectual function of elderly persons living in the community. *Am. J. Psychiat.*, 126, 1205–1212.

WARNER, S. J. (1950) The Wechsler–Bellevue psychometric pattern in anxiety neurosis. *J. Consult. Psychol.*, 14, 297–304.

WARREN, S. A. and KRAUS, M. J. (1961) WAIS Verbal minus Performance IQ comparisons in mental retardates. *J. Clin. Psychol.*, 17, 57–59.

WATKINS, J. T. and KINZIE, W. B. (1970) Exaggerated scatter and less reliable profiles produced by the Satz–Mogel abbreviation of the WAIS. *J. Clin. Psychol.*, 26, 343–345.

WATSON, C. G. (1965a) WAIS profile patterns of hospitalized brain-damaged and schizophrenic patients. *J. Clin. Psychol.*, 21, 294–295.

WATSON, C. G. (1965b) Intratest scatter in hospitalized brain-damaged and schizophrenic patients. *J. Consult. Psychol.*, 29, 596.

WATSON, C. G. (1965c) WAIS error types in schizophrenics and organics. *Psychol. Rep.*, 16, 527–530.

WATSON, C. G. (1966) Evidence on the utilities of three WAIS short forms. *J. Consult. Psychol.*, 30, 181.

WATSON, C. G. (1972) Cross-validation of a WAIS sign developed to separate brain-damaged from schizophrenic patients. *J. Clin. Psychol.*, 28, 66–67.

WATSON, C. G. and THOMAS, R. W. (1969) Differentiation of organics from schizophrenics with the Trail Making, dynamometer, Critical Flicker Fusion, and light-intensity matching test. *J. Clin. Psychol.*, 25, 130–133.

WATSON, C. G., DAVIS, W. E. and McDERMOTT, M. T. (1976) MMPI–WAIS relationships in organic and schizophrenic patients. *J. Clin. Psychol.*, 32, 539–540.

WEBB, A. P. (1963) A longitudinal comparison of the WISC and WAIS with educable mentally retarded Negroes. *J. Clin. Psychol.*, 19, 101–102.

WEBB, E. (1915) Character and intelligence. *Br. J. Psychol., Monogr. Suppl.*, No. 3.

WEBB, W. B. (1947) A note on the Rabin ratio. *J. Consult. Psychol.*, 11, 107–108.

WEBSTER, R. E. (1974) Predictive applicability of the WAIS with psychiatric patients in a vocational rehabilitation setting. *J. Commun. Psychol.*, 2, 141–144.

WEBSTER, R. E. (1979) Utility of the WAIS in predicting vocational success of psychiatric patients. *J. Clin. Psychol.*, 35, 111–116.

WECHSLER, D. (1932) Analytic use of the Army Alpha examination. *J. Appl. Psychol.*, 16, 254–256.

WECHSLER, D. (1935) *The Range of Human Capacities*. Baltimore: Williams & Wilkins.

WECHSLER, D. (1939) *Measurement of Adult Intelligence*. Baltimore: Williams & Wilkins.

WECHSLER, D. (1940) Nonintellective factors in general intelligence. *Psychol. Bull.*, 37, 444–445. (Abs.)

WECHSLER, D. (1941a) *The Measurement of Adult Intelligence*. 2nd Ed. Baltimore: Williams & Wilkins.

WECHSLER, D. (1941b) The effect of alcohol on mental activity. *Q. J. Stud. Alcohol*, 2, 479–485.

WECHSLER, D. (1943) Nonintellective 'factors in general intelligence. *J. Abnorm. Psychol.*, 38, 101–103.

WECHSLER, D. (1944) *The Measurement of Adult Intelligence*. 3rd Ed. Baltimore: Williams & Wilkins.

WECHSLER, D. (1946) *The Wechsler–Bellevue Intelligence Scale, Form II*. New York: Psychological Corporation.

WECHSLER, D. (1949) *Wechsler Intelligence Scale for Children*. New York: Psychological Corporation.

WECHSLER, D. (1950) Cognitive, conative, and non-intellective intelligence. *Amer. Psychol.*, 5, 87–91.

WECHSLER, D. (1955) *Manual for the Wechsler Adult Intelligence Scale*. New York: Psychological Corporation.

WECHSLER, D. (1963) *Manual for the Wechsler Preschool and Primary Scale of Intelligence.* New York: Psychological Corporation.

WECHSLER, D. (1974) *Manual for the Wechsler Intelligence Scale for Children – Revised.* New York: Psychological Corporation.

WECHSLER, D. and JAROS, E. (1965) Schizophrenic patterns on the WISC. *J. Clin. Psychol.*, 21, 288–291.

WECHSLER, D., HALPERN, F. and JAROS, E. (1940) Psychometric study of insulin-treated schizophrenics. *Psychiat. Q.*, 14, 466–476.

WECHSLER, D., ISRAEL, H. and BALINSKY, B. (1941) A study of the subtests of the Bellevue Intelligence Scale in borderline and mental defective cases. *Am. J. Ment. Defic.*, 45, 555–558.

WEHLER, R. and HOFFMAN, H. (1978) Intellectual functioning in lobotomized and non-lobotomized long term chronic schizophrenic patients. *J. Clin. Psychol.*, 34, 449–451.

WEIDER, A. (1943) Effects of age on the Bellevue Intelligence Scales in schizophrenic patients. *Psychiat. Q.*, 17, 337–346.

WEISGERBER, C. A. (1955) A note on Diamond's method of scoring the Wechsler–Bellevue Intelligence Scale for vocational aptitude. *J. Clin. Psychol.*, 11, 311.

WELLS, F. L. (1927) *Mental Tests in Clinical Practice.* New York: World Book.

WELLS, F. L. and KELLEY, C. M. (1920) Intelligence and psychosis. *Am. J. Insanity*, 77, 17–45.

WELLS, F. L. and MARTIN, H. A. A. (1923) A method of memory examination suitable for psychotic cases. *Am. J. Psychiat.*, 3, 243–257.

WENDT, R. A. and BURWELL, E. (1964) Test performance of Jewish day-school students. *J. Genet. Psychol.*, 105, 99–103.

WENER, B. D. and TEMPLER, D. I. (1976) Relationship between WISC Verbal-Performance discrepancies and motor and psychomotor abilities of children with learning disabilities. *Percept. Motor Skills*, 42, 125–126.

WESNER, C. E. (1973) The relationship between WISC and WAIS IQs with educable mentally retarded adolescents. *Educ. Psychol. Measure.*, 33, 465–467.

WENTWORTH, M. M. (1924) Two hundred cases of dementia pracecox tested by the Stanford revision. *J. Abnorm. Psychol.*, 18, 278–384.

WENTWORTH-ROHR, I. and MACINTOSH, R. (1972) Psychodiagnosis with WAIS intrasubtest scatter of scores. *J. Clin. Psychol.*, 28, 68.

WEST, P. V. (1924) The significance of weighted scores. *J. Educ. Psychol.*, 15, 302–308.

WHEATON, P. J. and VANDERGRIFF, A. F. (1978) Comparison of WISC and WISC-R scores of highly gifted students in public school. *Psychol. Rep.*, 43, 627–630.

WHEELER, J. H. and WILKINS, W. L. (1951) The validity of the Hewson ratios. *J. Consult. Psychol.*, 15, 163–166.

WHIPPLE, G. M. (1909) A range of information test. *Psychol. Rev.*, 16, 347–351.

WHIPPLE, G. M. (1921) The National Intelligence Tests. *J. Educ. Res.*, 4, 16–31.

WHITE, W. A. (1926) The language of schizophrenia. *Arch. Neurol. Psychiat.*, 16, 395–413.

WHITEHEAD, A. (1973) The patterns of WAIS performance in elderly psychiatric patients. *Br. J. Soc. Clin. Psychol.*, 12, 435–436.

WHITMYRE, J. W. and PISHKIN, V. (1958) The abbreviated Wechsler Adult Intelligence Scale in a psychiatric population. *J. Clin. Psychol.*, 14, 189–191.

WIENER, G. (1957) The effect of distrust on some aspects of intelligence test behavior. *J. Consult. Psychol.*, 21, 127–130.
WIENS, A. N., MATARAZZO, J. D. and GAVER, K. D. (1959) Performance and Verbal IQ in a group of sociopaths. *J. Clin. Psychol.*, 15, 191–193.
WIGHT, B. W. and SANDRY, M. (1962) A short form of the Wechsler Intelligence Scale for Children. *J. Clin. Psychol.*, 18, 166.
WILDMAN, R. W. and WILDMAN, R. W., II. (1977) Validity of Verbal IQ as a short form of the Wechsler Adult Intelligence Scale. *J. Consult. Clin. Psychol.*, 45, 171–172.
WILSON, R. C., GUILFORD, J. P., CHRISTENSEN, P. R. and LEWIS, D. J. (1954) A factor-analytic study of creative-thinking abilities. *Psychometrika*, 19, 297–311.
WINFIELD, D. L. (1953) The relationship between IQ scores and Minnesota Multiphasic Personality Inventory scores. *J. Soc. Psychol.*, 38, 299–300.
WINNE, J. F. and SCHOONOVER, S. M. (1972) Diagnostic implications of WISC scores: A reanalysis. *Psychol. Rep.*, 30, 823–828.
WITTENBORN, J. R. (1949) An evaluation of the use of Bellevue–Wechsler subtest scores as an aid in psychiatric diagnosis. *J. Consult. Psychol.*, 13, 433–439.
WITTENBORN, J. R. and HOLZBERG, J. D. (1951) The Wechsler–Bellevue and descriptive diagnosis. *J. Consult. Psychol.*, 15, 325–329.
WOLFENSBERGER, W. P. (1958) Construction of a table of the significance of the difference between Verbal and Performance IQ's on the WAIS and the Wechsler–Bellevue. *J. Clin. Psychol.*, 14, 92.
WOLFF, B. B. (1960) The application of Hewson ratios to the WAIS as an aid in the differential diagnosis of cerebral pathology. *J. Nerv. Ment. Dis.*, 131, 98–109.
WOLFSON, W. and BACHELIS, L. (1960) An abbreviated form of the WAIS Verbal Scale. *J. Clin. Psychol.*, 16, 421.
WOODROW, H. (1939) The common factors in fifty-two mental tests. *Psychometrika*, 4, 99–108.
WOODWORTH, R. S. and WELLS, F. L. (1911) Association tests. *Psychol. Rev. Monogr.*, No. 57.
WOODY, R. H. (1968) Diagnosis of behavioral problem children: Mental abilities and achievement. *J. Sch. Psychol.*, 6, 111–116.
WOO-SAM, J., ZIMMERMAN, I. L. and ROGAL, R. (1971) Location of injury and Wechsler indices of mental deterioration. *Percept. Motor Skills*, 32, 407–411.
WRIGHT, R. E. (1939) A factor analysis of the original Stanford–Binet Scale. *Psychometrika*, 4, 209–220.
WYLIE, A. R. T. (1902) On some recent work in mental pathology. *J. Psycho-Asthenics*, 7, 1–5.
WYSOCKI, B. A. and WYSOCKI, A. C. (1969) Cultural differences as reflected in Wechsler–Bellevue Intelligence (WB II) test. *Psychol. Rep.*, 25, 95–101.
YACORZYNSKI, G. K. (1941) An evaluation of the postulate underlying the Babcock deterioration test. *Psychol. Rev.*, 48, 261–267.
YATER, A. C., BOYD, M. and BARCLAY, A. (1975) A comparative study of WPPSI and WISC performance of disadvantaged children. *J. Clin. Psychol.*, 31, 78–80.
YERKES, R. M. (1917) The Binet versus the point scale method of measuring intelligence. *J. Appl. Psychol.*, 1, 111–122.
YERKES, R. M. and ANDERSON, H. M. (1915) The importance of social status as indicated by the results of the Point-Scale method of measuring mental capacity. *J. Educ. Psychol.*, 6, 137–150.

YERKES, R. M., BRIDGES, J. W. and HARDWICK, R. S. (1915) *A Point Scale for Measuring Mental Ability*. Baltimore: Warwick & York.

YOAKUM, C. A. and YERKES, R. M. (1920) *Army Mental Tests*. New York: Holt.

YOUNG, F. M. and BRIGHT, H. A. (1954) Results of testing 81 Negro rural juveniles with the Wechsler Intelligence Scale for Children. *J. Soc. Psychol.*, 39, 219–226.

YOUNG, F. M. and PITTS, V. A. (1951) The performance of congenital syphilitics on the Wechsler intelligence scale for children. *J. Consult. Psychol.*, 15, 239–242.

YUDIN, L. W. (1966) An abbreviated form of the WISC for use with emotionally disturbed children. *J. Consult. Psychol.*, 30, 272–275.

ZIMMERMAN, S. F., WHITMYRE, J. W. and FIELDS, F. R. J. (1970) Factor analytic structure of the Wechsler Adult Intelligence Scale in patients with diffuse and lateralized cerebral dysfunction. *J. Clin. Psychol.*, 26, 462–465.

ZIMMERMAN, I. L., WOO-SAM, J. W. and GLASSER, A. J. (1973) *Clinical Interpretation of the Wechsler Adult Intelligence Scale*, New York: Grune & Stratton.

ZIMMERMAN, W. S. (1953) A revised orthogonal rotational solution for Thurstone's original primary mental abilities test battery. *Psychometrika*, 18, 77–93.

ZUNG, W. W. and GIANTURCO, J. (1968) Further validation of the Ohio Literacy Test: Correlation with the Wechsler Adult Intelligence Scale and grade achieved in school. *J. Clin. Psychol.*, 24, 197–198.

ZYTOWSKI, D. G. and HUDSON, J. (1965) The validity of split-half abbreviations of the WAIS. *J. Clin. Psychol.*, 21, 292–294.

Author Index

184   AUTHOR INDEX

Rabin, A.   2, 23, 24, 37, 42, 58, 64,
    71, 80, 82, 83, 120, 124
Radcliffe, J.   86
Ramanaiah, N.   86
Ramanauskas, S.   46
Ramsay, R.   16
Randolph, M.   73
Rankin, R.   114
Rapaport, D.   32, 41, 43, 50, 62, 65,
    67, 68, 90, 92
Rardin, M.   82
Rasbury, W.   27
Raskin, L.   46
Rasof, B.   45
Ravenette, A.   38
Rawan, H.   100
Rawlings, E.   62
Reed, H.   52, 54
Reed, J.   46, 86
Reichard, S.   92
Reid, W.B.   27
Reid, W.R.   46
Reitan, R.   50, 52, 86, 99
Rennick, P.   86, 103, 109
Reschley, D.   86
Resnick, R.   27
Reynell, W.   50
Reynolds, C.   86
Reznikoff, M.   25
Ribich, F.   86
Rice, D.   84
Richard, W.   52
Richardson, H.   73
Richman, J.   69
Ricker, G.   27
Riegel, K.   86
Riegel, R.   86
Ries, H.   27
Rimoldi, H.   86
Robeck, M.   114
Roberts, T.   38
Robertson, J.   82
Rockwell, G.   99
Roe, A.   32
Rogal, R.   53
Rogers, L.   34, 35, 50, 64
Rosenberg, M.   114
Rosenthal, D.   38
Rosman, B.   109

Ross, R.   20
Roth, R.   122
Rourke, B.   38, 39
Rourke, D.   52
Rowley, V.   26, 38, 75
Royer, F.   69
Rubin-Rabson, G.   120
Rugel, R.   86
Ruml, R.   13, 32
Russell, E.   52, 54
Rust, J.   37

Saccuzzo, D.   38, 74, 80
Sanderson, M.   120
San Diego, E.   82
Sandry, M.   24
Sanford, N.   32
Sannito, T.   76
Sarason, I.   99
Sarason, S.   35, 76
Sartain, A.   113
Saslow, G.   75
Sattler, J.   122
Satz, P.   26, 27, 52
Saunders, D.   50, 87, 93, 97
Savage, R.   25, 35, 38
Savage, W.   115
Schafer, R.   32, 41, 42, 60, 65, 67, 68,
    69, 90, 92
Scheerer, M.   32
Scherer, I.   89
Schill, T.   75, 97, 99, 100
Schiller, B.   87
Schlosser, J.   35
Schnadt, F.   16, 81
Schneider, B.   16
Schneyer, S.   25
Schoer, L.   46
Schofield, W.   80
Schoonover, S.   38, 66
Schroeder, H.   122
Schulman, J.   122
Schultz, W.   27, 28
Schwartz, L.   26
Schwartz, M.   55, 94, 122
Seaquist, M.   15, 16
Sears, R.   32
Seashore, H.   39

Williams, M.   24, 26
Williams, R.   25
Wilson, R.   86
Wilson, W.   27
Winfield, D.   102
Winget, B.   122
Winne, J.   66
Winter, K.   25
Winters, S.   106
Wisser, R.   38
Wittenborn, J.   65, 72
Wittman, P.   42, 67
Wolfensberger, W.   41
Wolff, B.   50
Wolfson, W.   26
Woodrow, H.   13, 32, 86
Woodward, J.   38
Woodworth, R.   11
Woody, R.   38, 73
Woo-Sam, J.   53, 93
Wright, C.   64
Wright, F.   24, 28
Wright, H.   24, 28
Wright, R.   87

Wylie, A.   32
Wysocki, A.   82, 83
Wysocki, B.   82, 83

Yacorzynski, G.   69
Yater, A.   21
Yerkes, R.   8, 9, 10, 11, 12, 13, 79,
    82, 117, 118
Yoakum, C.   8, 9, 10, 11, 12, 13
Young, F.   39, 82
Young, G.   38, 39
Yudin, L.   27

Zeigler, M.   113
Ziebell, P.   52
Zimmerman, I.   53, 93
Zimmerman, S.   86
Zimmerman, W.   86
Zuibelman, B.   81
Zung, W.   113
Zytowski, D.   27

Subject Index

189

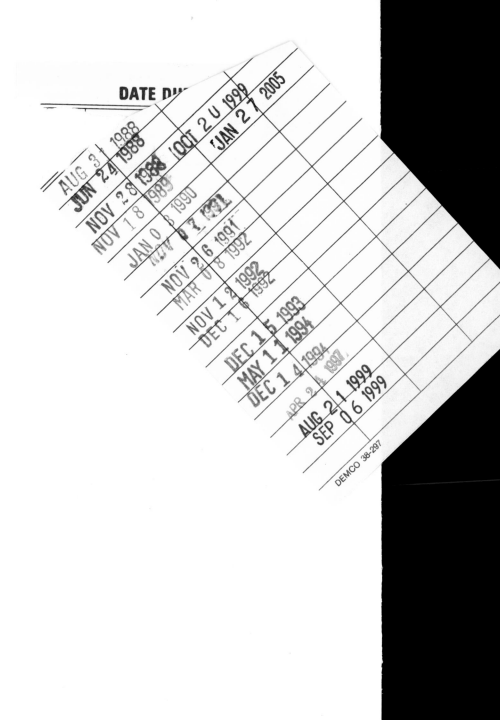